m-TOEFL
LINK
문법편

LinguaForum™

ⓜ~TOEFL® LINK [문법편]

지은이 링구아포럼 리서치센터   **발행인** 이길호   **발행처** 링구아포럼   **등록번호** 제2000-000335호   **등록일자** 2000. 5. 17
전화 교재구입 02) 3480-6627 / 대표전화 02) 590-6900   ISBN 978-89-5563-180-7 (54740)   **가격** 15,000원

Printed in the Republic of Korea SS 1506

R/N (CRmTFGMI): 08010830KB/08250830KB/12170830KB/01300930KB/03270930KB/06220930KB/10280930KB/01141030KB/03191030KB/09171030KB/01141130KB/03301130KB

본 교재에 대하여

본 교재의 수준

본 교재는 TOEFL 기초가 취약한 대학생, 성인은 물론 신세대 중고등 학생들의 기본 영어 총정리를 위하여 제작하였다. 영어를 보다 쉽게 이해할 수 있도록 내용의 분류 및 설명에 대하여 새로운 방향을 제시하였으며, 영어의 기본에 대한 중요성을 부각시켜, 원리에 대한 설명을 강화하였다.

Structure

1 Grammar Up - 문법 향상

꼭 알아 두어야 할 문법 사항과 더불어 보다 나은 영어 실력을 위해 필요한 문법의 기본 원리까지 정리하였다. 또한 Check Up 문제를 실어 학습한 사항들을 바로 확인해 볼 수 있게 하였다.

2 Power Up Test - 실력 향상 연습

Grammar Up에서 공부한 내용을 바탕으로 다양한 형태의 문제를 풀어봄으로써 학습내용을 완전히 익힐 수 있도록 하였다.

3 Pattern Drill

영어 학습의 기본이 되는 영어 문장의 structure를 총 67가지 유형으로 분류하고, 그 유형별로 문제를 실어 집중적으로 연습할 수 있게 하였다.

4 Pattern Review

5 Mini Test

Introductory Contents

STRUCTURE

CHAPTER 1

품사, 구, 절, 문장

Grammar Up / Power Up Test / Pattern Drill / Pattern Review / Mini Test

영어의 8 품사

1 명사: 명사는 사람, 사물, 장소 등에 이름을 부여한다. 따라서 명사를 '이름을 정하는 단어(Naming Word)' 라 부르기도 한다. 주어, 보어, 목적어, 전치사의 목적어로 쓰인다.

> Frank, Mrs. Lloyd, rabbit, mountain, train, love, idea, ...

Fred likes to play computer games.

A horse is a **mammal**.

My boy friend wrote this **letter**.

❋ 명사 상당어구: 대명사, to 부정사(명사적 용법), 동명사, 명사절

2 대명사: 명사를 대신하여 주어, 보어, 목적어, 전치사의 목적어로 쓰인다. 종류로는 인칭대명사, 의문대명사, 부정대명사 등이 있다.

> I, she, him, it, ours, this, that, myself, ...

This is made in Scotland.

Nancy wants to see **him**.

3 동사: 문장의 중심 단어로서 주어의 동작과 상태를 나타낸다. 문장에서 술어 동사로 쓰인다.

> be, have, do, make, laugh, think, know, ...

The boys usually **play** basketball after school.

Annie **was** sick last night.

❋ to make, making과 같이 동사는 형태를 바꾸어 명사, 형용사, 부사로 쓰일 수 있다.

4 형용사: 사람과 사물의 성질이나 상태를 나타낸다. 명사를 꾸미거나 보어로 쓰여 명사를 설명해준다.

> many, deep, nice, new, cute, seven, first, ...

Mr. Jones is **kind and humorous**.

Shall We Dance is a very **interesting** movie.

❋ 형용사 상당어구: to 부정사(형용사적 용법), 현재분사, 과거분사, 형용사절, 전치사구

5 부사: 때, 장소, 원인, 방법 등을 나타낸다. 동사, 형용사, 부사, 문장 등을 꾸미는 수식어로 쓰인다.

> very, too, quickly, hard, differently, ...

She speaks **fast** and walks **fast**.

My mother told me to stay **here**.

❋ 부사 상당어구: to 부정사(부사적 용법), 분사구문, 부사절, 전치사구

6 전치사: 전치사 다음에는 명사 또는 명사 상당어구가 따라와야 하며 전치사+명사(명사 상당어구)가 하나의 구를 이루며 그 구는 형용사나 부사의 역할을 한다.

■ in, on, at, with, from, to, for, ...

They are **in the living room**. (부사의 역할)

The cup **on the table** is my sister's. (형용사의 역할)

7 접속사(등위 접속사, 종속 접속사): 단어와 단어, 어구와 어구, 문장과 문장을 연결한다.

■ and, but, or, because, when, if, as, ...

Paul likes rain, **but** Susan doesn't like it.

I always listen to the radio **when** I am at home.

8 감탄사: 감탄하는 기분을 나타낸다.

■ oh(놀람), alas(슬픔, 한탄), hurrah(기쁨), ...

Hurrah! My boy friend won the contest.

❋ 주요 품사의 쓰임

	주요 역할	보조 역할
명사	주어, 보어, 목적어	전치사의 목적어
동사	술어	·
형용사	보어	명사 수식
부사	·	동사, 형용사, 부사, 구, 절, 문장수식

❋ 단어와 품사 하나의 단어가 하나의 품사로만 쓰이지는 않는다.

→ I **walk** to school every day. (동사)

→ Taking a **walk** is one of my hobbies. (명사)

→ **This** is New York. (대명사)

→ **This** notebook computer is mine. (형용사)

Vocabulary

□ **mammal**: 포유동물   □ **contest**: 경기, 경연

A-1   밑줄 친 단어들의 품사를 쓰세요.

(1)   I went to the grocery store <u>then</u>.

(2)   Steve is the <u>tallest</u> man in the office.

(3)   We painted the wall <u>in</u> sky blue.

(4)   They did their best, <u>but</u> they lost the game.

(5)   Nancy was late for school <u>because</u> she missed the bus.

(6)   Let's have a <u>break</u> when we finish this.

(7)   She walked down the steps very <u>quietly</u>.

(8)   I like <u>her</u> beautiful brown eyes.

(9)   He is <u>so</u> kind and handsome.

(10) I feel <u>blue</u> when it rains.

A-2   알맞은 낱말에 동그라미 하세요.

(1)   The man is a very (fame, famous) actor.

(2)   She is very (kind, kindly).

(3)   I will (gift, give) her this ring.

(4)   Come here (quickness, quickly).

(5)   I want to be (health, healthy).

(6)   (Though, Despite) Annie was very sick, she came to school.

(7)   It has been raining (heavy, heavily).

(8)   The team has (won, winning) the Korean Series.

(9)   I like him (because, because of) his kindness.

(10) Marie and Pierre Curie (discovery, discovered) radium.

A-3 밑줄 친 단어를 바르게 고치세요.

(1) Diane studies very <u>hardly</u>.

(2) The cook prepares a <u>deliciousness</u> dinner.

(3) A dog is barking <u>loudness</u>.

(4) The moon is shining brightly <u>when</u> the sky.

(5) You should <u>obedience</u> your parents.

A-4 두 경우의 품사를 비교하세요.

(1) ① I don't **doubt** that he will win.

② There is some **doubt** whether it will snow.

(2) ① Today was a **long** day.

② Stay here as **long** as you want.

(3) ① She left at the **end** of October.

② How does the film **end**?

(4) ① Please **close** the window.

② My birthday is very **close**.

(5) ① Brown leaves are **falling** from the trees.

② Of all the four seasons, I like **fall** most.

Vocabulary

□ deliciousness: 맛있음   □ bark: 짖다   □ obedience: 복종

 문장 성분

1 주어(~은/는, ~이/가): 문장의 주체가 되는 말. 명사와 그 상당어구.

> **Corey** is a middle school student.
> **To take pictures** is my hobby.
> **Eating too much** is bad for health.
> **Whether he will come or not** is important.

2 동사(~다): 주어의 행동이나 주어의 상태를 나타내는 말.

> Boys **were playing** baseball there.
> I **know** the rules of the game.
> This **was written** by Mr. Anderson.

3 보어(동사와 함께: ~이다): 문법상 동사를 보충하고 의미상으로 주어나 목적어를 보충하는 말. 동사에 어구가 수반되어 그 어구가 없으면 동사가 불완전하게 되어 제 기능을 잃게 된다. (문법적으로 문장이 성립되지 않거나 전혀 다른 뜻이 된다.)

> I am **happy**.　　　→ 보이기 없으면: I am. (뜻이 통하지 않는다.)
> He made me **happy**.　→ 보어가 없으면: He made me. (말이 안 되거나 전혀 다른 뜻이 된다.)

보어가 될 수 있는 것은 명사와 그 상당어구, 형용사와 그 상당어구(형용사절 제외)이다.

- **명사가 보어인 경우**: She is a nice girl. (She = a nice girl)
- **형용사가 보어인 경우**: He made me happy. (happy는 me의 상태 표시)

	명사	형용사
주격보어	주어의 다른 표현 My mother is **a cook**. (my mother = a cook)	주어의 상태, 성질 표시 Melons are very **sweet**. (Melons ≒ sweet)
목적격 보어	목적어의 다른 표현 They called him '**one-eyed Jack**'. (him = one-eyed Jack)	목적어의 상태, 성질 표시 The man made me **angry**. (me ≒ angry)

4 목적어(~을, ~를): 동사의 행동의 대상이 되는 말. 직접목적어(~을/를), 간접목적어(~에게)

> Mrs. Johnson teaches **us history**.
> My sister sent **me this book**.

Vocabulary

□ **one-eyed**: 한쪽 눈의, 애꾸의

Check-Up

B-1   밑줄 친 부분의 각 문장 성분(주어, 동사, 보어, 목적어)을 쓰세요.

(1)   There is a tower on top of the mountain.

(2)   It is raining outside.

(3)   He gave me a pretty yellow flower.

(4)   What are you going to do this Christmas?

(5)   The food smells good.

(6)   I met the boy during my trip to London.

(7)   Who made this cream soup?

(8)   It is important to keep one's promise.

(9)   The computer enables us to do many things easily.

(10)   This is what I wanted.

B-2   알맞은 낱말이나 어구에 동그라미 하세요.

(1)   A lot of Japanese students (go, going) to school by bicycle.

(2)   My brother gave (me, mine) this CD.

(3)   The TV show was very (interest, interesting).

(4)   (Take, Taking) trips is my favorite hobby.

(5)   The woman is (a kind, a kindness) lady.

B-3   괄호 안에 알맞은 단어를 적어 빠진 성분을 보충하세요.

(1)   There (   ) no school on Saturday and Sunday.

(2)   He is so kind that I like (   ).

(3)   What beautiful scenery this (   )!

(4)   Did you (   ) your homework?

(5)   My only wish (   ) to meet him.

Vocabulary

□ **keep one's promise**: 약속을 지키다

 **구와 절**

1 **구:** 두 개 이상의 단어가 하나의 무리를 이루어 명사, 형용사, 부사 중 한 가지 품사 구실을 하되
주어와 동사가 들어있지 않은 어군. 구는 하나의 사고 단위(thought unit)를 형성한다.

❋ 구가 만들어지는 두 가지 방법과 구의 쓰임 세 가지

구분	형태	명사구	형용사구	부사구
전치사구	전치사＋(형용사)＋명사		○	○
준동사구	to 부정사＋α	명사적 용법	형용사적 용법	부사적 용법
	-ing＋α	동명사	현재분사	
	-ed＋α		과거분사	

1) **명사구:** (명사처럼) 주어, 보어, 목적어로 쓰임. to 부정사구, 동명사구.

Loving one another is important. (주어)

My only wish is **to live happily.** (보어)

I want **to drink some cool water.** (목적어)

2) **형용사구:** 명사를 꾸미거나 보어로 쓰임. to 부정사구, 분사구, 전치사구.

She is a person **of great ability.** (명사 수식)

This machine will be **of some use.** (주격 보어)

I want a magazine **to read on the train.** (명사 수식)

We are **to meet in front of the clock tower.** (주격 보어)

Look at the bird **singing in the tree.** (명사 수식)

Love is an emotion **experienced by the many** and **enjoyed by the few.** (명사 수식)

3) **부사구:** 동사, 부사(구), 문장 등을 꾸밈. to 부정사구, 전치사구.

We ate dinner **in an Italian restaurant.**

I went there **to meet Mr. Watson.**

2   **절:** 두 개 이상의 단어가 하나의 무리를 이루어 쓰이되 주어와 동사가 있는 어군. 특히 문장 안에서 명사, 형용사, 부사 중 한 가지 품사 구실을 하는 절을 종속절이라 한다.

✛ **종속절의 종류**

1) **명사절:** (명사처럼) 주어, 보어, 목적어로 쓰인다. 전치사의 목적어로 쓰이기도 한다.

What I want is some food.

The question is **whether it will be fine tomorrow or not.**

I believe **that he is innocent.**

2) **형용사절:** (형용사처럼) 명사를 수식한다.

This is the book **that he gave me as a present.**

That is the place **where we first met.**

2) **부사절:** (부사처럼) 문장을 수식하며 때, 이유, 조건, 양보, 상태 등을 나타낸다.

When I was young, I was slim.

She couldn't come **because she had a cold.**

If it is fine tomorrow, we will go to the zoo.

✳ **구와 (종속)절의 차이점과 공통점**

	구	(종속)절
차이점	주어와 술어동사가 없다.	주어와 술어동사가 있다.
	전치사와 준동사에 의해 이끌린다.	접속사, 관계사, 의문사에 의해 이끌린다.
공통점	두 개 이상의 낱말이 집합하여 쓰인다.	
	하나의 품사(명사, 형용사, 부사)의 역할을 한다.	

준동사(Verbals): to 부정사, 동명사, 분사

Vocabulary

□ **innocent**: 결백한, 무죄의   □ **slim**: 날씬한

✳ **문장이 시작되는 세 가지 기본 방식** (의문문인 경우에는 다양한 변경이 있음)

- 주어 (+ 수식어구) + 동사 + …

  명사, 대명사, 명사구, 명사절로 시작한다.

  The problem with all of his poems **is** that they are sentimental.

  → 주어에 걸리는 동사를 찾으며 문장을 읽어간다.

- 부사(구 · 절) + 주어 (+ 수식어구) + 동사 + …

  전치사, 접속사로 시작한다.

  Although our television was broken, **we** still **heard** the game on the radio.

  → 주어를 찾으며 문장을 읽어간다.

- 형용사(구) + 주어 + 동사 + …

  Never **afraid** of controversy, **McCarthy was known** for her irony and sharp wit.

  Having finished work, **I went** to the movies.

  Compared with New York, **Seattle is** not so big a city.

  * 한국에서는 위의 두 예문에서 밑줄 친 부분이 부사구(분사구문)로 인식되는 경우가 많은데, 대부분의 미국 문법학자들은 이 부분을 주어를 수식하는 형용사구로 분류하고 있다.

Check-Up

C-1 밑줄 친 구가 어떤 품사의 역할을 하는지 쓰세요. (명사구, 형용사구, 부사구)

(1) Austin is in Texas.

(2) To learn a foreign language is difficult but interesting.

(3) He came to America at the age of 11.

(4) I like listening to classical music.

(5) The man in black is my business partner.

(6) Playing computer games is a lot of fun.

(7) The meeting is to begin at 4 p.m.

(8) I have something to tell you.

(9) He didn't know what to do.

(10) She is learning French to study in France.

C-2   밑줄 친 절이 어떤 품사의 역할을 하는지 쓰세요. (명사절, 형용사절, 부사절)

(1)   She started ballet dancing <u>when she was seven years old</u>.

(2)   <u>Whether he will come or not</u> is not certain.

(3)   I hope <u>that it will snow on Christmas Eve</u>.

(4)   He is the man <u>who directed the movie</u> *Fancy Dance*.

(5)   <u>As it became dark</u>, we climbed down the mountain.

(6)   This is <u>what I wanted to have</u>.

(7)   <u>Though she is an American</u>, she speaks Korean very well.

(8)   1970 is the year <u>when I was born</u>.

(9)   I want to know <u>if it will be fine tomorrow</u>.

(10) She did <u>as her mother had told her</u>.

Chapter • 1

Vocabulary

□ **business partner**: 업무(사업), 동료, 협력자   □ **certain**: (be동사 뒤에서) 확실한   □ **direct**: (영화를) 감독하다

1   밑줄 친 단어의 품사와 역할(주어, 보어, 술어, 목적어, 수식어, 연결어)을 쓰세요.

(1) One day a <u>truck</u> hit a person.

(2) I saw a <u>pretty</u> blue bird flying.

(3) I played badminton <u>with</u> my father last Sunday.

(4) <u>Alas</u>! My dog ran out of the house and never came back.

(5) Ms. Lee is my teacher. <u>She</u> is kind to all students.

(6) Time <u>flies</u> like an arrow.

(7) I know <u>that</u> the Earth is round.

(8) Yesterday I got to school <u>late</u>.

2   다음 문장들을 보기와 같이 바꾸세요.

> 보기   She plays tennis well. → She is a <u>good tennis player</u>.

(1) He makes a box well. → He is a _____.

(2) You sing beautifully. → You are a _____.

(3) I run fast among the students in our school.

　　→ I am a _____ among the students in our school.

3   각 문장에서 밑줄 친 부분의 형태를 바꾸어 어법에 맞는 품사로 바꾸세요.

(1) He showed me a <u>differently</u> house.

(2) The <u>hunger</u> child is looking for food.

(3) Children can learn <u>easy</u> both in school and at home.

(4) His uncle <u>death</u> last year.

(5) Sara has a <u>meet</u> in the afternoon.

(6) <u>At</u> the guests arrived, we began the New Year's party.

(7) <u>Windy</u> is necessary to dry clothes.

Vocabulary

□ **arrow:** 화살   □ **get to ~:** ~에 가다, 도착하다   □ **look for ~:** ~를 찾다   □ **necessary:** 필요한

[4-7] 다음의 괄호 안에 들어갈 알맞은 단어를 보기 중에서 찾으세요.

4 My father (   ) the ball in the wrong direction.

(A) throwing　　　(B) to throw　　　(C) threw　　　(D) thrown

5 (   ) fell off the ladder.

(A) I　　　(B) me　　　(C) mine　　　(D) my

6 I believe (   ) you will come back home again.

(A) at　　　(B) that　　　(C) in　　　(D) by

7 (   ) my friend lied to me, I still like and trust him.

(A) Because　　　(B) Despite　　　(C) Because of　　　(D) Though

8 아래의 우리말에 맞게 주어진 영어 단어들을 배열하세요. (첫 단어는 반드시 대문자로 시작하세요.)

(1) 자전거를 타는 사람은 반드시 안전 규칙을 지켜야 한다.

　(should, bikers, rules, safety, follow)

→ _____ .

(2) 성공한다는 것이 반드시 부유하다는 것을 의미하는 것은 아니다.

　(successful, to be, always, does, to be, mean, not, rich)

→ _____ .

(3) 나는 내 친구가 내 셔츠를 빌려가도록 허락했다.

　(my, shirt, friend, I, to, allowed, my, borrow)

→ _____ .

Vocabulary

□ **fall off:** 떨어지다　　　　□ **ladder:** 사다리　　　　□ **biker:** 자전거 타는 사람 (bike: 자전거)

유형 1   형용사 – 명사 혼동

1 The greatness years of Hollywood were from 1918 to 1948.
         A   B   C   D

2 In every cultural, people eat certain kinds of food on special holidays.
             A   B   C   D

유형 2   형용사 – 부사 혼동

1 We can use road maps very easy.
         A   B   C   D

2 Las Vegas is the most famously city for gambling in the United States.
                 A   B   C   D

유형 3   동사 – 명사 혼동

1 The Statue of Liberty was a give from the people of France to the United States.
   A   B   C   D

유형 4   부사 – 명사 혼동

1 Almost everyone in the world wants to live peace.
    A   B   C   D

유형 5   전치사 – 접속사 혼동

1 Despite it has changed since 1970, the New York City Marathon is always
      A   B   C
   exciting.
     D

2 While his lifetime, Pasteur studied how germs cause diseases in animals
     A   B   C   D
   and people.

유형 6   주어 찾기

1 _____ is a funny drawing.

(A) Its   (B) For a cartoon

(C) A cartoon   (D) A cartoon has

2 _____ is one key to writing well.

(A) Write often   (B) Writing often

(C) Often write   (D) You often write

3 _____ would be safest to wear boots.

(A) It is   (B) It

(C) When it   (D) According to him

유형 7   동사 찾기

1 The hamburger _____ no connection to ham.

(A) to have   (B) having

(C) have   (D) has

2 Smoking _____ of developing lung cancer.

(A) increases   (B) increases and

(C) increases the risk   (D) the risk increases

1 When _____ sports for money, they are professional.

(A) play teams   (B) teams play

(C) teams that play   (D) teams playing

2 _____ usually very cold in New York in January.

(A) Its   (B) They are

(C) The weather   (D) It is

1 *Uncle Tom's Cabin* was _____ that helped change history.

(A) as the book   (B) a book

(C) a book of   (D) which book

2 Amelia Earhart's dream was _____ the world.

(A) flew around   (B) a flight

(C) to fly around   (D) she flew around

3 The music was really _____.

(A) beautiful   (B) beautifully

(C) beautify   (D) beauty

유형 10   보어와 목적보어 찾기

1 All living things contain _____ called carbon 14.

(A) are

(B) a substance

(C) a substance is

(D) that a substance

2 Today most scientists believe _____ .

(A) the moon from the Earth

(B) the moon to be the Earth

(C) because the moon formed from the Earth

(D) that the moon formed from the Earth

유형 11   문장 성분이 빠진 경우

1 Jesse Owens the star of the Ohio State track team.
　　　　　　 A 　　　　　 B C 　　　　　　 D

Vocabulary

□ **contain**: 지니고 있다　　　□ **carbon**: 탄소　　　□ **substance**: 물질　　　□ **track**: 트랙 경기(달리기, 허들 등)

1   Ants and butterflies _____ insects.

    (A) are   (B) is   (C) being   (D) be

2   You <u>should</u> know <u>that</u> <u>healthy</u> is more important <u>than money</u>.
             A   B   C   D

3   <u>As</u> I was <u>a stranger</u> in that city, I couldn't <u>find</u> the way <u>ease</u>.
       A   B   C   D

4   Poor old _____ ship disappeared in the middle of the sea.

    (A) Kingstone   (B) Kingstone is

    (C) Kingstone's   (D) Kingstone who

5   To know world history is partly _____ ourselves.

    (A) knowledge   (B) to know

    (C) known   (D) that know

6   <u>When</u> he finished <u>his</u> work, he <u>kind</u> helped me <u>with mine</u>.
        A   B   C   D

7   Rome is an Italian city, and it has _____.

    (A) of a mild climate   (B) that a mild climate

    (C) a mild climate is   (D) a mild climate

8   <u>While</u> the summer season, various <u>kinds</u> of birds <u>fly</u> to <u>our</u> country.
        A   B   C D

9 My doctor advised _____ in the hospital.

(A) that I am resting   (B) me to rest

(C) me rested   (D) whether I rest

10 I find many students _____ English now.

(A) has learned   (B) learned

(C) learning   (D) learns

11 The two <u>Koreas</u> should <u>become</u> one nation again <u>for</u> future <u>develop</u>.
              A   B   C   D

12 In America, <u>there a</u> holiday <u>in May</u> for mothers, and <u>it</u> <u>is called</u> Mother's Day.
                  A   B   C D

13 _____ won the Nobel Peace Prize in 1964.

(A) Martin Luther King Jr.   (B) If Martin Luther King Jr.

(C) Because Martin Luther King Jr.   (D) When Martin Luther King Jr.

14 I saw the <u>happiness</u> puppy <u>walk along</u> <u>the street</u> with <u>its</u> friend.
                 A   B   C   D

15 Huckleberry Finn, the hero of the famous novel, _____ with his family.

(A) not to live   (B) who doesn't live

(C) and doesn't live   (D) doesn't live

Vocabulary

□ **the Nobel Peace Prize:** 노벨 평화상   □ **along ~:** ~를 따라서   □ **hero:** (시·극·소설 등의) 주인공, 영웅

1 The body of the jellyfish looks like a bell or a umbrella.
        A   B   C   D

2 We should not allow children _____ in dangerous places.

(A) play   (B) to play   (C) played   (D) playful

3 Good stories teach a lot of values, and in many countries they are considered
              A   B

as gifts of wise.
C   D

4 Inertia is a name for the way things behave when they are stopped and when
            A   B   C

they are move.
     D

5 Brian must have a cold, for he has a nose red and has been coughing.
        A   B   C   D

6 There _____ a real William Tell, but he was also possibly
a legendary hero.

(A) have been   (B) may have been

(C) to be   (D) be

7 Patrick Henry spoke against the Stamp Act, a British law that it forced
                A   B   C

Americans to pay taxes on newspapers.
        D

8 _____ Sam and Jane try to get along, they are different in many ways.

(A) Although　　　(B) If　　　　　(C) Despite　　　(D) Because

9 Many cultures have their own legends _____ the appearance of humans on earth.

(A) that explain　　(B) explain　　　(C) explain that　　(D) to explain that

10 Agriculture is one of <u>the world's</u> most <u>important industry</u> because everyone
　　　　　　　　　　　　　A　　　　　　　　B
<u>depends upon</u> plants <u>for food</u>.
　　　C　　　　　　　D

11 A veto is the right of an <u>executive</u> to forbid or withhold <u>his</u> assent to <u>act</u>
　　　　　　　　　　　　　　A　　　　　　　　　　　B　　　　　　C
passed by <u>a lawmaking</u> body.
　　　　　D

12 _____ no forces except gravity were at work, the world's water would settle into the ocean basins and remain there.

(A) When　　　　(B) There are　　　(C) Despite　　　(D) If

Vocabulary

□ jellyfish: 해파리	□ look like ~: ~처럼 보이다	□ value: 가치
□ be considered as ~: ~라 여겨지다	□ inertia: 관성, 타성	□ behave: 행동하다, 움직이다, 반응을 나타내다
□ have a cold: 감기 걸리다	□ have a red nose: (코를 많이 풀어서) 코가 빨갛다	
□ cough: 기침하다	□ possibly: 아마, 어쩌면	□ legendary: 전설의
□ force: 강요하다	□ get along: 사이좋게 지내다	□ legend: 전설
□ appearance: 출현, 등장	□ agriculture: 농업	□ industry: 산업
□ depend on[upon] ~: ~에 의존하다	□ plant: 식물	□ executive: 행정부
□ withhold: (허락하지) 않고 두다	□ assent: 동의	□ gravity: 중력　　□ basin: 웅덩이

STRUCTURE

CHAPTER 2

명사와 관사

Grammar Up / Power Up Test / Pattern Drill / Pattern Review / Mini Test

A 셀 수 있는 명사와 셀 수 없는 명사

1 **셀 수 있는 명사:** 복수형이 가능하고 단수인 경우 부정관사 a, an이 붙을 수 있다.

1) 보통명사

boy, girl, dog, apple, star, book, train, pencil 등

2) 셀 수 있는 집합명사

family, class, crowd 등

※ 집합명사와 군집명사: 많은 수의 사람이나 동물을 뜻하는 다음과 같은 명사는 <u>집합명사</u>로 여겨 일반적으로 단수 취급한다. 그러나 그 집단의 구성원을 개별적인 것으로 볼 때는 <u>군집명사</u>로 간주하여 복수 취급한다. family, class, crowd등이 이에 해당한다.

ex) **His class is** large. / **All the class are** diligent.

3) 셀 수 있는 추상명사

■ 측정의 단위: meter, gram, inch, pound, degree(도) 등

■ 돈의 단위: dollar, penny 등

■ 구체화될 수 있는 개념: idea, plan 등

2 **셀 수 없는 명사:** 복수형이 불가능하고, 부정관사 a, an이 붙을 수 없다.

1) 고유명사: 세상에 하나뿐이므로 셀 수 없다.

Tom, Mary, Mr. Anderson, the White House, Kimpo Airport 등

2) 물질명사: 모양이 자연적/인위적으로 바뀔 수 있는 물질

■ 음식물: bread, meat, butter, biscuit 등

■ 자연의 물질: water, ice, smoke, oxygen(산소), grass 등

■ 액체: milk, tea, coffee, juice, oil, ink 등

■ 기타: hair, wood, iron, glass, sand 등

3) 셀 수 없는 집합명사

money, fruit, clothing(의류), furniture(가구), traffic(교통) 등

4) 추상명사

■ 추상적인 개념: time, work, beauty, news, information, health, knowledge 등

■ 언어, 학문: English, Korean, literature, mathematics, history 등

■ 여가, 운동: baseball, football, walking, driving, shopping, traveling 등

■ 자연 현상: weather, rain, snow, wind, light, sunshine 등

Check-Up

A-1 밑줄 친 단어 중 셀 수 있는 명사에는 C, 셀 수 없는 명사에는 U를 쓰세요.

(1) She has lots of <u>work</u> to do.

(2) How much <u>money</u> do you have?　I have only one <u>dollar</u>.

(3) I like <u>fruit</u>, but my husband doesn't.

(4) This <u>desk</u> is made of <u>wood</u>.

(5) Do you have <u>time</u>?　Yes, maybe about an <u>hour</u>.

(6) What kind of <u>sports</u> do you like?　I like <u>baseball</u> and basketball.

(7) She can speak four <u>languages</u>.　They are <u>Korean</u>, English, French, and Japanese.

(8) We have much <u>snow</u> in this province.

(9) Have you done your <u>homework</u>?

(10) You know, I have a wonderful <u>idea</u>.

A-2 다음 문장에서 틀린 부분을 바르게 고치세요.

(1) There are some rose in the vase.

(2) All our family gets up early.

(3) We eat too many butter.

(4) I don't have times to talk with you.

(5) Mr. Wilson wrote a lot of poem.

(6) Kelly is one of the tallest girl in the school.

(7) He has few friend.

(8) They bought new furnitures for their new house.

┤ 혼동하기 쉬운 셀 수 있는 명사(Countable Noun), 셀 수 없는 명사(Uncountable Noun) ├

• CN: hour	dollar	jewel	poem	fact
• UN: time	money	jewelry	poetry	knowledge

Vocabulary

☐ **language**: 언어　　　☐ **poem**: (한 편의) 시　　　☐ **furniture**: 가구　　　☐ **province**: 지방

33

B 셀 수 없는 명사를 세는 방법

1 셀 수 없는 명사는 자체로는 셀 수 없으므로 단위를 이용하여 양을 표시한다.

- 추상적인 개념: a piece of advice/ news / information
- 조각: a piece of bread / paper / cake / toast / meat
- 쪽: a slice of bread / cheese
- (종이) 장: a sheet of paper
- 덩어리: a loaf of bread / meat
- 병: a bottle of milk / juice / wine / ink
- 단지: a jar of jam
- 종이 팩: a carton of milk
- 튜브: a tube of toothpaste
- (비누) 덩어리: a cake / bar of soap

Check-Up

B-1 괄호 안에 알맞은 단어를 쓰세요.

(1) I ordered four (   ) of coffee.

(2) My sister gave me a good (   ) of advice.

(3) I need several (   ) of paper to print it on. 「프린트할 종이가 몇 장 필요합니다.」

(4) I ate several (   ) of bread for lunch. 「점심에 빵 몇 조각을 먹었다.」

(5) He took a (   ) of wine to the party. 「그는 파티에 와인 한 병을 가져갔다.」

B-2 주어진 낱말을 알맞게 배열하여 문장을 만드세요.

(1) of, me, give, a, coffee, cup.

→ _____.

(2) a, eat, we, of, bread, for, loaf, lunch.

→ _____.

(3) will, I, piece, news, tell, a, surprising, you, of.

→ _____.

Vocabulary

□ **advice**: 충고   □ **information**: 정보   □ **toothpaste**: 치약   □ **soap**: 비누   □ **order**: 주문하다

명사의 수

1 항상 복수로 쓰이는 명사

1) 짝을 이루어 쓰이는 낱말

glasses(안경), socks, shoes, pants, gloves, scissors(가위) 등

※ a pair of ~, two pairs of ~ 등을 이용하여 센다.

2) 관습적으로 복수로 쓰이는 낱말

clothes(옷), arms(무기), contents(목차), outskirts(변두리, 교외) 등

2 형태는 복수이지만 단수 취급하는 명사

1) 학문

mathematics, politics, economics, physics 등

2) 복수 나라이름/연방국이름

the United States, the Netherlands, the Philippines 등

3) 놀이

billiards(당구), darts(화살 던지기 놀이) 등

3 명사가 복합 형용사(Compound Adjectives)의 한 부분으로 사용되는 경우: 단수로 쓴다.

My office is in a **ten-story** building.

She has a **five-year-old** son.

※ 'five-year-old'는 복합 형용사로서 son을 수식하고 있다. 복합 형용사는 복수의 의미가 있는 수 형용사를 포함하고 있어도 뒤의 명사는 단수를 써야 한다. 복합 형용사의 단어들 사이에 −(하이픈)을 쓴다.

cf) Her son is **five years old**.

4 명사의 복수형

history class → history class**es**   woman writer → **women** writer**s**

grown-up → grown-up**s**   passer-by → passer**s**-by,

※ 두 단어 이상이 (하이픈을 이용하여) 하나의 명사로 사용되는 경우에는 마지막 단어를 복수형으로, 또는 중요한 단어를 복수형으로 하거나 모두 복수형으로 바꾸기도 한다.

5 명사와 수량 형용사

수 (셀 수 있는 명사 앞)		양 (셀 수 없는 명사 앞)	두 경우 모두
셀 수 있는 명사의 단수형 앞	셀 수 있는 명사의 복수형 앞		
each every	few (거의 없는) a few (몇몇의) a couple of (두 개의) several (몇몇의) many a number of (= a lot of) various (여러 개의) a dozen of (12개의) a score of (20개의) hundreds of (수백 개의) thousands of (수천 개의)	little (거의 없는) a little (약간의) much a great deal of (많은 양의) a large amount of (많은 양의)	some any most (대부분의) a lot of (= lots of) all no (아무도, 어느 것도 ~아닌)

Check-Up

C-1 다음 중 틀린 문장을 골라 바르게 고치세요.

(1) She asked me several question.

(2) They showed me various sample.

(3) Each persons has a name.

(4) I bought a pair of shoe.

(5) There are a lot of cars in the streets of New York.

(6) Billiards are my favorite pastime.

(7) Hundreds of bird were flying in the sky.

(8) We have a fourteen-years-old daughter.

(9) She is one of the best dancer in the country.

(10) Tommy has few hobby.

C-2 알맞은 단어에 동그라미 하세요.

(1) I have (a little, a few) friends in the United States.

(2) There are few (book, books) in his room.

(3) I saw a large (number, amount) of horses.

(4) (Thousand, Thousands) of people came to the beach.

(5) All the students (was, were) silent.

명사의 복수형

1 규칙변화

1) -s

- [f, k, p, t, θ] 발음 뒤의 s는 [s] 발음: books, cups, cats, months, handkerchiefs(손수건) 등
- 나머지는 [z] 발음: dogs, boys, things, pens 등

2) s, x, ch, sh로 끝나면 → -es

buses, boxes, benches, dishes 등

3) 자음+y → -ies

baby → babies   lady → ladies   city → cities   story → stories 등

cf) 모음 + y → -s: boys, days, toys 등

4) 자음+o → -oes

potatoes, tomatoes, echoes 등

❋ 예외: pianos, radios, zoos, studios 등

5) -f(e) → -ves

leaf → leaves   life → lives   wife → wives   knife → knives   wolf → wolves 등

❋ 예외: roofs(지붕), chiefs(장, 우두머리), beliefs(신조), cliffs(절벽), safes(금고) 등

6) 복합명사의 복수형

- 명사가 있을 때 : 주요 명사를 복수로 만든다.

lookers-on(방관자), passers-by(지나가는 사람), mothers-in-law(장모, 시어머니) 등

- 명사가 없을 때 : 단어의 끝에 s를 붙인다.

grown-ups(성인), forget-me-nots(물망초), merry-go-rounds(회전목마) 등

2 불규칙변화

1) 어미변화

child → children   ox → oxen 등

2) 모음변화

man → men   woman → women   foot → feet   tooth → teeth   goose → geese 등

3) 외래어의 복수형

datum → data   oasis → oases   stimulus(자극) → stimuli

phenomenon(현상) → phenomena 등

3 단수 복수 형태가 같은 명사

fish, sheep, means(수단), species(종 ; 種), series, deer(사슴), salmon(연어) 등

D-1   다음 명사들의 복수형을 쓰세요.

(1) foot   (11) woman

(2) taxi   (12) month

(3) tomato   (13) datum

(4) video   (14) story

(5) fish   (15) father-in-law

(6) cow   (16) thesis

(7) bench   (17) roof

(8) lady   (18) photo

(9) leaf   (19) house

(10) merry-go-round   (20) phenomenon

D-2   다음 중 틀린 문장을 골라 바르게 고치세요.

(1) I should wash the dishs after dinner.

(2) There is a childrens' park near the station.

(3) There are a lot of passer-bys in this street.

(4) She likes to read short storys.

(5) He is five foots tall.

 **명사의 소유격**

1 생물 + 's

my best **friend's** wedding, **Billy's** car, the **lady's** shoes, my **dog's** house

❋ s로 끝나는 단어: '만 붙인다

  a **girls'** middle school, the **students'** books

2 무생물

1) of + 무생물

  the door of the room, the cover of the book

2) 시간, 거리, 가격, 무게: 's

  today's newspaper, an hour's walk

  ten thousand miles' journey

  one hundred dollars' profit

  ten pounds' weight of salt

Check-Up

E 다음 밑줄친 부분을 바르게 고치세요.

(1) I painted my room's wall in blue.
         _____

(2) She bought sugar of two pounds.
                   _____

(3) The store is walk of thirty minutes from here.
              _____

(4) These are girls's shoes.
             _____

(5) David is looking for newspaper of yesterday.
                   _____

❋ **관사의 기본 의미**

• 관사는 명사에 생명력을 불어 넣는다. 예를 들어, 'apple'은 '사과'라는 단어에 불과하며,
'an apple'은 '먹을 수 있는 사과'라는 의미를 지니게 된다. 관사의 사용에 무관심할 수 있겠는가?

Vocabulary

□ **journey**: 여행   □ **profit**: 이익   □ **weight**: 무게

F 부정관사 a, an의용법

1	셀 수 있는 명사의 단수 앞. (특히 '하나의' 라고 해석할 필요 없음)
2	하나의
3	어떤
4	~ 마다
5	같은
6	종족 전체
7	관습적인 쓰임들

Jenny is **a girl**.

A day has twenty-four hours.

A man came to see you.

We work eight hours **a day**.

Albert and I are of **an age**.

A dog(= The dog) is the most popular pet.

as **a** rule(대체로), in **a** hurry(허둥지둥, 급히), make it **a** rule to ~ (~를 규칙으로 삼다) 등

※ a와 an: 뒤에 오는 단어의 첫 '발음' 에 따라 결정된다.

• a + 자음 발음: 빌음기호 [j]과 [w]는 자음으로 취급된다.

one, useful, university, universal(전세계의), unique(독특한), year, yellow, young, European, usual(보통의, 평상시의) 등

• an + 모음 발음: hour, honest, heir(상속인), X-ray 등

Check-Up

F-1 다음 문장을 해석하세요.

(1) We eat three meals a day.

(2) These two boxes are of a size.

(3) A Miss Jackson is waiting for you.

(4) Give me a glass of cold water.

(5) How many movies do you see in a month?

F-2 괄호 안에 a 또는 an을 넣으세요.

(1) She is (　　) honest girl.

(2) This is (　　) useful thing.

(3) There are 24 hours in (　　) day.

(4) He wears (　　) uniform.

(5) I want to go to (　　) university.

(6) Have you ever been to (　　) European city?

(7) English is (　　) universal language.

(8) There are twelve months in (　　) year.

G 정관사 the의 용법

1 앞에 한번 나왔던 명사가 다시 나왔을 때
2 서로 알고 있는 대상
3 뒤에서 수식 받고 있는 명사
4 최상급 형용사 앞
5 서수 앞
6 이 세상에서 유일한 것
7 단위 앞
8 종족 전체
9 관습적인 쓰임들

I bought a pen yesterday. **The pen** is very good.

He is waiting for you at **the gate**.

The food on the table is for you.

She is **the tallest** girl in our class.

January is **the first** month of the year.

The sun rises in the east and sets in the west.

They rent the bicycle by **the hour**.

The giraffe(= A giraffe) has a long neck.

in **the** morning/afternoon/evening, in **the** past/future

be in **the** right(옳다) / wrong(그르다)

in **the** dark, in **the** country, in **the** center(중앙에) / front(앞에) / back(뒤에) of 등

 고유명사와 정관사

1) 정관사를 붙이는 경우
→ 복수형 고유명사: the Himalayas(산맥), the West Indies(군도), the Netherlands(국가), the Koreans(국민), the Lennons(레논 씨 가족, 부부)
→ 공공건물: the British Museum(영국 박물관)
→ 강, 바다, 운하: the Thames(템즈강), the Pacific(태평양), the Panama Canal(파나마 운하)
→ 반도, 사막, 해협: the Iberian Peninsula(이베리아 반도), the Sahara Desert(사하라 사막), the English Channel(영국 해협)
→ 열차, 배: the Orient Express(오리엔트 특급 열차), the Titanic(타이타닉 호)

2) 정관사를 붙이지 않는 경우
→ 역, 공원, 공항, 대학, 호수, 만, 항구 등: London Station, Central Park, J.F.K. Airport, Boston University, New York Harbor

G-1 괄호 안에 **a, an, the** 중에서 알맞은 것을 넣으세요.

(1) Jackie is ( ) second daughter.

(2) He works 10 hours ( ) day.

(3) This is ( ) postcard that she sent me from Paris.

(4) The hero was killed in ( ) end.

(5) She will be somebody in ( ) future.

(6) Which is ( ) shortest way to the post office?

(7) I want ( ) paper bag to carry these books.

(8) Could you please open ( ) window?

(9) ( ) month has 30 or 31 days.

(10) ( ) doll is made in China.

G-2 다음 중 관사가 잘못 쓰인 것을 골라 바르게 고치세요.

(1) This is an oldest tower In Korea.

(2) They sell candy by a pound at the store.

(3) The boys were in the hurry.

(4) He studied law at the Harvard University.

(5) She keeps a dog. A dog is a four-year-old Maltese.

G-3 필요한 곳에 정관사 **the**를 넣으세요.

(1) The students visited ( ) Korean National Folk Museum.

(2) Sandy will meet him at ( ) Heathrow Airport.

(3) This is ( ) same watch that I lost.

(4) ( ) Pacific Ocean is the largest ocean in the world.

(5) I want to go to ( ) Netherlands to see windmills.

┤ play + the + 악기이름 / play + 운동이름 ├

• John is **playing the** cello.

• Mee-Hyun Kim **plays golf** well.

Vocabulary

□ **keep a dog**: 개를 기르다　　□ **Maltese**: 몰티즈(개의 일종)　　□ **Heathrow Airport**: (런던의) 히드로우 공항　　□ **windmill**: 풍차

H 관사의 생략

1 건물, 기구가 본래의 목적으로 쓰일 때
2 신분이나 관직을 나타내는 말이 보어로 쓰일 때
3 by + 교통, 통신 수단
4 운동, 식사, 계절
5 짝을 이뤄 쓰이는 말
6 소유격 대명사가 쓰일 때

We **go to school** 5 days a week.   She **is in hospital**.   I usually **go to bed** at midnight.

She is **mayor** of this city.   They elected him **chairman**.

I go to school **by bus**.   cf) in a bus, in a train   She sent the letter **by airmail**.

They are **playing baseball**.   We **ate lunch** at 12 p.m.   I like **winter**.

day and night, hand in hand(손을 잡고), right and left, day by day(나날이),

step by step(단계적으로), side by side(나란히), from morning till night

Nancy is **my friend**. (a my friend: ×) He is **my first love**. (the my first love: ×)

❊ 관사와 소유격은 함께 쓸 수 없기 때문에 관사 a, an을 쓰려면 이중 소유격을 이용한다.

• 이중 소유격 (of): a(an), this, that, some, any, no 등을 소유격과 함께 쓸 때
  [a(this, some, ...) + 명사 + of + 소유대명사 / 명사소유격]으로 쓰는 것.
  Tommy is **a friend of mine**.   I'll borrow **this book of Jane's**.

Check-Up

H 다음 중 필요한 곳엔 괄호 안에 알맞은 관사를 넣고 필요 없는 곳엔 X표를 하세요.

(1) What time did you go to (   ) bed last night?

(2) I went there by (   ) ship.

(3) There is (   ) church on the hill.

(4) Mr. Baker was elected (   ) chairman of the committee.

(5) They will go to London in (   ) airplane.

(6) We were at (   ) table when he came home. (식사 중이었다)

(7) I usually play (   ) basketball on weekends.

Vocabulary

□ **mayor**: 시장   □ **chairman**: 의장   □ **committee**: 위원회

Ⅰ 관사의 위치

1 원칙: 관사＋부사＋형용사＋명사

This is **a very funny movie**.

2
such ⎫
quite ⎬ ＋ a/an ＋ 형 ＋ 명
what ⎭

I have never seen **such** a tall man.
She is **quite a** good girl.
What a beautiful day it is!

3
so ⎫
too ⎬ ＋ 형 ＋ a/an ＋ 명
how ⎭

He is **so kind a** man.
That is **too heavy a** bag for me to carry.
How beautiful a day it is!

4
all ⎫
both ⎬ ＋ the ＋ 명
half ⎭

All the students will take part in the contest.
I have met **both the sisters**.
I haven't read **half the book**.

Check-Up

I-1 다음 문장에서 알맞은 자리에 필요한 관사를 넣으세요.

(1) I want to buy small bag.

(2) It is too good chance to lose.

(3) Did you buy book that I told you about?

(4) What small car it is!

(5) Kevin is quite good student.

I-2 다음 중 틀린 문장을 골라 바르게 고치세요.

(1) This is very a useful machine.

(2) What a pretty flower it is!

(3) He is so a nice man that I like him so much.

(4) The all boys play football after school.

(5) I have never seen a such funny guy.

Chapter • 2

1 다음 문장들을 보기와 같이 바꾸세요.

> 보기 I have one child. → You have two children.

(1) I met one man in the park.

→ You met two _____ in the park.

(2) I have one rotten tooth.

→ You have two rotten _____ .

(3) I caught one fish in this lake.

→ You caught two _____ in this lake.

(4) I saw one mouse in the kitchen.

→ You saw two _____ in the kitchen.

(5) The police officer met a couple: a wife and her husband.

→ The police officer met two couples: two _____ and their husbands.

2 다음 빈칸에 들어갈 말을 보기에서 찾아 쓰세요. (한 단어를 두 번 이상 선택할 수 있습니다.)

> 보기 a few   a little   a piece   a glass

(1) I need _____ water to wash my hands.

(2) She bought me _____ of furniture.

(3) I saw _____ cats near my house.

(4) I drink _____ of milk before I go to bed.

(5) I feel like listening to _____ music tonight.

(6) We sang _____ songs at the party.

(7) I haven't finished my work. I need _____ more time.

3 다음 제시된 각각의 두 문장을 비교해 보고 관사가 쓰인 이유를 설명하세요.

(1) Money means everything to him.

→ The money in my purse is only 5 dollars.

Vocabulary

☐ **rotten**: 썩은   ☐ **police officer**: 경찰관

(2) My favorite writer is <u>Herman Melville</u>.

    → I'm reading <u>a Herman Melville</u> now.

(3) Soldiers think <u>courage</u> is most important.

    → I was surprised at <u>the courage</u> of the soldier.

[4-6] 다음 중 밑줄 친 부분이 어법상 올바른 문장을 고르세요.

4
(A) <u>Mathematics are</u> my favorite subject.

(B) I have <u>several friend</u> in U.S.

(C) <u>Your new pants look</u> so good.

(D) <u>Five peoples were hurt</u> in the traffic accident.

5
(A) <u>The camel</u> can be seen in the desert.

(B) <u>Sun</u> is always shining above us in the sky.

(C) <u>The happiness</u> is in your mind.

(D) I like playing <u>piano</u> in the afternoon.

6
(A) I was invited to the <u>Jane birthday party</u>.

(B) <u>A my teacher</u> lives here.

(C) She is <u>a fastest runner</u> in our school.

(D) <u>The water in this glass</u> tastes good.

7 주어진 문장을 우리말로 해석하세요.

(1) There were a dozen pieces of mail for me in my mailbox today.

→ _____.

(2) A one-dollar bill has the picture of the president of the United States. It is the picture of George Washington.

→ _____.

Vocabulary

□ **courage**: 용기   □ **be hurt**: 다치다   □ **traffic accident**: 교통사고

□ **camel**: 낙타   □ **taste ~**: 맛이 ~하다

유형 12   명사의 수가 잘못된 경우

1 A dozen is <u>a</u> group <u>of</u> 12, so twelve <u>egg</u> are <u>a dozen</u> eggs.
              A   B   C   D

2 There <u>are</u> 12 a.m. <u>hours</u> and 12 p.m. hours <u>in</u> each <u>days</u>.
           A   B   C   D

유형 13   명사의 복수형이 잘못된 경우

1 Henry Ford <u>built</u> <u>a</u> car <u>with</u> bicycle <u>wheeles</u>.
                A B   C   D

2 The role of <u>womens</u> <u>is</u> <u>changing</u> in many <u>parts</u> of the world.
                  A   B   C   D

유형 14   필요한 관사가 빠진 경우

1 A group <u>of</u> people <u>that</u> play together <u>is</u> <u>team</u>.
              A   B   C D

2 <u>First</u> movie studio <u>was</u> <u>built</u> in Hollywood <u>in</u> 1918.
       A   B C   D

유형 15   불필요한 관사가 쓰인 경우

1 People <u>who</u> <u>write</u> history <u>are called</u> <u>a historians</u>.
               A   B   C   D

2 Levi Strauss <u>made</u> his <u>the first</u> jeans <u>from</u> <u>canvas</u> for tents.
                   A   B   C D

유형 16   관사를 잘못 쓴 경우

1 A person <u>that</u> <u>is</u> not a <u>child</u> is <u>a</u> adult.
               A B   C   D

2 John Adams <u>was</u> <u>the first</u> president <u>to live</u> in <u>a</u> White House.
               A   B   C   D

1   Inside its red mouth is rows of teeth.
    A   B C   D

2   Phil sings his favorite sings in the shower.
     A   B C D

3   A person who grows food is called a farm.
 A   B   C   D

4   It will be a last chance for you to win the MVP title.
   A   B   C   D

5   In the 1800s, there were several million wild horse in North America.
    A   B   C   D

6   In autumn, the streets are covered with fallen leafs.
 A   B   C   D

7   Milk that we bought yesterday may have gone bad, so you'd better not drink it.
 A   B   C   D

8   *Dooly* is one of my favorite movie, and I have seen it five times.
       A   B   C   D

9   Best way to lose weight is to eat and exercise regularly.
  A   B   C   D

10 A doctor asks a patient a lot of question and finds out her/his disease.
    A   B   C   D

11 I usually have a breakfast at 8 o'clock in the morning.
  A   B C   D

12 My child has two bright eye and she always smiles brightly.
    A   B   C   D

13 Teachers help each students to do his/her best in his/her studies.
     A   B   C   D

1   The English author Lewis Carroll introduced the strange and
              A   B

     interest world to a girl named Alice.
       C   D

2   Grammar is _____ language, and should be connected with
spelling and composition.

(A) a part only of   (B) of only a part

(C) a part of only   (D) only a part of

3   Writing and reading are for everybody, so everyone have to use
                             A   B   C

     the same rules in writing and reading.
       D

4   Anne Frank wrote a famous autobiography _____ she hid from
enemies during wartime.

(A) which   (B) when   (C) during   (D) whose

5   Tomorrow is my sister's birthday, but I cannot figure out what give her.
            A   B   C   D

6   Gandhi _____ a movement of nonviolent resistance to British rule
in 1918.

(A) began   (B) who began

(C) he began   (D) beginning

7 In winter, Seoul's temperature falls to -10℃ at the night.
　　　A　　　　B　　　　　　　　C　　　　　D

8 _____, an African-American man, wrote a book about his own life.

(A) If Frederick Douglass　　　(B) Frederick Douglass

(C) Frederick Douglass who　　(D) Frederick Douglass and

9 The bigger of all nine planets in the solar system is Jupiter.
　　　　A　　　　　　　B　　　　　C　　　　D

10 People have tried to make strange machines what will run
　　　　　　　　　　　A　　　　　　B　　　C

themselves.
　　D

11 Locating in the picturesque Kaministikwia River valley, Thunder
　　　A　　　　　　B

Bay is surrounded by forests, lakes, and streams that offer
　　　　　　　　　　　　　　　　　　　　　　　　　C

abundant hunting and fishing.
　　　D

12 The great predators of the Silurian period were the scorpion like eurypterids,

_____ were more than three feet long.

(A) which some　　　　　(B) some of whom

(C) some　　　　　　　　(D) some of which

Vocabulary

□ author: 작가　　　　□ grammar: 문법　　　　□ be connected with ~: ~와 관계가 있다

□ composition: 구성, 조직　□ autobiography: 자서전　　□ hid: hide(숨기다)의 과거　　□ enemy: 적

□ figure out: 생각해내다, 이해하다　　　　□ nonviolent: 비폭력의　　□ resistance: 저항

□ temperature: 기온　　□ Jupiter: 목성　　　　□ picturesque: 그림과 같은　　□ abundant: 풍부한

□ predator: 육식 동물, 포식자, 약탈자

※ scorpion, eurypterids와 같이 모르는 단어가 나올 때 문장의 구조 분석을 통하여 문제를 해결하는 연습도 매우 중요하다.

STRUCTURE

CHAPTER 3

대명사

Grammar Up / Power Up Test / Pattern Drill / Pattern Review / Mini Test

Grammar Up

Power Up Test   Pattern Drill   Pattern Review   Mini Test

 A 사람을 가리키는 인칭대명사

1 인칭대명사의 격변화

	수	주격	소유격	목적격	소유대명사	재귀대명사
1인칭	단	I	my	me	mine	myself
	복	we	our	us	ours	ourselves
2인칭	단	you	your	you	yours	yourself
	복	you	your	you	yours	yourselves
3인칭 단 여성		she	her	her	hers	herself
남성		he	his	him	his	himself
중성		it	its*	it		itself
복		they	their	them	theirs	themselves

※ 소유격 its를 '주격+be동사'인 it's와 혼동하지 않도록 한다.

2 소유의 의미 + 대명사 = 소유대명사: '~의 것'으로 해석되며, '대명사의 소유격 + 명사'를 줄인 형태로 볼 수 있다.

■ mine, yours, his, hers, ours, theirs

This is his bag, and that is **mine**(= my bag).

Is this floppy disk **yours**(= your floppy disk)?

3 it의 특별 용법(it은 해석하지 않는다)

1) 비인칭 주어: 날씨, 날짜, 요일, 시간, 계절, 거리, 밝기 등을 나타내는 it

It is snowing in Seoul.

What day is **it** today?   It is Friday.

What time is **it**?   It is half past twelve. (12시 30분이다.)

It is a hundred miles to the next gas station.

2) 가주어, 가목적어

It is good to travel a lot when we are young. (진주어: to travel a lot)

(= To travel a lot when we are young is good.)

I found **it** easy to make a sandwich. (진목적어: to make a sandwich)

(= I found to make a sandwich easy: 샌드위치 만드는 게 쉽다는 걸 알았다.)

※ 가목적어 it은 5형식에서 명사절, 부정사구, 동명사구가 긴 경우 이를 대신한다.

Vocabulary

☐ **floppy disk**: 플로피 디스크, 디스켓(diskette)   ☐ **gas station**: 주유소

3) It is ~ that 강조구문

It was Sally **that(who)** sent me this card.

It was in London **that(where)** Sue met him.

※ 강조되는 대상이 사람일 때는 who/whom, 시간일 때는 when, 장소일 때는 where로 바꿔 쓸 수 있다.

4) It takes time to 부정사: ~하는 데 시간이 ~ 걸리다

It takes about 20 minutes **to walk** to school.

It takes two hours **to go** to Tokyo by plane.

4 행동이 자신에게 돌아가는 재귀대명사

■ myself, yourself, herself, himself, itself, ourselves, yourselves, themselves

1) 재귀적 용법: 주어의 행동의 대상(목적어)이 주어 자신일 경우.   → 생략 불가능

2) 강조적 용법: 주어나 목적어를 강조하기 위해 씀.   → 생략 가능

3) 관용적 용법: 재귀대명사가 전치사의 목적어로 관용적 의미를 가짐.   → 생략 불가능

Kevin looked at **himself** in the mirror.
You should love **yourself** first.

You have to tell her about it (**yourself**). ← 생략 가능
The job (**itself**) is not bad, but the salary is poor. ← 생략 가능

Nina was taking a walk **by herself**. (= alone: 혼자서)
Cindy **overworked herself** and got sick. (과로하다)

cf) oversleep(늦잠자다), overeat(과식하다)은 재귀대명사를 써도 되고 쓰지 않아도 된다.

Money is not important **in itself**. (그 자체로)
Between ourselves, I don't like the man. (우리끼리 얘긴데)

Check-Up

A-1 알맞은 낱말에 동그라미 하세요.

(1) The man asked (me, my) name.

(2) Did she go out with (she, her) husband?

(3) People came to the party with (his, their) family.

(4) Every rose has (its, it's) thorn.

(5) Where does (he, his) live?

A-2 대명사가 잘못 쓰인 것을 골라 바르게 고치세요.

(1) Andrew went there with him brother.

(2) Every girl got their uniforms and books.

(3) I don't know what her name is.

(4) Do that to I one more time.

(5) She made hers daughter a doll.

A-3 틀린 문장을 골라 옳게 고치세요.

(1) These are hers shoes and those are mine.

(2) Have you finished your homework?

(3) *Casablanca* is my favorite movie. What is your?

(4) The house with a red roof is ours house.

(5) The poet spent the vacation in hers hometown.

A-4 괄호 안에 알맞은 말을 넣으세요.

(1) What's the date today? ( ) is November 7th.

(2) ( ) is very cold in Beijing in winter.

(3) Is ( ) possible to get there in an hour?

(4) It took about 30 minutes ( ) go there by bus.

(5) ( ) was in 1998 that I first met him.

A-5 두 문장의 뜻이 같도록 빈칸에 알맞은 낱말들을 넣으세요.

(1) To exercise regularly is good for health.

= It _____ .

(2) I think to tell a lie bad.

= I think _____ bad _____ .

(3) Whether she knows it or not is not important.

= _____ is not important _____ .

A-6 알맞은 재귀대명사를 넣으세요.

(1) I can't make ( ) understood in French. 「나는 불어로 의사소통을 할 수 없다.」

(2) He often says to ( ). 「그는 종종 혼잣말을 한다.」

(3) Can you go there by ( )? 「혼자 거기 갈 수 있니?」

(4) Heaven helps those who help ( ). 「하늘은 스스로 돕는 자를 돕는다.」

(5) During the last class, we painted ( ). 「지난 시간에 우리는 자화상을 그렸다.」

A-7 생략할 수 있는 재귀 대명사에 동그라미를 치세요.

(1) Did you make this cake yourself?   (2) Don't overwork yourself.

(3) The door opened of itself.   (4) I want to talk to him myself.

(5) To love others, we must love ourselves.

지시대명사 this/these, that/those

1 이것/이것들(this/these), 저것/저것들(that/those)

This is a desk and **that** is a table.

I like **this**, but I don't like **that**.

These are from the United States, but **those** are from Canada.

2 한 문장에서 반복되는 명사를 대신하는 that/those

The area of England is larger than **that** of Ireland.
　　　　　　　　　　　　　　　(the area)

The cows of Mr. James are bigger than **those** of Mr. Watson.
　　　　　　　　　　　　　　　(the cows)

3 앞, 뒤의 절을 대신하는 this

His mother bought him a toy gun, and **this** made him happy.

(this가 가리키는 것은 앞의 절 'His mother bought him a toy gun')

I want to tell you **this**: don't enter my room.

(this가 가리키는 것은 뒤의 절 'don't enter my room')

4 전자: that(앞의 것), 후자: this(뒤의 것)

this는 가까이 있는 것을 가리키고 that은 멀리 있는 것을 가리킨다. 따라서, 나중에 나왔기에 가까이에 있는 '후자'는 this, 먼저 나왔기에 멀리 있는 '전자'는 that이다.

I have been to Paris and London; **this** is more beautiful than **that**.
　　　　　　　　　　　　　　(London)　　　　　　　(Paris)

5 지시 대명사 those는 구나 절의 수식을 받을 수 있다.

Those with young children were invited to the meeting.

We send the pamphlet to **those** who have showed interest in the program.

❋ 오늘/이번 ~: this ~

this morning, this afternoon, this evening, this Sunday, this week, this month, this summer, this year

cf) 오늘: today (this day ×), 오늘밤: tonight (this night ×)

• 지난 ~: last ~

last night, last week, last Friday, last month, last Christmas, last year 등

• 다음 ~: next ~

next week, next month, next spring, next year 등

⇒ 앞에 전치사가 필요 없다.

❋ 명사를 수식하는 지시 형용사로도 쓰인다

This room has a fine view.　　　　　　**That woman** is my English teacher.

These dogs are Mrs. Anderson's.　　　**Those people** are tourists from China.

B-1   괄호 안에 알맞은 지시대명사/지시형용사를 넣으세요.

(1)   I will go to see a doctor (   ) afternoon.

(2)   The eyes of Nancy are bigger than (   ) of George.

(3)   He didn't say anything, and (   ) made me more angry.

(4)   I can speak English and German; this is easier than (   ).

(5)   The salary of Miss Johnson is bigger than (   ) of Miss Lewis.

B-2   잘못된 문장을 골라 옳게 고치세요.

(1)   This books are written in English.

(2)   The area of Vermont is smaller than it of Maine.

(3)   You should remember this: time is the most important thing.

(4)   Those animal is from Africa.

(5)   That man is our mathematics teacher.

 의문대명사

의문사에는 의문대명사, 의문형용사, 의문부사가 있는데 그중에서 대답으로 요구하는 것이 명사인 것을 의문대명사라 한다. 한편, 대답으로 요구하는 내용이 언제, 어디서, 어떻게, 왜에 해당하는 부사인 경우는 의문부사라 한다.

위의 질문에 대한 대답은 정보를 제공하는 문장이 나오게 되며 Information Question이라고 한다. 조동사나 be 동사로 시작하는 의문문의 대답은 Yes/No로 시작하게 되며 Yes/No Question이라고 칭한다.

who (누가) **whose** (누구의, 누구의 것) **whom** (누구를)	**Who** wrote this? **Whose** bag is this? **Whose** is this? **Whom** do you like?	**Olivia** did. That is **Tom's bag**. That is **Tom's**. I like **Andy**.
what (무엇이, 무엇을)	**What** made you happy? **What** did you buy?	**His present** made me happy. I bought **a book**.
which (어느 것이, 어느 것을)	**Which** is your pen? **Which** did you choose?	**The blue pen** is my pen. I chose **the blue one**.

❋ 의문문이 다른 문장 뒤에 붙어서 간접의문문이 될 때는 조동사 do는 빠지고, 평서문의 어순(주어-동사)이 된다.

Do you know ~ + What does she learn?　→ 대답은 Yes / No로 시작

　→ Do you know **what she learns**?

Do you think ~ + How old am I ?　→ 대답은 Information 제공. 의문사로 시작해야함

　→ **How old** do you think **I am**? (guess, believe, imagine 등의 동사가 포함된 간접의문문 경우)

　cf) I can guess **how old you are**.

❋ 의문부사: **When** were you born?　　I was born **in October, 1970**.

　　　　　 How do you go to school?　I go to school **by subway**.

　　　　　 Why are you angry?　　　It is **because of his rude behavior**.

Check-Up

C　괄호 안에 알맞은 의문사를 넣으세요.

(1) (　　　) did you do yesterday? I went on a picnic with my family.

(2) (　　　) car is the biggest? Mr. Jameson's is.

(3) (　　　) made this? My mother did.

(4) To (　　　) did she tell the secret?

(5) (　　　) is the weather like?

D 특별히 정해지지 않은 것을 가리키는 부정대명사

부정(不定: 정해지지 않음)이란 말에서 알 수 있듯이 특별히 정해지지 않은 대상을 가리킨다.

1 one

1) 셀 수 있는 명사를 대신할 수 있다. 복수형은 ones: 수식어가 앞/뒤에 붙을 수 있으며, 그런
   경우 관사 the도 붙을 수 있다.

   Here are a white shirt and a pink shirt. Which **one** do you like? (= a shirt)

   I have several American friends and two Japanese **ones**. (= friends)

   This skirt is the **one** I bought in Japan.

2) 앞에 나온 명사를 받되 특정하지 않은 것을 가리킨다

   Do you have a bicycle?   Yes, I have **one**.

   cf) 특정한 것을 받을 때는 it: Do you have **the** bicycle?   Yes, I have it.

3) 일반인

   One should keep **one's** promise. (소유격은 one's)

2 other/another

1) 다른 ~: other + 복수명사, another + 단수명사

   I want to visit many **other countries**.

   Would you have **another cup** of green tea?

2) 두 개일때: one, the other
   세 개일때: one, another, the third
   여러 개일때: one, another, a third, ...

   She has **two** brothers.   **One** is Tim and **the other** is Jeff.

   There are **three** boys.   **One** is Jimmy, **another** is Andy, and **the third** is Tommy.

3) others: other people

   You can't live for yourself. You should live with **others**(= **other people**).

4) another: 또 다른 하나

   I don't like this ring. Could you show me **another**?

3 some/any: some은 긍정문에, any는 부정문 · 의문문 · 조건문에 쓰이며, 둘 다
       부정형용사로도 쓰인다.

I have **some** chocolate.   Do you want **any**?   Yes, give me **some**.

I don't have **any** money.   If you have **any**, lend me **some**.

※ some이 의문문에 쓰일 때는 권하는 의미이거나 긍정의 답을 예상하는 경우임.
   Would you have **some** coffee? (커피 마실 것을 권하고 있음)

4   **all:** all이 단독으로 쓰일 경우 일반적으로 '모든 사람'을 가리킬 때는 복수로, '모든 것'을
가리킬 때는 단수로 취급한다.

all/every + 부정어: 부분 부정

All were present at the meeting.   **All was** silent.

I **didn't** know **all** the people at the party. (모두를 다 알지는 못했다)

Check-Up

D-1   알맞은 낱말에 동그라미를 치세요.

(1)   I like the blue shirt more than the black (one, it).

(2)   Do you have the letter that I sent you?   Yes, I have (one, it).

(3)   One should listen to (ones, one's) parents.

(4)   There are a white dog and a brown dog. Which (one, ones) do you like?

(5)   This pen is the (one, it) he gave me.

D-2   알맞은 낱말에 동그라미를 치세요.

(1)   Paul has (other, another) things to do.

(2)   I have (some, any) money to spend.

(3)   There are two men. One is skinny and (another, the other) is fat.

(4)   This is too big for me. Please show me (other, another).

(5)   Will you have (other, another) glass of water?

1 다음 문장들을 보기와 같이 바꾸세요.

> 보기 Ms. Lee wrote a letter to Ms. Lee's husband.
> → She wrote a letter to her husband.

(1) My grandfather lives in my grandfather's house and I live in my house.

→ _____ lives in _____ house and I live in _____ .

(2) My brother and I ate dinner in the room of my brother and me.

→ _____ ate dinner at _____ room.

(3) Nick and Robertson went on a trip with Mr. Simpson.

→ _____ went on a trip with _____ .

2 밑줄에 들어갈 말을 보기에서 찾아 쓰세요. (한 단어를 두 번 이상 사용할 수 있으며, 필요한 경우 대문자로 시작하세요.)

> 보기 that   it   one   others   some   any   by

(1) The climate of Korea is milder than _____ of Japan.

(2) You have a good dictionary. Could you lend _____ to me?

(3) _____ of my best friends works for this company.

(4) _____ was in this hall that my mother played the violin yesterday.

(5) _____ of my friends sometimes visit me.

(6) Did your father buy _____ gift for you?

(7) Some like summer, but _____ do not.

(8) My aunt didn't marry and lives _____ herself.

[3-4] 밑줄 친 단어의 쓰임이 나머지 셋과 다른 한 문장을 고르세요.

3

(A) <u>It</u>'s a mile from here to my house.

(B) <u>It</u>'s too late. Let's go back home.

(C) <u>It</u> rained heavily last night.

(D) <u>It</u> is important to take care of yourself.

4

(A) She prides <u>herself</u> on her beauty.

(B) We enjoyed <u>ourselves</u> at the party.

(C) I did my homework <u>myself</u>.

(D) The man killed <u>himself</u> because he was too poor.

5 다음 중 밑줄 친 단어의 쓰임이 잘못된 문장을 고르세요.

(A) There are two colors. One is white, and <u>the other</u> is black.

(B) You must be kind to <u>another</u>.

(C) Tommy is my brother, and Kevin is <u>another</u>.

(D) To know is one thing; to teach is <u>another</u>.

6 아래의 우리말에 맞게 주어진 영어 단어들을 배열하세요. (첫 단어는 반드시 대문자로 시작하세요.)

(1) 한국의 국기에는 4가지 색깔이 있다.

(Korean, are, the, four, there, in, colors, flag)

→ _____ .

(2) 색깔 중 하나는 빨간색이고 또 하나는 파란색이며 나머지는 검은색과 흰색이다.

(blue, is, the, black and white, others, are, another, and)

→ One of the colors is red, _____ .

(3) 나는 나 혼자의 힘으로 이 문제를 해결할 것이다.

(for, solve, this, will, problem, myself, I)

→ _____ .

Vocabulary

□ **pride oneself on**: ~를 자랑스러워하다

유형 6   주어 찾기

1 Do you know how _____ feels to walk in space?

    (A) it   (B) its

    (C) itself   (D) it's

2 When Jane Wright was very young, _____ wanted to be an artist.

    (A) and she   (B) hers

    (C) it was she   (D) she

유형 10   목적어와 목적보어 찾기

1 You will meet them when you visit _____ next month.

    (A) I   (B) my

    (C) me   (D) mine

2 People eat _____ raw.

    (A) they   (B) them

    (C) their   (D) there

유형 17 명사와 대명사의 일치

1 A tornado is <u>so</u> strong <u>that</u> <u>they</u> can <u>pull up</u> trees.
                 A   B   C   D

2 <u>American</u> leaders wanted the eagle <u>to be</u> a symbol <u>of</u> <u>its</u> country.
    A   B   C D

유형 18 인칭대명사의 격이 잘못된 경우

1 Mozart <u>is</u> also <u>famous</u> <u>for</u> <u>him</u> operas.
          A   B   C D

2 In <u>hers</u> <u>first</u> job, Rachel Carson <u>worked</u> <u>for the</u> U.S. Government.
    A   B   C   D

유형 19 대명사를 잘못 쓴 경우

1 <u>Time</u> tells us <u>how long</u> <u>that</u> takes <u>for</u> something to happen.
    A   B   C   D

2 Coyotes are not popular <u>because</u> <u>those</u> <u>sometimes</u> kill chickens and <u>sheep</u>.
                             A   B   C   D

1   Rosa Parks didn't give up hers place on the bus.
        A   B   C   D

2   When we talk to each another, we have to use easy and clear words.
        A   B   C   D

3   Tom made a sandwich, and sat down to eat its lunch.
        A   B   C   D

4   I have two native countries: one is France, and another is Spain.
        A   B   C   D

5   The squirrel has a long tail and uses it tail for many things.
        A   B   C   D

6   While I was shopping at the department store, I met a friend of mc.
        A   B   C   D

7   Them who live in big cities should be careful when they cross the street.
        A   B   C   D

8   Everyone in my class will do their best to pass the college entrance examination.
        A   B   C   D

9   The history of the United Kingdom is much longer than one of the United
        A   B   C   D
        States.

10 Our college had a very good football team, and his best player was my friend,
        A   B   C   D
        Jimmy.

Vocabulary

□ native: 출생지의   □ native country: 모국   □ squirrel: 다람쥐

□ college entrance examination: 대학 입학 시험

1 Great Britain <u>separates</u> from <u>the rest</u> of Europe <u>by</u> the English Channel <u>and</u> the
                        A   B   C   D
North Sea.

2 _____ the name of "Indians" to Native Americans.

(A) Columbus giving mistakenly   (B) Columbus mistakenly to give

(C) Columbus who gave mistakenly   (D) Columbus mistakenly gave

3 <u>Beginning</u> in the <u>later</u> <u>eighth</u> century, many Europeans lived <u>in fear of</u> Vikings.
          A   B   C   D

4 _____ from Europe, people couldn't reach Asia without bumping
into North or South America first.

(A) Is sailing westward   (B) They were sailing westward

(C) Sailing westward   (D) Sailing westward where

5 Both word language <u>or</u> body language <u>are</u> <u>the most</u> important <u>means of</u>
                            A   B   C   D
communication.

6 Jennifer wore boots, jeans, a long-sleeved shirt, and gloves _____
in her garden.

(A) work   (B) worked   (C) she worked   (D) to work

7 <u>In the</u> United States, inches and <u>feets</u> are <u>still used</u> <u>as</u> units of
    A   B   C   D

measurement.

8 <u>Wind power</u> is an <u>ancient source</u> of energy <u>which</u> people may depend in
      A   B   C

<u>the near</u> future.
  D

9 The American Academy of Poets _____ in the 1930s to support

poets.

(A) was founded   (B) found

(C) which was founded   (D) was founded when

10 When Louis Armstrong moved to <u>north to</u> Chicago, <u>it was</u> surprised <u>to find</u> that
                                          A   B   C

<u>people</u> in Chicago loved jazz so much.
  D

11 The camel's nostrils are slanting slits <u>that</u> can <u>open wide</u> to draw <u>breathe</u> or
                                        A   B   C

close to keep out <u>blowing sand</u>.
                D

12 When scientists learned a century ago _____ cause infection, they

soon found a germ killer in carbolic acid.

(A) when germs   (B) germs have

(C) germs in which   (D) that germs

Vocabulary

□ **separate**: 분리하다	□ **rest**: 나머지	□ **the English Channel**: 영국 해협	□ **mistakenly**: 실수로
□ **in fear of ~**: ~를 무서워하여	□ **westward**: 서쪽으로	□ **bump into**: 부딪치다, 마주치다	□ **means**: 수단
□ **long-sleeved**: 긴 소매의	□ **unit**: 단위	□ **measurement**: 측정, 측량	□ **source**: 근원, 원천
□ **found**: 설립하다(found-founded-founded)		□ **nostril**: 콧구멍	□ **blow**: (바람이) 불다
□ **infection**: 전염	□ **carbolic**: 탄소의		

STRUCTURE

CHAPTER 4

형용사, 부사, 비교

Grammar Up / Power Up Test / Pattern Drill / Pattern Review / Mini Test

A 형용사

1 형용사의 두 가지 종류

1) 성질이나 상태를 나타내는 형용사

big, nice, red, ... ← 원래 형용사

American, Korean, ... ← 고유명사에서 온 것

this, that, each, all, other, another, ... ← 대명사에서 온 것

interesting, excited, ... ← 분사에서 온 것

2) 수와 양을 나타내는 형용사

one, two, three, ... ← 기수 (수효)

first, second, third, ... ← 서수 (순서)

few, little, some, any, many, much, ...

2 형용사의 두 가지 쓰임

1 명사 수식	← 한정적 용법
2 보어(주격, 목적격)	← 서술적 용법

Julia is a very **kind** girl.

Neil is very **kind and humorous**. (주격 보어)

I thought Neil **kind and humorous**. (목적격 보어)

❋ 대부분의 형용사는 두 가지(한정적, 서술적) 용법에 모두 쓰인다

✳ 형용사의 두 가지 용법

1) 한정적 용법으로만 쓰이는 형용사들

chief(최고의), main(주된), live(살아있는), total(전체의), principal(주요한), drunken(술취한), golden(금으로 된) 등

2) 서술적 용법으로만 쓰이는 형용사들

afraid, alike, alive(살아있는), alone(혼자인), ashamed(부끄러워하는), asleep(잠든), awake(깨어있는), aware, glad, sorry, well(건강한) 등

* This crab is live. [X] ➜ This is a **live crab**. This crab **is alive**.

3 형용사의 어순

1) 관사/대명사의 소유격 + 부사 + 형용사 + 명사

This is my very proud son, John.

2) 형용사가 여러 개일 때

'판단+크기/품질/모양/나이+색깔+분사+기원+재료+유형+용도' 형용사+명사

※ 일반적으로 '의견, 크기, 품질, 모양, 나이' 등의 등급화 할 수 있는 형용사(gradable adjectives)는 '분사나 기원, 재료, 유형, 용도' 등을 나타내는 등급화 할 수 없는 형용사(ungradable adjectives)보다 앞에 위치한다. 단, 이 순서가 반드시 고정된 것은 아니므로 꼭 암기할 필요는 없으며 논리적으로 합당한 어순을 생각해 본다.

an **old plastic** container	(나이+재료+명사)
a **hard red** ball	(품질+색깔+명사)
a **frightening Korean** mask	(판단+기원+명사)
a **round biscuit** tin	(모양+용도+명사)
a **small broken** plate	(크기+분사+명사)
a **useful digital alarm** clock	(판단+유형+용도+명사)

3) something, anything, everything, nothing은 형용사가 뒤에서 수식

I want **something hot** to drink.

cf) thing은 앞에서 수식: This is a strange thing.

4 수와 양을 나타내는 형용사

수(셀 수 있는 명사 앞)		양(셀 수 없는 명사 앞)	두 경우 모두
셀 수 있는 명사의 단수형 앞	셀 수 있는 명사의 복수형 앞		
each every	few (거의 없는) a few (몇몇의) a couple of (두 개의) several (몇몇의) many a number of (= a lot of) various (여러 개의) a dozen of (12개의) a score of (20개의) hundreds of (수백 개의) thousands of (수천 개의)	little (거의 없는) a little (약간의) much a great deal of (많은 양의) a large amount of (많은 양의)	some any most (대부분의) a lot of (= lots of) all no (아무도, 어느 것도 ~아닌)

• Chapter 2의 p.36에 나왔던 것과 같은 표임.

I ate **a few eggs** and **a little bread** for lunch.

Mr. Baker buys **many books**, but he doesn't have **much time** to read them.

Each person has his or her own name.

Every nation has its own name and territory.

Vocabulary

□ **territory**: 영토

5 여러 가지 수 읽기

1) **연도**: 원칙적으로 두 자리씩 끊어 읽는다.

   1979: nineteen seventy-nine

   2001: two thousand (and) one

2) **날짜**: 날은 서수로 읽는다.

   11월 7일: November 7th(seventh), the 7th of November

   5월 1일: May 1st(first), the 1st of May

3) **시간**: 시간과 분을 따로 읽는다.

   5:24: five twenty-four, twenty-four past five (분 past 시: ~시 ~분)

   11:50 (12시 10분 전): eleven-fifty, ten to twelve (분 to 시: ~시 ~분 전)

4) **전화번호**: 한자리씩 읽거나 두자리씩 끊어 읽는다.

   310-1552: three one zero - one five five two 또는 three ten - fifteen fifty two

5) **분수**: 분자는 기수로 분모는 서수로 쓰고, 분자가 2이상일 때 분모에 -s를 붙인다.

   $\frac{1}{2}$: a half, one half $\frac{1}{4}$: one fourth, a quarter $\frac{1}{5}$: one fifth

   $\frac{3}{4}$: three fourths $2\frac{2}{3}$: two and two thirds

6) **소수**: • 은 point라 읽고, 소수점 뒤는 한 자리씩 읽는다.

   1.24. one point two four   0.97. zero point nine seven

7) **기타**

   2차 대전 (World War II): World War Two, the Second World War

   엘리자베스 2세 (Elizabeth II): Elizabeth the Second

6 -ly 형용사(= 명사 + -ly)

-ly로 끝나더라도 형용사로 쓰이는 단어들이 있는데, 이들은 주로 명사에 -ly를 붙인 것들이 많다.
또한, 이들 중 형용사와 부사로 사용되는 단어들도 있다.

✳ lovely, friendly, lively, costly, manly, elderly 등

   Annie is a very **lovely** girl.

✳ daily, weekly, monthly, yearly, early 등은 형용사와 부사로 사용된다.

   National Geographic is a **monthly** magazine.

   I exercise **daily**.

Vocabulary

□ **costly**: 값이 비싼   □ **manly**: 남자다운   □ **elderly**: 나이가 지긋한   □ **magazine**: 잡지

Check-Up

A-1 형용사에 동그라미를 치세요.

(1) My elder sister made me a delicious lunch.

(2) I first met him in the early spring of my second year at the university.

(3) This mountain is higher than any other mountain in this country.

(4) I was tired after the hard and long day.

(5) An American man asked me a few questions.

A-2 형용사에 밑줄을 긋고 쓰임을 말하세요.

(1) February is the shortest month in the year.

(2) That was a very interesting movie.

(3) He always makes me happy.

(4) Her eyes are blue, and her hair is brown.

(5) I am afraid of all animals.

A-3 형용사의 위치가 잘못된 것을 골라 옳게 고치세요.

(1) Do you have exciting anything?

(2) Give me white that sweater on the table.

(3) I want to show you a thing interesting.

(4) He gave me this ring gold as a present.

(5) There is new nothing.

A-4a 알맞은 말에 동그라미를 치세요.

(1) There were (a few, a little) people in the theater.

(2) I don't have (many, much) time to sleep.

(3) He likes every (woman, women) in the office.

(4) We have a large (number, amount) of books.

(5) They grow (much, many) rice in the country.

Chapter · 4

A-4b 괄호 안에 알맞은 말을 넣으세요.

(1) She bought a (   ) of eggs. 「그녀는 달걀을 스무 개 샀다.」

(2) He has a large (   ) of money. 「그는 돈이 아주 많다.」

(3) I have (   ) hobbies. 「나는 다양한 취미를 갖고 있다.」

(4) She has (   ) friends to talk with. 「그녀는 함께 이야기할 친구가 거의 없다.」

(5) (   ) one could answer the question. 「아무도 그 질문에 답하지 못했다.」

A-5 다음을 읽는 대로 써보세요.

(1) 1998년

(2) 오전 10시 25분

(3) 1과 3분의 1

(4) 011-730-1234

(5) 5시 10분 전

(6) 3.14

(7) 3월 12일

 # B 부사 (Adverb)

1 부사의 쓰임

Mr. Russell <u>talks</u> **slowly**.　　　　　　(동사 수식)

Jimmy looks **very** <u>young</u> for his age.　(형용사 수식)

She walks **very** <u>fast</u>.　　　　　　　(부사 수식)

Happily, <u>he didn't hurt much</u>.　　　(문장 전체 수식)

2 부사(구)의 어순

부사는 종류에 따라 문장 앞(front), 중간(mid), 뒤(end position)에 위치할 수 있다.

대게 ⓐcertainly, obviously, sadly, personally, kindly등과 같은 '일반적인 부사'는 경우에 따라 문장의 앞, 중간, 뒤에 위치할 수 있으며, ⓑ '시간의 부사'는 앞 또는 뒤에, ⓒ '장소의 부사'는 주로 뒤에 (앞에 위치할 수도 있음) 위치한다.

As a result, Japan faces a crisis.

Yesterday I went to Paris.

I went to Paris **yesterday**.

He studied the problem **briefly**.*

1) 문장의 중간에 위치하는 주요 부사들: 빈도(frequency), 정도(degree), 집중(focus) 부사

① 빈도부사는 기본적으로 조동사와 be동사 뒤에 그리고 일반동사 앞에 위치한다.

always (100%)　　　- <u>usually</u>, frequently　　- <u>regularly</u>(규칙적으로)

- often　　　　　　- <u>sometimes</u>　　　　　- <u>occasionally</u>(가끔)

- seldom, hardly　　- never (0%)

She <u>is</u> **often** late for work.

My family **usually** <u>goes</u> on a picnic once a month.

I <u>can</u> **hardly** <u>hear</u> you.

　※ sometimes, usually, occasionally, normally는 문장의 앞 또는 뒤에 올 수도 있다.

　　I **normally** get up at 6 o'clock, but **sometimes** I have to be up by 5.

② only, just, nearly, hardly, almost, scarcely

동사를 수식하는 경우는 ①과 같고, 형용사나 부사를 수식하는 경우에는 수식하고자 하는 단어 바로 앞에 위치한다.

Mary **only** <u>saw</u> John. She did not talk to him. (동사 수식)

Mary knows **hardly** <u>any</u> Japanese. (형용사 수식)

----

* briefly가 studied를 수식한다. He studied **briefly** the problem은 틀린 문장이다. 하지만 목적어가 긴 경우에는 수식 관계에 있는 studied와 briefly가 너무 멀리 떨어지게 되어 수식 관계에 혼동을 유발시킬 가능성이 있으므로 다음과 같이 부사(briefly)를 동사 옆에 위치시킬 수 있다. We considered the long-term solution to the problem **briefly**. = We considered **briefly** the long-term solution to the problem. 영어 구조의 첫번째 근본은 명확성(clarity)이다.

2) 여러 개의 부사가 쓰일 때: 장 (-방) -시

(장소-방법-시간에 관한 부사(구)의 순으로. 방법의 부사 위치는 경우에 따라 변동 가능)

David arrived **here safely yesterday**. (장-방-시)

They left **at 3:00 with a great deal of noise**. (시-방)

3) 비슷한 부류의 부사(구)가 여럿 있는 경우: 세부적인 내용이 포괄적인 내용보다 먼저 온다

Mr. Kim stayed **at the Ritz-Carlton Hotel in Osaka**.

3 동사 + 부사

pick up(집어올리다, 차에 태우다), turn on(켜다), turn off(끄다), turn down(볼륨을 줄이다, 거절하다), put on(입다), take off(벗다) 등

목적어가 **명사**일 경우	: <u>동사 + **명사** + 부사</u>, <u>동사 + 부사 + **명사**</u>
목적어가 **대명사**일 경우	: <u>동사 + **대명사** + 부사</u> (반드시 동사와 부사의 사이에)

Please **turn the TV off**. = Please **turn off the TV**.

My father will come to **pick me up**. (pick up me는 틀림!)

4 주의할 부사들

1) very / much (very: 원급, 최상급, 현재분사 수식 / much: 비교급, 최상급, 과거분사 수식)

Andy is **very** handsome.   Tony is **much** more handsome than Andy.

Leslie is **the very most handsome** of all.   Leslie is **much the quickest worker** of all.

The baseball game was **very exciting**.   I am **much concerned** about your health.

2) ago / before

ago: 현재를 기준으로 ~ 전에 (과거 시제에만 쓰며 반드시 숫자와 함께 쓰인다.)

They got married **three days ago**.

before: ① 예전에 (단독으로. 과거, 현재완료, 과거완료와 함께)

I **visited** Japan **before**. I **have seen** the movie **before**.

② 과거를 기준으로 ~ 전에 (시간 + before. 과거완료와 함께)

She said that she **had seen** it **a week before**.

3) already / yet

already: 긍정문(이미, 벌써), 의문문(놀람) / **yet:** 부정문(아직), 의문문(이미/벌써)

I have **already** finished the work. (벌써 다 했다)

Have you finished the work **already**? (우와, 벌써 다 했어?)

I have **not** finished the work **yet**. (아직 안 했다)

Have you finished the work **yet**? (벌써 다 했나?)

4) too / either

'역시' 라는 의미로 too는 긍정문에, either는 부정문에 쓰이며 문장 끝에 놓인다.

I like Radiohead, **too**.

I don't like Radiohead, **either**.

Check-Up

B-1 부사에 밑줄을 긋고 쓰임을 말하세요.

(1) Tom tried hard to solve the math problem.

(2) I was very happy to get the letter.

(3) Even the teacher didn't know the answer.

(4) My sister likes the actor very much.

(5) Fortunately, he didn't die.

B-2 부사의 위치가 잘못된 것을 골라 옳게 고치세요.

(1) I will meet him tomorrow on 2nd Street.

(2) Danny never listens to his parents.

(3) My family eats out seldom.

(4) She fully was misunderstood by the people.

(5) I go often to the beach alone.

B-3a 괄호 안에 주어진 단어 중에서 알맞은 것에 동그라미 하세요.

(1) I don't want to go out, (too, either).

(2) Her daughter is (very, much) cute.

(3) The store closed two hours (ago, before).

(4) Paul is (very, much) taller than he was last year.

(5) She has (already, yet) finished reading the book.

B-3b 다음을 해석하거나 영작하세요.

(1) William said that he had come back two days before.

→ _____.

(2) Have you already eaten the sandwich?

→ _____.

(3) 나도 딸기를 무척 좋아해.

→ _____.

Vocabulary

□ **math:** 수학(= mathematics)   □ **2nd Street:** 2번가   □ **eat out:** 외식하다

□ **fully:** 완전히   □ **misunderstand:** 오해하다

Chapter • 4

비교급, 최상급의 형태

1 규칙 변화: -(e)r / -(e)st 모든 1음절과 일부 2음절의 형용사와 부사

 1) tall - taller - tallest   wise - wiser - wisest

 2) 원급이 "단**자**음+단**모**음+단**자**음"으로 끝나면 자음 알파벳을 한 번 더 쓴다.
   big - bigger - biggest   hot - hotter - hottest (공식: 자모자는 자모자자라)
   ※ 마지막 자음이 -w로 끝나는 경우는 예외 (예: new, slow 등)

 3) '자음+y'로 끝나는 단어는 y를 i로 고치고 -er, -est를 붙인다. (dry, crazy, funny 등)
   pretty - prettier - prettiest

2 more, most를 앞에 붙여서 비교급, 최상급을 만드는 경우

 대부분의 2음절과 모든 3음절의 형용사와 부사
   more famous, more foolish, more useful, more careless 등
   more important, more beautiful, more intelligent 등
   more quickly, more easily 등 (형용사 + ly로 끝나는 모든 부사)
   more boring, more tired 등 (-ed, -ing로 끝나는 모든 분사)

3 -er, -est 및 more, most가 겸용되어 사용되는 경우

 2음절의 단어 중 "-er, -ow, -le(-ble, -dle, -ple, -tle), -some"등으로 끝나는 경우
   clever, idle, handsome, narrow, noble, simple 등

4 불규칙 비교급, 최상급

good				old	older – oldest	(나이)	
well	} better – best				elder – eldest	(손 위)	
bad				late	later – latest	(시간)	
badly	} worse – worst				latter – last	(순서)	
ill				far	farther – farthest	(거리)	
many					further – furthest	(정도)	
much	} more – most			little – less – least			

Check-Up

C   다음 단어들의 비교급, 최상급을 쓰세요.

 (1) wide   (2) thin   (3) careful   (4) little

 (5) necessary   (6) free   (7) curious   (8) well

 (9) pleased   (10) diligent

주요 원급, 비교급, 최상급 구문

1 원급 구문

as 원급 as   This room is **as large as** that room.

                                           She sings **as well as** Linda.

not so(as) 원급 as   Peter is **not so(as) tall as** Dennis.

2 비교급 구문

우등 비교   Dennis is **taller than** Peter.

                                           This is **more useful than** that.

열등 비교   Peter is **less tall than** Dennis.

3 최상급 구문

최상급 + {
of 복수 명사   Dennis is **the tallest of** all the boys.

in 장소/집합체/the world   Tokyo is **the largest city in** Japan.

that ~ ever   This is **the biggest hamburger that I have ever** seen.
}

Check-Up

D   다음을 영작하세요.

(1) 크리스(Chris)는 앤디(Andy)만큼 키가 크지 않다.

→ _____.

(2) 에베레스트 산(Mt. Everest)이 세계에서 가장 높은 산이다.

→ _____.

(3) 한나(Hannah)가 학생들 중 가장 똑똑하다.

→ _____.

(4) 대서양(the Atlantic Ocean)은 태평양(the Pacific Ocean)보다 좁다.

→ _____.

(5) 이것은 이제껏 내가 보았던 것 중 가장 작은 컴퓨터이다.

→ _____.

E 원급, 비교급을 이용한 최상급 표현

Scott is **the tallest boy** in his class. (최상급)

= Scott is **taller than any other boy** in his class. (비교급 + than any other + 단수명사)

= **No boy** in his class is **taller than** Scott. (부정 주어 ~비교급)

= **No other boy** in his class is **as(so) tall as** Scott. (부정 주어 ~원급)

E 주어진 문장과 같은 뜻이 되도록 빈칸에 알맞은 어구를 써넣으세요.

> New York is the biggest city in the United States.

(1) New York is _____ city in the United States.

(2) _____ city in the United States is _____ than New York.

(3) _____ other city in the United States is _____ big _____ New York.

원급, 비교급, 최상급의 특별 용법

1 배수 표현

~ times as 원급 as = ~ times 비교급 than

This box is **three times as large as** that one.

= This box is **three times larger than** that one.

2 as 원급 as possible(= as 원급 as 주어 can)

Please call me **as soon as possible** (= as soon as you can).

3 비교급

1) 비교급 and 비교급: 점점 더 ~한

It is getting **colder and colder**.

2) the 비교급~, the 비교급~: ~하면 할수록 점점 더 ~한

The more you eat, **the fatter** you will become.

3) 비교급 앞에 the가 붙는 경우: 뒤에 of the two, because가 있을 때

This doll is **the prettier of the two**. (이 인형이 둘 중 더 예쁘다.)

I like him **the better because** he is smart. (나는 그가 똑똑하기 때문에 더 좋아한다.)

4) 비교급을 강조하는 부사: much, even, still, far, a lot 등

This is **much bigger** than that.

5) 라틴어에서 온 단어의 비교급: than 대신 to를 씀

senior to(연상의), junior to(연하의), superior to(우수한), inferior to(열등한), prior to(앞선)

4 최상급

1) one of the 최상급 + 복수명사

Seoul is **one of the biggest cities** in the world.

2) 최상급에 the가 붙지 않는 경우

The lake is **deepest** at this point. (동일물 안에서 비교)

I am **happiest** when I'm with him. (동일인의 성질 비교)

My mother gets up **earliest** in my family. (부사의 최상급)

Her best friend is Nancy. (최상급 앞에 소유격이 있을 때)

Vocabulary

□ **senior**: 연상의   □ **junior**: 연하의   □ **superior**: 우수한   □ **inferior**: 열등한

✳ 비교가 불가능한 형용사

perfect는 이미 완전한 상태를 이야기 하기 때문에 '더 완벽하다', '가장 완벽하다'는 논리적으로 모순이다. 이처럼 비교 자체가 불가능한 형용사들이 있다. 이 형용사들은 very로 수식할 수 없다. absolute, complete, empty, enough, final, full, perfect, sufficient, total, unique, universal 등이 이에 해당한다.

Check-Up

F-1 주어진 의미가 되도록 괄호 안에 알맞은 말을 넣으세요.

(1) Come home as early as (　　　). = Come home as early as (　　　) (　　　).
「가능한 한 일찍 집에 오렴.」

(2) This is four (　　　) (　　　) than that. = This is four (　　　) (　　　) (　　　)
as that. 「이것은 저것보다 네 배는 크다.」

(3) (　　　) (　　　) you study, (　　　) (　　　) your score will be.
「공부를 더 열심히 하면 할수록 점수가 더 좋아질 것이다.」

F-2 다음을 해석하세요.

(1) Robin is the smarter of the two boys.

→ _____.

(2) Jupiter is 1,300 times bigger than the Earth.

→ _____.

(3) Draw a circle as large as this.

→ _____.

1 괄호 안에 주어진 단어 중에서 알맞은 것을 고르세요.

(1) It may sound (strange, strangely), but it is true.

(2) The train moves (slow, slowly).

(3) She is wearing a (beautiful, beautifully) dress.

(4) The child looks (happy, happily) on seeing his mother.

(5) The movie seems to be (interesting, interested).

(6) My father doesn't smoke, and my mother doesn't, (too, either).

(7) The book has (few, little) mistakes.

2 밑줄 친 단어들의 어순이 올바르지 않은 것을 고르세요.

(A) There stand <u>large two buildings</u>.

(B) I received <u>a letter written in English</u>.

(C) My little brother <u>is always sleeping</u> with my mother.

(D) This lake is <u>twice as large as</u> that one.

3 주어진 그림을 보고, 보기와 같이 원급, 비교급, 최상급의 문장을 만들어 보세요.

I   my brother   my father   my mother   my grandmother

보기 I am <u>taller</u> than my brother. (tall)

(1) My brother is not _____ as I. (tall)

(2) My mother is _____ as my father. (tall)

(3) My father is _____ than my grandmother. (old)

(4) My grandmother is the _____ in my family. (old)

(5) I am much _____ my grandmother. (young)

Vocabulary

□ **strange**: 이상한   □ **lake**: 호수

4   다음 단어들 중 비교급, 최상급의 형태가 잘못 짝지어진 것을 고르세요.

(A) well - better - best   (B) bad - worse - worst

(C) much - more - most   (D) little - later - latest

5   다음 문장의 밑줄 친 부분이 어법상 올바르지 않은 것을 선택하세요.

(A) Hot water freezes <u>more quickly than</u> cold.

(B) His brother is <u>very brighter than</u> he.

(C) Admiral Lee is <u>one of the most famous soldiers</u> in Korea.

(D) You must go home <u>as soon as possible</u>.

6   비교급 표현에 유의하며 다음 문장을 해석하세요.

(1) Which do you like better, spring or fall? I like spring better, and I'm very happy now, because winter has gone, and it's getting warmer and warmer.

→ _____

_____

(2) I respect the great scientist Thomas Edison, and I want to be a scientist like him. My mother says that the harder I study, the more I will learn.

→ _____

_____

Vocabulary

□ **admiral:** 장군   □ **soldier:** 군인   □ **respect:** 존경하다

유형 9   보어 찾기

1 Sounds can be measured to find out how _____ they are.

(A) loudness   (B) loud   (C) loudly   (D) aloud

2 Everybody kept _____ in the hall of the museum.

(A) to be silent   (B) silently   (C) silent   (D) silence

유형 20   형용사를 혼동하여 쓴 경우

1 <u>July</u> is the <u>seven</u> month <u>of</u> the year, and it has <u>thirty-one</u> days.
    A   B   C   D

2 There are <u>lots</u> of <u>alive</u> <u>fish</u> <u>in</u> the market.
            A   B C D

3 You <u>should</u> not eat so <u>much</u>. You will <u>get</u> <u>fatly</u>.
       A   B   C D

유형 21   부사(구), 형용사(구) 찾기

1 All living things are born, grow, and _____ die.

(A) final   (B) are final   (C) finally as   (D) finally

2 _____ musical instruments like the piano and organ use a keyboard.

(A) A   (B) Any   (C) Some   (D) It is

유형 22   원급, 비교급, 최상급 찾기

1 Utah is _____ as Idaho.

(A) large   (B) larger   (C) as large   (D) larger than

2 Pyramids are many times _____ a house.

    (A) big   (B) big as   (C) the biggest   (D) bigger than

3 In fact, one of _____ ways to learn about music is to sing.

    (A) the better   (B) the best   (C) better than   (D) best

---

유형 23   원급, 비교급, 최상급의 쓰임이 잘못된 경우

1 Eating properly is as important than exercising regularly for our health.
    A   B   C   D

2 The number 3 is less as the number 4.
    A   B   C   D

3 The Statue of Liberty is most famous statue in America.
    A   B   C   D

유형 24   원급, 비교급, 최상급의 형태가 잘못된 경우

1 Clouds are much more commoner than rainbows, and we see them nearly
                A   B   C   D
every day.

2 The Nile is the most longest river in the world.
    A   B   C   D

1   I need your help right <u>away</u>, <u>so</u> please come as <u>sooner</u> as <u>possible</u>.
       A   B   C   D

2   Linda is _____ girl in town.

(A) as beautiful   (B) beautiful than

(C) most beautiful   (D) the most beautiful

3   <u>We</u> can't see a <u>bright</u> star than <u>the sun</u> <u>in</u> the sky.
       A   B   C   D

4   You should go _____ to arrive at the station.

(A) much farther   (B) farther than

(C) farthest   (D) the farther

5   The more you love yourself, _____ you can love other people.

(A) easily   (B) more easily

(C) and more easily   (D) the more easily

6   Coins <u>have been</u> used <u>for</u> <u>a long</u> time than paper <u>money</u>.
              A   B   C   D

7   <u>Of</u> our national <u>holidays</u>, Samiljeol falls on <u>the one</u> of <u>March</u>.
       A   B   C   D

8   The dress in the window was _____ expensive that I can't buy it for
       you.

(A) too much   (B) so

(C) very   (D) too

9   My neighbors are _____ my old friends.

(A) more friendly than   (B) friendly as

(C) friendly than   (D) as friendly

10 She wants to buy me a new watch, but I have an old one _____ for me.

(A) enough good   (B) enough well

(C) good enough   (D) well enough

11 Mars is not so close to the sun _____ the earth is.

(A) than   (B) as

(C) that   (D) more

12 The lion <u>may</u> be the king of the beasts, <u>but</u> the whale is the <u>most largest</u> animal
            A   B   C
    <u>of all</u>.
        D

13 The U.S. consists of more various peoples than _____ in the world.

(A) any other nation   (B) any of nation

(C) every other nation   (D) the other nation

14 <u>Some</u> people believe <u>that</u> Elvis Presley is <u>still live</u> <u>somewhere</u>.
         A   B   C   D

15 Our teacher always explains the directions very _____.

(A) clear   (B) clearly

(C) to clear   (D) clearness

Vocabulary

□ **direction**: 지시 사항

1 Many <u>languages</u> <u>speaking</u> today in Europe and America <u>grew</u> out of <u>the Latin</u>
             A   B   C   D
language.

2 The word "nature" means all the things in the universe that _____
made by humans.

(A) were not   (B) they were not

(C) it was not   (D)because it was not

3 <u>Many of</u> today's <u>civilizations</u> received from Rome <u>only not</u> their languages, but
         A   B   C
also some of <u>their</u> habits and ideas.
               D

4 Pizarro, _____, came for gold and defeated the Incas in South
America.

(A) who the Spanish conqueror   (B) and the Spanish conqueror

(C) the Spanish conqueror had   (D) the Spanish conqueror

5 I have several <u>idea</u> <u>to make</u> the world a <u>better</u> place <u>to live</u> in.
                    A   B   C   D

6 <u>Both</u> moths and butterflies <u>have</u> a <u>keen sense</u> of sight, smell, and <u>tasting</u>.
      A   B   C   D

7 Heat makes gases _____.

(A) to expand   (B) expand

(C) expanded   (D) be expanded

Chapter · 4

8   The Pueblo Native Americans buried a <u>dead</u> fish in <u>each hill</u> of corn <u>makes</u> the

          corn grow <u>well</u>.
               D

9   My friend and I were tired, so we went home _____ dinner.

(A) enough early for   (B) for enough early

(C) early for enough   (D) early enough for

10   Thomas Edison is <u>remembered</u> <u>chiefly</u> as the man <u>whose</u> invented the <u>light bulb</u>.
                      A   B   C   D

11   Until the late 1930's, _____ only in black and white, doing

          lithographs and drawings illustrating stories and magazine articles.

(A) Adolf Dehn working   (B) Adolf Dehn worked

(C) Adolf Dehn's works   (D) when Adolf Dehn worked

12   Alaska's forests are capable <u>to supply</u> a <u>sustained</u> production of several billion
                                          A   B

          <u>board feet</u> of timber <u>annually</u>.
              C   D

Vocabulary

□ civilization: 문명	□ conqueror: 정복자	□ defeat: 무찌르다
□ the Incas: 잉카족, 잉카 사람	□ moth: 나방	□ keen: 예리한, 날카로운
□ sense of sight[smell][taste]: 시각 [후각] [미각]	□ chiefly: 주로	□ light bulb: 전구
□ lithograph: 석판 인쇄	□ illustrate: 삽화를 넣다	□ article: (신문, 잡지의) 기사
□ sustained: 지속된	□ annually: 해마다	□ timber: 재목

STRUCTURE

동사, 시제

Grammar Up / Power Up Test / Pattern Drill / Pattern Review / Mini Test

A 동사와 문장의 형식

	주어	동사	주격 보어	목적어	목적격 보어	수식어구	
1형식	She	dances				with a man.	완전 자동사
2형식	He	is	a dentist.				불완전 자동사
3형식	Fleming	discovered		penicillin		in 1928.	완전 타동사
4형식	Mother	bought		me a book. 간접 직접			수여 동사
5형식	We	believe		him	innocent.		불완전 타동사

• 자동사(1, 2형식 동사) – 목적어 불필요 / 타동사(3, 4, 5 형식 동사) – 목적어 필요

• 많은 동사들은 의미에 따라 자동사와 타동사로 모두 쓰인다. 예를 들어 흥얼대는 것은 인간의 본능이므로 sing은
자동사이지만, 특정한 노래를 부른다고 치면 타동사로 쓰인다. 또한 타동사로 사용되는 경우에도 동사들이 3, 4,
5형식에 모두 사용되는 경우가 있다.

✹ 5가지 형식과 품사의 역할

1) 1형식: 주어 + 동사   [n + v (+부사)]

   Alice sat by her brother.

2) 2형식: 주어 + 동사 + 보어   [n + v + a 또는 n1 + v + n2 (n1 = n2)]

   I am feeling better today.

3) 3형식: 주어 + 동사 + 목적어   [n1 + v + n2 (n1 ≠ n2)]

   She put the basket on the table.

4) 4형식: 주어 + 동사 + 간접목적어 + 직접목적어   [n1 + v + n2 + n3 (n1 ≠ n2 ≠ n3)]

   She knitted her grandson a wool sweater.

5) 5형식: 주어 + 동사 + 목적어 + 목적격 보어   [n1 + v + n2 + a 또는 n1+ v + n2 + n3 (n2 = n3)]

   A little alcohol can make you feel better. (feel better는 부정사 형용사적 용법)

✻ 4형식과 5형식의 구별

「주어(n1) + 동사 + 목적어(n2) + 명사(n3)」에서

• 목적어(n2) = 명사(n3) → 5형식   • 목적어(n2) ≠ 명사(n3) → 4형식

   She made her daughter a doll. (her daughter ≠ a doll → 4형식)

   She made her daughter a pianist. (her daughter = a pianist → 5형식)

   cf) 「주어 + 동사 + 목적어 + 형용사」는 5형식

     My mother made us happy. (형용사 happy는 us의 상태 표시, ∴목적보어)

1 **1형식:** 주어 + 동사 (+ 부사)

1형식 동사는 보어나 목적어가 필요 없다. 부사구의 수식을 받을 수는 있다. 특히,

(1) come, go, walk, move, arrive, leave, live, stay 등과 같은 왕래 발착, 거주, 이전에 관한 동사들,

(2) rise, set, rain, snow, exist, appear, die 등과 같은 자연 현상의 동사들,

(3) talk, speak, sing, sleep, breathe, drink, study, lie(거짓말하다), brag(잘난체하다) 등과 같은 인간 본능에 관한 동사들이 이에 속한다.

> Sandy **lives** in New York.

2 **2형식:** 주어 + 동사 + 주격 보어(보어가 될 수 있는 품사는 명사와 형용사)

주요 2형식 동사: be(~이다), look, seem, keep, feel, become/get/grow(~되다) 등

> She **looks happy** today. (형용사 happy는 She의 상태표시, ∴주격보어)
>
> My brother **is an English teacher**. (My brother = an English teacher, ∴주격보어)

3 **3형식:** 주어 + 동사 + 목적어(목적어가 될 수 있는 품사는 명사)

> I **like coffee**. (주어 ≠ 목적어)
>
> He **bought the CD** for me. (=He **bought me the CD**. ← 4형식으로 전환 가능)
>
> ※ 주의해야 할 3형식 동사(4형식으로 전환 불가): explain, introduce, suggest, describe
>   I **introduced John** to Mary last year.

4 **4형식:** 주어 + 동사 + 간접목적어 + 직접목적어

4형식 동사는 '~에게 ~를 주다/해주다' 라는 의미를 갖기 때문에 수여동사(주는 동사) 라고도 부른다. give, tell, send, make, buy, teach, show, lend 등

> My boyfriend **bought me a lovely dress**. (=~ bought a lovely dress **for** me. ← 3형식)
>   • 동사의 종류에 따라 전치사 to, for, of를 사용하여 3형식으로 전환할 수 있다.

5 **5형식:** 주어 + 동사 + 목적어 + 목적격 보어

> We **call her Snow White**. (대명사 her = 명사 Snow White, ∴목적 보어)
>
> The movie **made me sad**. (형용사 sad는 목적어 me의 상태표시, ∴목적 보어)
>
> ※ make, have, let 및 see, notice, watch, observe, hear, smell, feel 등은 1~5형식 중 대부분에 사용되는데, 사역동사 및 지각동사란 용어로 사용되는 경우는 5형식의 문장을 구성하는 경우이며, 부정사가 따라 나오게 되면 원형 부정사(또는 현재 분사형)의 형태로 사용된다.
>   • 사역동사: make, have / let
>   The sad movie **made** me *cry*.
>   • 지각동사: see, notice, watch, observe, hear, smell, feel 등
>   Do you **smell** something *burning*? (5형식)
>   It **smells** like garlic. (1형식)
>   It **smells** wonderful. (2형식)
>   I can **smell** a flower. (3형식)
>   I enjoyed **watch**ing the children *play* soccer. (3형식 문장. 밑줄친 부분은 5형식의 형태)
>   * play 대신 playing을 사용하여도 됨. 의미의 차이는 거의 없으나 현재분사형이 움직임의 느낌이 강함.

❋ 용법을 혼동하기 쉬운 '말하는' 동사들

tell	주로 타동사로서 3, 4형식 문장에 쓰인다. 직접화법에는 쓰지 않는다.
say	that절, how절, 명사를 목적어로 취한다. (사람을 목적어로 갖지 않는다.) 직접, 간접화법에 모두 쓰인다.
speak	언어를 쓰다, 연설하다, 정보 및 내용을 전달하다.
talk	주로 자동사로 전치사 about, over, of, to등과 함께 쓰인다. 타동사로 쓰일 때는 사람을 목적어로 갖지 않는다.

He's good at **telling** jokes. / **Tell** me all about your new job.

He **said** that he was tired. / He **said** a few words.

English is **spoken** in New Zealand. / Actions **speak** louder than words.

I don't know what you're **talking** about! / I want to **talk** to you.

❋ 혼동하기 쉬운 자동사, 타동사 (암기하지 말고 논리적으로 접근하여 이해하도록 한다.)

I must **apologize** to her for his rudeness.

She **discussed** her plans with her mother.

Will you **join** me for a drink? (join with를 사용하면 안됨)

Please **answer** me. (answer to를 사용하면 안됨)

The President **answered** the reporters' questions.

Will you be **attending** the meeting?

Please let us know if you are able to **attend.**

The thieves **entered** the building by the back door. (enter into를 사용하면 안됨)

Knock before you **enter.**

He **kissed** her on the forehead. (kiss to her를 사용하면 안됨)

In the final scene of the film, they **kiss.**

She wanted to **marry** a rich man. (marry with로 사용하면 안됨. 논리적으로 살펴보면, 결혼하기 위해서는 상대를 필요로 하고, 상대는 목적어임)

He **married** late in life. (결혼 상태를 말함)

Please **open** the window.

The door **opened,** and people came out.

How can I **reach** you? (어떻게 하면 당신에게 연락할 수 있을까요?)

We could see nothing but houses as far as the eye could **reach.**

*as far as the eye could reach = to the horizon

❋ rise - rose - risen - rising / raise - raised - raised - raising

Smoke **rose** from the factory chimneys.

He **raised** the lid of the box.

❋ lie - lay - lain - lying (재 눕다, 놓여있다) / lay - laid - laid - laying (타 눕히다, 놓다, 알을 낳다)

lie - lied - lied - lying (재 거짓말 하다)

They just **lie** on the beach all day.

He **laid** his coat on a chair.

❋ sit - sat - sat - sitting / set - set - set - setting

He usually **sits** at the back of the class.

Please **set** the alarm at 7 o'clock.

Let's **set aside** my personal feelings for now.(지금은 내 개인적인 감정은 제껴둡시다.)

*set aside: to ignore, to save for a special purpose

Check-Up

A-1   각 문장의 성분들을 표시하고 몇 형식인지 쓰세요.

(1)   She is a teacher of history in my school.

(2)   They eat lunch at a fast food restaurant.

(3)   Who wrote this novel?

(4)   Tom and I were walking along the beach.

(5)   Keeping early hours is good for health.

(6)   I want to know if he will come.

(7)   Did you buy him a bicycle?

(8)   He must be a foreigner.

(9)   They consider the man honest.

(10)   You mean everything to me.

A-2   밑줄친 부분이 틀린 문장을 골라 옳게 고치세요.

(1)   This is a sunflower, and that <u>being</u> a lily.

(2)   Andy <u>wants</u> to become a rock singer.

(3)   Mr. Wilson <u>to work</u> for the company.

(4)   Roger and Nick <u>been</u> in New York now.

(5)   Please <u>to talk</u> more loudly.

 **영어의 기본 시제**

1 현재 – 현재의 행동, 상태, 사실, 습관, 반복적인 일, 진리, 격언

Tommy **plays** basketball with his friends.

It **is** warm today.

New York **is** not the capital city of the United States.

Mr. and Mrs. Brown **take** a walk every evening.

Light **travels** fastest of all.

2 과거 – 과거의 행동, 상태, 사실, 습관

I didn't **go** there because of the rain.

Jenny **was** sick last week.

There **was** a white house on the hill.

3 미래

1) 미래에 발생할 것 같은 일에 대한 일반적인 예측(prediction): *will* or *be going to*

   I think I **will** (= **am going to**) enjoy the trip to Africa.

   I **will** (**am going to**) be eighteen years old next week.

2) 말하는 순간에 미래의 일에 대한 의지 표현(willingness) 및 계획되지 않은 미래의 행동: *will*

   A: The telephone is ringing.   B: I **will** get it.

   Call me next week. Maybe I'**ll** be free. (maybe는 계획되어진 의미가 아니므로 be going to와
                                     함께 사용하지 않는다.)

3) 말하는 순간 이전에 계획된 미래의 일에 대한 표현: *be going to*

   A: Why did you buy this paint?

   B: I'**m going to** paint my room this afternoon.

   A: Do you have any plan this evening?

   B: Yes, I **am going to** meet my brother at eight.

 **shall**

- shall이 의문문의 형태로 1인칭에 사용되는 경우는 "공손한 제안"을 표현한다. 그 이외에는 현대의 American English에서는 shall을 거의 사용하지 않는다.

  Shall I (= Do you want me to) set the table for you?

  Shall we dance? (같이 춤을 추시겠어요?) Yes, let's.

- shall이 2, 3인칭에 사용될 수는 있는데, 이때는 강력한 결정(strong determination) 및 피할 수 없음, 필연성(inevitability)을 표현한다. (이 경우도 현대의 미국 영어에서는 will을 쓰는 경우가 많다.)

  You're laughing now, but you **shall** regret your mistake when you're older.

Check-Up

B-1 괄호 안의 동사를 알맞은 시제로 바꾸어 넣으세요.

(1) Angie usually (read) books in the subway on her way to work.

(2) He (be) in university in 1993.

(3) Miss Anderson (return) to Chicago next Friday.

(4) What (be) you going to do this evening?

(5) Sacramento (be) the capital of California State.

(6) My mother (make) a cheese cake on my birthday every year.

(7) We (have) a very good time at the party yesterday.

(8) Peter (go) back to Iowa a month from now.

(9) I already (see) that movie.

(10) At the moment, I (be) with my friend John.

 **진행 시제**

형태는 be + -ing(현재분사). 말하는 시점 전에 시작되어, 말하는 시점을 지나, 말하는 시점보다 약간 미래에도 지속될 것임을 나타낸다.

1 현재/과거/미래진행

We **are watching** *Terminator II* on TV.

They **were eating** dinner when I came home.

I **will be sleeping** then.

✽ always + 진행형 = 불평하는 감정 (회화에서 자주 쓰이는 표현)

- My husband always leaves his dirty socks on the floor. (사실표현)
- My husband is always leaving his dirty socks on the floor for me to pick up!
  Who does he think I am? His maid? (불평하는 감정의 표현)
- My sister is always borrowing my clothes without asking me. (불평하는 감정의 표현)

2 진행시제를 쓸 수 없는 동사들

have(가지고 있다), know, like, love, think, want, believe, need, remember 등 정신적 상태를 나타내는 동사들, see, hear 등의 지각 동사들. (논리적으로 생각해 보면 이해가 쉽다.)

He **is having** lots of sisters and brothers. (X) → He **has** lots of sisters and brothers.

I **am knowing** his name. (X) → I **know** his name.

Are you **needing** someone? (X) → Do you **need** someone?

✽ 하지만 위의 동사들도 사용되는 상황의 의미에 따라 진행형으로 사용될 수도 있다.

- I am thinking about my hometown. (구체적이고 일시적인 행동을 의미)
- They are having lunch on the grass.
- We were having a good time.

Check-Up

C-1 틀린 문장을 골라 옳게 고치세요.

(1) I am needing a girlfriend.

(2) She is having a cup of coffee.

(3) We are having little time.

(4) Jimmy is remembering the day.

(5) I don't know his phone number or e-mail address.

C-2 다음을 영작하세요.

(1) 나는 지금 TV를 보고 있는 중이다.

(2) 엄마가 돌아오셨을 때 나는 혼자 저녁을 먹고 있는 중이었다.

(3) 내일 이맘때면 나는 시험을 보고 있을 것이다. (내일 이맘때: **this time tomorrow**)

완료 시제

1 **현재완료(have + 과거분사)** – 과거와 현재가 연결되고 있는 시제

1) **완료**: 과거부터 해오던 동작을 현재 막 끝냈음을 나타낸다.
- 주로 쓰이는 부사: already, just

I **have** already **finished** writing the paper.

They **have** just **arrived** at the station.

2) **계속**: 어떤 일이 과거부터 현재까지 계속되고 있음을 나타낸다.
- 주로 쓰이는 전치사, 접속사: for, since

It **has snowed** for three days.

We **have lived** in this house since 1982.

> **cf)** 현재완료진행: 현재완료의 계속 용법과 비슷하나, 진행의 의미가 더 강하다.
> They **have been playing** soccer for 2 hours.

3) **경험**: 과거의 경험을 현재에 지니고 있음을 나타낸다.
- 주로 쓰이는 부사: ever, never, often, before, once, twice, ~ times 등

I **have met** him many times.

Have you ever **seen** a real tiger?

- have been to ~: ~에 가본 적이 있다(경험), 갔다 왔다(완료)

I **have been to** Japan twice. (경험)

> **cf)** I **have been in** Japan for six months. (계속)
> I **have** just **been to** the station to see her off. (완료)

4) **결과**: 과거에 있었던 일의 결과가 현재에 영향을 미치고 있음을 나타낸다.

She **has lost** her umbrella. (우산을 잃어버려서 현재 갖고 있지 않다)

> **cf)** She **lost** her umbrella. (과거에 잃어버렸으나 그 뒤에 찾았는지 아닌지를 모름)

5) 현재완료에 쓸 수 없는 단어들

과거임을 알 수 있는 부사들(~ ago, yesterday, last month 등), when, in + 연도 등

I have been there last Saturday. (X) → I **went** there **last Saturday**.

When have you come? (X) → **When did** you come?

2 **과거완료(had + 과거분사)**

과거보다 앞선 일(대과거)을 나타내며, 과거를 기준으로 완료, 경험 등을 나타낼 수도 있다.

I **lost** the purse that my sister **had bought** for me on my birthday. (대과거)

He **had** already **left** when I **arrived** at his home. (완료)

She **had been** in Seoul for 2 years when I **met** her on the street. (계속)

She **knew** the man, since she **had seen** him before. (경험)

They **found** that the man **had gone** to a foreign country. (결과)

D-1   괄호 안의 동사를 알맞은 시제로 바꾸세요.

(1)   I (be) to the National Library many times.

(2)   She (wash) the dishes already, and now she is watching TV.

(3)   Miss Ulman (live) in Seattle since 1994.

(4)   We (go) to see the movie yesterday.

(5)   Mr. James (work) on the subject for 2 years.

(6)   I burned the letter which I (write) the night before.

(7)   They (learn) English for over 10 years.

(8)   What you (do) since he went out?

(9)   When I got there, he (leave) already.

(10) My girl friend (go) to the city to make money.

D-2   다음을 해석하세요.

(1)   Mrs. Harris has been in Germany for 5 years.

→ _____ .

(2)   It has been raining since last Thursday.

→ _____ .

(3)   The movie had already begun when I entered the theater.

→ _____ .

(4)   Henry recognized her, for he had seen her before.

→ _____ .

D-3   틀린 문장을 골라 옳게 고치세요.

(1)   When have you gone to Australia?

(2)   I have arrived in Hong Kong last night.

(3)   Miss Lewis has been sick for three days ago.

(4)   The train has already left when I got to the station.

 **주의해야 할 시제**

1 미래인데 현재를 쓰는 경우

1) 시간과 조건의 부사절에서는 의미상 미래여도 현재를 써야 한다. ← 반드시!

- 시간의 부사절: when, until, as soon as, after, before 등의 접속사가 이끄는 절
- 조건의 부사절: if, unless 등의 접속사가 이끄는 절

I will go home **as soon as** my boss **returns**.

If it **snows** on Christmas, I will meet my boy friend.

cf) 명사절과 형용사절에는 미래 시제를 쓴다.

I'm not sure if Susan will marry James. (명사절)

2004 is the year when I will enter a university. (형용사절)

2) 왕래발착 동사는 현재, 현재진행 시제로 미래를 나타낼 수 있다.

← 미래임을 알 수 있는 부사가 필요하다.

- 왕래발착 동사: go, come, start, leave, arrive 등

She leaves for New York <u>tomorrow morning</u>.

They are coming <u>tonight</u>.

2 과거의 일들을 순서대로 쓸 때는 과거완료를 쓰지 않고 모두 과거를 쓴다.

Janice **bought** the book yesterday and **read** it last night.

cf) Janice **read** the book last night which she **had bought** yesterday.

Check-Up

E-1 괄호 안의 동사를 알맞은 시제로 바꾸세요.

(1) I will go to bed after the TV show (end).

(2) You have to stay here until the captain (return).

(3) We don't know when the professor (have) us take a test.

(4) I will give you 100 dollars if you (make) it happen.

(5) I want to know if you (have) time on the 5th of April.

E-2 틀린 문장을 옳게 고치세요.

(1) Mr. Smith will leave tomorrow morning if it will be fine then.

(2) Helen will go home as soon as her boss will leave.

(3) I have no idea if he will win the game.

 시제의 일치

1 시제의 일치

주절과 종속절이 있는 경우 종속절의 시제에 제한이 있는 것을 말한다.

주절의 시제		종속절의 시제
현재, 현재완료, 미래	→	모든 시제가 다 올 수 있음
과거, 과거완료	→	과거, 과거완료

I think she is sick. → I **thought** she **was** sick.

She says she has been sick for a week. → She **said** she **had been** sick for a week.

2 시제 일치의 예외

불변의 진리, 현재의 습관, 지속적인 사실: 항상 현재

역사적인 사실: 항상 과거

He **told** them that the Earth **is** round.

She **said** that she **runs** for about 30 minutes every morning.

He **said** that World War I **ended** in 1918.

F-1 괄호 안에 동사의 알맞은 형태를 넣으세요.

(1) He says that he will study abroad.

→ He said that he (   ) (   ) abroad.

(2) She says that her mother has been ill for a month.

→ She said that her mother (   ) (   ) ill for a month.

F-2 틀린 문장을 골라 옳게 고치세요.

(1) Mr. Baker said that he will go to the United States next year.

(2) He said that the Earth was round.

(3) I believed he had left Korea.

(4) The teacher told us that light traveled fastest in the universe.

(5) She said that it would rain that night.

✳ 동사의 불규칙 변화형

bear	bore	born/borne	go	went	gone
beat	beat	beaten/beat	grow	grew	grown
become	became	become	hang	hung/hanged	hung/hanged
begin	began	begun	have	had	had
bite	bit	bitten	hear	heard	heard
blow	blew	blown	hide	hid	hidden
break	broke	broken	hit	hit	hit
bring	brought	brought	hold	held	held
broadcast	broadcast	broadcast	hurt	hurt	hurt
build	built	built	keep	kept	kept
buy	bought	bought	know	knew	known
catch	caught	caught	lay	laid	laid
choose	chose	chosen	lead	led	led
come	came	come	leave	left	left
cost	cost	cost	lend	lent	lent
cut	cut	cut	let	let	let
do	did	done	lie	lay	lain
draw	drew	drawn	lie	lied	lied
eat	ate	eaten	light	lit/lighted	lit/lighted
fall	fell	fallen	lose	lost	lost
feed	fed	fed	make	made	made
feel	felt	felt	mean	meant	meant
fight	fought	fought	meet	met	met
find	found	found	mistake	mistook	mistaken
fit	fit	fit	pay	paid	paid
fly	flew	flown	put	put	put
forbid	forbade	forbidden	quit	quit	quit
forecast	forecast	forecast	read	read	read
forget	forgot	forgotten	ride	rode	ridden
forgive	forgave	forgiven	ring	rang	rung
freeze	froze	frozen	rise	rose	risen
get	got	gotten	run	ran	run
give	gave	given	say	said	said

see	saw	seen	strike	struck	struck/stricken
seek	sought	sought	swear	swore	sworn
sell	sold	sold	sweep	swept	swept
send	sent	sent	swim	swam	swum
set	set	set	take	took	taken
shake	shook	shaken	teach	taught	taught
shine	shone/shined	shone/shined	tear	tore	torn
shoot	shot	shot	tell	told	told
show	showed	shown/showed	think	thought	thought
shut	shut	shut	throw	threw	thrown
sing	sang	sung	understand	understood	understood
sit	sat	sat	upset	upset	upset
sleep	slept	slept	wake	woke/waked	woken/waked
speak	spoke	spoken	wear	wore	worn
spend	spent	spent	weep	wept	wept
stand	stood	stood	win	won	won
steal	stole	stolen	withdraw	withdrew	withdrawn
stick	stuck	stuck	write	wrote	written

1

보기와 같이 각 문장의 구성요소를 표시하세요. (주어는 S, 동사는 V, 목적어는 O, 주격 보어는 SC, 목적격 보어는 OC로 표시하세요.)

(1) Debbie woke up in the morning.

(2) Tim can't reach the ceiling.

(3) I like living in Cheju Island in winter.

(4) I saw the little girl playing with her pretty doll.

(5) The baby sleeping in the bed looks happy.

(6) My friend sent me a present by mail.

(7) It is important to keep one's promise.

(8) You know that you should stop at the red traffic light.

(9) There are two students in the classroom.

(10) My mother always calls me 'baby.'

[2-4] 동사의 변화형이 잘못 제시된 것을 찾으세요.

2

(A) bear - bore - born

(B) blow - blew - blown

(C) break - broke - broken

(D) choose - cheese - chosen

3

(A) cut - cut - cut

(B) feel - feel - feel

(C) cost - cost - cost

(D) put - put - put

4

(A) eat - ate - ate

(B) fight - fought - fought

(C) come - came - come

(D) meet - met - met

[5-6] 완료시제의 용법이 보기와 같은 것을 고르세요.

5

(보기) Bob has been in Chicago since last Tuseday.

(A) My parents have been married for forty years.

(B) Mike has already eaten breakfast.

(C) I have been to that theater five or six times.

(D) Peter is not here. He has gone to Paris.

6 I <u>have never heard</u> such a beautiful song.

    (A) I <u>have just finished</u> my homework.

    (B) Jane <u>has been</u> out of town for two days.

    (C) <u>Have you ever fallen</u> in love?

    (D) I <u>have moved</u> into a new apartment.

[7-8] 어법상 올바르지 않은 문장을 고르세요.

7

    (A) I learned that two and three makes five.

    (B) Mother said that the Korean War broke out in 1950

    (C) When I arrived there, the meeting already ended.

    (D) The teacher says that there will be a test in the afternoon.

8

    (A) If you come tomorrow, I will wait for you at your house.

    (B) She has met her teacher two hours ago.

    (C) I am leaving Seoul tomorrow morning.

    (D) I have been studying for an hour.

9 아래의 우리말에 맞게 주어진 영어 단어들을 배열하세요. (첫 단어는 대문자로 시작하세요.)

    (1) 나는 내 여동생에게 오랫동안 편지를 쓰지 않았다.

       (written, I, long, a, haven't, to, sister, my, for, a letter, time)

    → _____ .

    (2) 나는 그제 그 책을 샀다.

       (I, the, before, book, yesterday, the, bought, day)

    → _____ .

Vocabulary

□ **break out**: (전쟁이) 발발하다

유형 3   동사–명사 혼동

1 Leaf-cutting ants <u>building</u> <u>their</u> nests <u>under</u> the ground.
        A   B   C   D

유형 7   동사 찾기

1 In the 1972 Olympics Mark Spitz _____ a record seven gold
medals.

(A) to win   (B) winning   (C) winner   (D) won

유형 25   동사 자리에 준동사를 쓴 경우

1 The sunlight <u>leaving</u> the <u>sun's</u> surface eight minutes <u>before</u> we see <u>it</u>.
               A   B   C   D

2 <u>In</u> some ways the ancient Olympics <u>to be</u> much <u>like</u> <u>today's</u> Olympic games.
  A   B   C   D

유형 26   진행 시제의 형태가 맞지 않을 경우

1 <u>The</u> <u>number</u> of bald <u>eagles</u> is <u>increase</u> in the United States.
   A   B   C   D

유형 27   완료 시제의 형태가 잘못된 경우

1 Throughout <u>time</u>, maps have <u>be</u> important <u>to</u> <u>people</u> around the world.
             A   B   C   D

2 <u>Have</u> you <u>ever</u> <u>broke</u> <u>your</u> arm?
    A   B   C   D

Chapter · 5

1 In 1849, thousands of men come to California because they wanted to find
             A   B   C   D
gold.

2 Originally the White House was gray, but now it was white.
      A   B   C   D

3 I sit in class at this exact same time yesterday.
  A B   C   D

Vocabulary

□ **originally:** 원래

1 I met <u>my</u> boyfriend yesterday and <u>tell</u> him <u>that</u> I love <u>him</u>.
　　　　 A 　　　　　　　　　　　　 B 　　 C 　　　 D

2 I visited <u>New York</u> <u>during</u> the summer vacation and <u>to meet</u> my brother <u>there</u>.
　　　　 A 　　　　 B 　　　　　　　　　　　　　 C 　　　　　　 D

3 The teacher <u>is</u> <u>listen</u> to the tape, <u>and</u> the students <u>are, too</u>.
　　　　　　　　 A 　　 B 　　　　　 C 　　　　　　　 D

4 In old <u>times</u>, the Greek people <u>believe</u> that <u>their</u> gods lived <u>on</u> the tops of the
　　　　　 A 　　　　　　　　　　 B 　　　 C 　　　　　 D
mountains.

5 I have <u>keep</u> the door <u>open</u> <u>since</u> my daughter went out <u>to play</u>.
　　　　　 A 　　　　　 B 　　 C 　　　　　　　　　　 D

6 When human beings began <u>to live</u>, other animals <u>were</u> <u>already</u> living <u>on earth</u>.
　　　　　　　　　　　　 A 　　 B 　　　　　　 C 　　　　 D

7 Since the <u>Korean War</u>, Korea <u>is separated</u> <u>into</u> two <u>different</u> nations.
　　　　　　 A 　　　　　　　 B 　　 C 　　　 D

8 <u>My</u> cousin Young, <u>who</u> lives in a small town <u>near</u> Seattle, <u>visiting</u> me yesterday.
　　 A 　　　　　　 B 　　　　　　　　　 C 　　　　 D

9 I regret <u>that</u> <u>my friend</u> John Whittier <u>has died</u> two weeks <u>ago</u>.
　　　　　 A 　　 B 　　　　　　　　 C 　　　　　 D

10 If the new millennium <u>will come</u>, I hope <u>there</u> <u>will be</u> no <u>more</u> wars.
　　　　　　　　　　 A 　　　　　　 B 　　 C 　　 D

Vocabulary

□ **separate A into B**: A를 B로 분리하다　　　　□ **millennium**: 천년

1   We clean our <u>clothes</u> by <u>wash</u> <u>them</u> in soap and <u>water</u>.
                       A   B   C   D

2   Plants use energy _____ chemicals from the air and soil to make food.

    (A) to take in   (B) when to take

    (C) being taken in   (D) takes in

3   So far, scientists <u>have discovered</u> more <u>than</u> a dozen <u>vitamin</u> important <u>for</u>
                                  A   B   C   D
  human beings.

4   For <u>our</u> environment, no <u>living thing</u> can <u>being allowed</u> to disappear and make
         A   B   C
  nature lose <u>its</u> balance.
               D

5   Only a few types of vegetables _____ more than two years.

    (A) that live   (B) of living

    (C) to live   (D) live

6   Alex <u>caught</u> my <u>attend</u> when he played the <u>leading</u> role in <u>that play</u>.
            A   B   C   D

7   It is thought _____ feelings.

    (A) since plants have   (B) it is plants that

    (C) that plants have   (D) plants to have

8 Half of earth is always covered with light from the sun.
          A   B   C   D

9 African elephants are larger, fiercer, and difficult to tame than Asian elephants.
          A   B   C   D

10 The dingo has a face like a wolf, howls like a wolf, and hunts in a pack the way

_____ .

(A) why wolves do   (B) when wolves do

(C) wolves doing   (D) wolves do

11 Just as steam becomes water if its temperature falls below 212°F,

_____ air becomes liquid when its temperature is reduced to

-312°F.

(A) at which   (B) so

(C) at such   (D) so does

12 Every nation grants its citizens certain rights and privileges and imposes on

their certain duties and responsibilities.

Vocabulary

- **chemical**: 화학약품(pl.)
- **fierce**: 사나운
- **howl**: (개, 늑대 등이) 소리를 길게 뽑으며 짖다
- **impose**: 부과하다
- **attention**: 주의, 주목
- **tame**: 길들이다
- **pack**: 한패
- **leading role**: 주연
- **dingo**: 오스트레일리아산 들개
- **privilege**: 특권

STRUCTURE

CHAPTER 6

EH

Grammar Up / Power Up Test / Pattern Drill / Pattern Review / Mini Test

A 수동태와 능동태

1 능동태는 주어가 직접 행동을 하고 수동태는 주어가 다른 대상으로부터 행동을 받거나 당한다.

능동태 Hemingway wrote *The Old Man and the Sea.*
          ③   ②   ①

수동태 *The Old Man and the Sea* was written by Hemingway.

① 능동태의 목적어 → 수동태의 주어
② 동사 → be + 과거분사
③ 능동태의 주어 → 문장 끝에 by + 행위의 주체 (목적격)

Check-Up

A 다음 문장의 태를 바꾸세요.

(1) Many singers sing the song *La Vie en Rose.*

→ _____.

(2) This picture was painted by Claude Monet.

→ _____.

(3) He hit me on the back.

→ _____.

(4) Snow covers the top of the mountain.

→ _____.

(5) Today most people use cellular phones.

→ _____.

 **수동태**

1 수동태가 가능한 동사

1) 목적어를 갖는 동사(타동사)
   – 목적어가 없으면 수동태의 주어가 있을 수 없기 때문에 문장이 불가능하다. 따라서 목적어가 없는
     자동사는 수동태를 만들 수 없다.
   – 타동사의 역할을 하는 '자동사 + 전치사' 의 어구도 수동태가 가능하다.

2) 기쁨, 놀람, 슬픔, 실망 등 '감정 유발 타동사' 가 수동태로 쓰이는 경우
   이 경우 전치사는 대부분 by가 아니다.
   The news **surprised** me. → I **was surprised at** the news.
   The present **pleased** Sue. → Sue **was pleased with** the present.

2 수동태의 시제: be 동사로 표현한다

She **will be** welcomed by the people.
The boy **has been** treated badly by the adults.
The song **is being** played by Lucy.

3 수동태의 부정문, 의문문, 명령문

The movie **is not screened** in this city.
Did her parents scold her? → **Was** she **scolded** by her parents?
Who **was elected** chairperson of the committee? (의문사는 그대로 문장 앞에)
Turn the TV off. → **Let** the TV **be turned off**.
Don't throw it away. → **Don't let** it **be thrown away**. = **Let** it **not be thrown away**.

4 4형식의 수동태

1) 대부분의 경우는 직접목적어, 간접목적어 둘 다 수동태의 주어가 된다.
   Scott gave **me this ring**.
   → **This ring was given** (to) me by Scott.
   → **I was given** this ring by Scott.

2) 직접목적어만 수동태의 주어가 되는 경우: buy, bring, get, make, pass(건네주다), send,
   sing, write 등
   Johnny sent me **a Christmas card**.
   → **A Christmas card was sent** to me by Johnny. (O)
   → I was sent a Christmas card by Johnny. (X)

Vocabulary

□ **treat badly:** 구박하다   □ **screen:** 상영하다   □ **scold:** 혼내다

Chapter • 6

3) 간접목적어만 수동태의 주어가 되는 경우: answer, envy(질투하다), refuse(거절하다) 등

I envied **him** (for) his talent.

→ **He was envied** (for) his talent by me. (O)

→ His talent was envied (for) him by me. (X)

5 **지각동사, 사역동사가 있는 문장의 수동태:** 능동태에서는 지각동사, 사역동사의 목적보어로 동사원형이 쓰이지만, 수동태에서는 to 부정사가 쓰인다.

The teacher **saw** the boys **play** baseball.

→ The boys **were seen to play** baseball by the teacher.

My mother **made** me **clean** my room.

→ I **was made to clean** my room by my mother.

6 **목적어가 that 절일 경우의 수동태:** 주어가 일반인인 They나 People이며, 동사 say, think, know, believe, feel, expect 등의 목적어가 that절일 때 두 가지 수동태가 가능하다.

People say that Tim is kind.

→ **It is said that** Tim is kind.

→ Tim **is said to** be kind.

They believe that she will pass the exam.

→ It **is believed that** she will pass the exam.

→ She **is believed to** pass the exam.

7 **by 외의 전치사를 쓰는 경우**

1) at: 놀라거나 무서운 경우

be amazed at, be frightened at(~에 겁먹다), be shocked at, be surprised at(or by) 등

2) with: 기쁘거나 실망한 경우

be pleased with, be satisfied with, be disappointed with(~에 실망하다)

기타) be covered with, be acquainted with(~와 아는 사이다)

3) about: 걱정하는 경우

be worried about, be concerned about(~을 걱정하다)

4) in, to 등

be interested in, be married to(~와 결혼하다), be known to 사람(~에게 알려지다), be known for 내용(~로 유명하다), be known as(~라고 알려지다), be known by(~에 의해 판단되다)

8 **행위자(by ~)가 생략되는 경우:** 행위의 주체가 일반인이거나 누구인지 확실하지 않을 때는 생략할 수 있다.

Pizza is eaten all over the world these days.

Her father was killed in the war.

Check-Up

B-1 수동태가 가능한 문장을 골라 수동태로 바꾸세요.

(1) They invented the motion picture.

(2) She understands what I tell her.

(3) She got angry at my behavior.

(4) The sight surprised me.

(5) They look down on the man.

B-2 다음을 영작하세요.

(1) 그 세탁기는 10년째 사용되고 있다.

→ _____.

(2) 우리는 무라카미 선생님으로부터 일본어를 배우게 될 것이다.

→ _____.

(3) 아이들에 의해 눈사람(snowman)이 만들어지고 있다.

→ _____.

B-3 다음을 수동태로 바꾸세요.

(1) Did she clean the house?

(2) Do it at once.

(3) Who directed the movie *Christmas in August*?

(4) Does she drive the car?

(5) Never close the door.

B-4 다음을 수동태로 바꾸세요.

(1) My husband will pick me up on his way home.

(2) We should look into the matter.

(3) She looks after her nephew.

(4) The bad boys laughed at the dwarf.

(5) He always speaks ill of his boss.

Chapter • 6

B-5 다음을 수동태로 바꾸세요. (두 가지가 가능한 것은 두 가지 방식으로 모두)

(1) He told me a surprising story.

(2) My father bought me a bicycle.

(3) They envy him his wealth.

(4) She made me a cushion.

(5) My sister gave me a skirt.

B-6 다음을 수동태로 바꾸세요.

(1) We all heard the baby cry.

(2) The mother was watching her son play on the playground.

(3) The teacher made the students read it aloud.

B-7 다음을 두 종류의 수동태 문장으로 바꾸세요.

(1) They say that Deborah is smart.

(2) They believe that Mr. Parker will be the president.

(3) People think that the man is guilty.

B-8a 괄호 안에 알맞은 전치사를 넣으세요.

(1) I was shocked (   ) the news.

(2) She is pleased (   ) the present.

(3) They are satisfied (   ) the result.

(4) What are you interested (   )?

(5) He is concerned (   ) the thing.

B-8b 틀린 문장을 골라 옳게 고치세요.

(1) She is worried by her husband's health.

(2) The man is known by all the people in the town.

(3) We all were frightened by it.

(4) I was disappointed by his attitude.

(5) He is annoyed with the matter.

Vocabulary

□ playground: 운동장   □ aloud: 소리를 내어

122

1

다음 문장들을 보기와 같이 바꾸세요.

> 보기 Bob mailed the package. → The package <u>was mailed by Bob.</u>

(1) Ms. Hopkins invited me to dinner.

→ I _____ .

(2) Mr. Cart kept the door key in the box.

→ The door key _____ .

(3) The doctor has examined the sick child.

→ The sick child _____ .

(4) The jeweler is going to fix my watch.

→ My watch _____ .

(5) A maid will clean our hotel room.

→ Our hotel room _____ .

2

다음 문장들을 보기와 같이 바꾸세요.

> 보기 Did you kill the bird? → <u>Was the bird killed by you?</u>

(1) My cat didn't kill the bird.

→ The bird _____ .

(2) Johnny cannot break the window.

→ The window _____ .

(3) Is your father repairing his car?

→ _____ ?

(4) Does the hotel provide clean towels?

→ _____ ?

(5) Who invented the radio?

→ _____ ?

(6) We saw him enter the room.

→ He _____ .

Vocabulary

□ **examine**: 진찰하다, 조사하다   □ **jeweler**: 보석상   □ **provide**: 공급하다, 제공하다

(7) Do your homework now.

　　→ _____ .

(8) They say that he is kind.

　　→ It _____ .

　　→ He _____ .

3　다음의 ( ) 안에 들어갈 알맞은 단어를 보기 중에서 찾으세요. (한 단어를 두 번 이상 선택할 수 있습니다.)

> 보기　　with　　　　to　　　　at　　　　by

(1) The boys are surprised _____ thunder.

(2) Ms. Brown is known _____ everybody in town.

(3) A man is known _____ the company he keeps.

(4) She is satisfied _____ her present apartment.

(5) The classroom is crowded _____ too many students.

[4-7]　( )에 가장 알맞은 것은?

4　One of my friends ( ) her brother's teacher.

(A) was married by　　　　　　(B) was married to

(C) was married for　　　　　　(D) was married with

5　Our mail ( ) before noon every day.

(A) is delivered　　　　　　(B) delivers

(C) is delivered by　　　　　　(D) is delivered to

6　This house ( ) me.

(A) belongs　　(B) is belonged　　(C) belongs to　　(D) is belonged to

7　George ( ) go abroad.

(A) says　　(B) is said　　(C) is said by　　(D) is said to

Vocabulary

□ thunder: 천둥

124

Pattern Drill

유형 29   능동태와 수동태를 혼동하여 쓴 경우

  1   <u>Mount</u> Kilimanjaro <u>knew to</u> local people <u>as</u> the "Mountain of Cold Devils."
       A   B   C   D

  2   <u>Ancient</u> people <u>were looked</u> into the night sky and <u>saw</u> <u>shapes</u> in the stars.
       A   B   C   D

유형 30   수동태의 형태가 잘못된 경우

  1   <u>The</u> seven <u>largest</u> pieces of land are <u>call</u> <u>continents</u>.
       A   B   C   D

  2   If something <u>is dividing into</u> 10 <u>equal parts</u>, <u>each</u> part is 1/10.
                   A   B   C   D

Chapter • 6

Vocabulary

☐ **Mount Kilimanjaro**: 킬리만자로 산   ☐ **local**: (특정한) 지방의   ☐ **devil**: 악마
☐ **continent**: 대륙   ☐ **divide**: 나누다

1   Cars, buses <u>and</u> trucks <u>are used</u> roads, <u>but</u> trains <u>run on</u> tracks.
                 A   B   C   D

2   Mother <u>didn't know</u> that the cake had <u>already</u> <u>eaten by</u> the <u>children</u>.
                A   B   C   D

3   *Romeo and Juliet* <u>was</u> <u>wrote</u> <u>not by</u> Hemingway, <u>but by</u> Shakespeare.
                    A   B   C   D

4   <u>Yesterday</u> our teacher <u>was arrived</u> five <u>minutes</u> <u>late</u>.
        A   B   C D

5   If I <u>post</u> this letter today, <u>it</u> will <u>deliver</u> <u>to</u> you tomorrow.
          A   B   C   D

6   <u>My old</u> TV set <u>is repairing</u> <u>by</u> my <u>girlfriend</u>, Sera.
        A   B   C   D

7   *Hangeul* was <u>first</u> <u>invent</u> by King Sejong, <u>the</u> greatest Korean king <u>of all</u>.
                  A   B   C   D

8   On <u>the</u> day <u>before</u> Christmas, the stores <u>crowd</u> with <u>a lot of</u> customers.
            A   B   C   D

9   I'm <u>very</u> <u>interesting</u> in science, and I want <u>to be</u> a great <u>scientist</u>.
          A   B   C   D

10   Janet, <u>a</u> smart African-American girl, <u>has chosen</u> as <u>the best</u> student by all
          A   B   C
     <u>students</u>.
      D

1 From end <u>to</u> end, <u>ours</u> solar system <u>measures</u> <u>trillions of</u> miles.
            A   B   C   D

2 Jake cuts <u>his own</u> hair <u>at</u> home <u>instead</u> going to <u>a</u> barber.
                A   B   C   D

3 An island _____ with water all around it.

(A) is a piece of land   (B) to be a piece of land

(C) which is a piece of land   (D) a piece of land

4 *The Little Prince* by Antoine de Saint-Exupéry is <u>so</u> a famous novel that both
    A   B
children <u>and</u> adults read <u>it</u>.
          C   D

5 The Mediterranean Sea _____ Europe from Africa.

(A) separates   (B) to separate

(C) separating   (D) be separated

6 When a bee <u>dies of</u> hard work, a young worker <u>immediate</u> takes <u>the place</u> of
               A   B   C
the dead <u>one</u>.
        D

7 Our heart weighs less than a kilogram, but it is _____ organs in our
body.

(A) the strongest one   (B) that the strongest one is

(C) the strongest one has   (D) one of the strongest

8 Canning is the most widely using method of food preservation.
  A   B   C   D

9 In the United States, _____ special programs that help the
  homeless.

(A) there are   (B) having

(C) to be   (D) has

10 These days, families are smaller, and more women are working as before.
  A   B   C   D

11 Pocket billiards is played on a table that has pockets in each corner and one in
                      A   B

center of each of the longer sides.
  C   D

12 The first schools in Hawaii were _____ established by
  missionaries; today most of the schools are secular, and education is
  compulsory.

(A) what   (B) those

(C) them   (D) they

Vocabulary

- solar system: 태양계
- take the place of ~: ~를 대신하다
- widely: 널리
- the homeless = homeless people: 노숙자들
- compulsory: 의무적인
- trillion: 1조(兆)
- organ: 기관, 조직
- method: 방법
- missionary: 선교사
- The Mediterranean Sea: 지중해
- canning: 통조림(법)
- preservation: 보존, 저장
- secular: 비종교적인, 세속의

STRUCTURE

CHAPTER 7

조동사

Grammar Up / Power Up Test / Pattern Drill / Pattern Review / Mini Test

조동사의 특징

조동사란 단독으로 사용되지 않으며, 동사 앞에 위치하여 미래를 나타내기 위하여 쓰이거나 <u>말하는 사람의 태도에 대한 강도</u>를 표현한다.

예를 들어 전달하고자 하는 내용에 대한 확신이 없거나 거짓말을 하는 입장이라면 말하는 사람의 태도에 자신감이 없을 것이며(태도의 강도가 약해짐), 확신이 없거나 거짓말일지도 모른다는 태도를 상대방에게 전달하려면 가정법을 사용하게 된다. 따라서 가정법의 주절에는 말하는 사람의 자신감 없는 태도를 표현하기 위하여 조동사가 필요하게 된다.

조동사의 종류에는 can, could, may, might, must, ought (to), shall, should, will, would, had better 등이 있다. 조동사와 유사한 역할을 하는 유사 조동사구(Phrasal modals)로는 be able to, be going to, be supposed to, have to, have got to, used to 등이 있다. 유사 조동사는 will be able to와 같이 조동사와 함께 사용되는 경우도 있다.

1 뒤에는 반드시 동사 원형이 온다.

You **may go** out and play.

2 주어가 3인칭 단수여도 -(e)s가 붙지 않는다.

Diane can swim better than I.

3 부정문은 조동사 + not

I **cannot** finish it in a week.   You **may not** enter the room.

4 의문문은 조동사만을 앞으로 보내서 만든다.

May I come in?   **Shall** we go to the movies?

5 조동사는 둘 이상을 함께 쓸 수 없다.

You **will can** speak English well soon. (×) → You **will be able to** speak English well soon. (○)

Check-Up

A 잘못된 문장을 골라 바르게 고치세요.

(1) She can makes pizza at home.   (2) The boy mays play with the toy.

(3) Do I should clean the room alone?   (4) The drunken man couldn't stand up.

(5) They will can have a vacation next week.

 **조동사의 종류**

1 CAN(cannot, can't, could, could not, couldn't)

1) 능력 (ability and possibility, ~할 수 있다)

I have some money. I **can** buy an ice cream.

She **will be able to** get there in time. (can의 미래형 표현)

The baby **could** read a book. = The baby **was able to** read a book. (can의 과거형 표현)

2 MAY(may not, might, might not)

1) 허가, 공손한 부탁(permission, polite request, ~ 해도 된다)

May I come in?　Yes, you **may**.

- 부정: may not(불가)/must not(강한 금지): ~해서는 안 된다

May I have these potato chips?

No, you **may not**. You have to diet. / No, you **must not**. They're not fresh.

❋ can과 may의 의미상 기본적 차이점

can은 physically able의 의미를 내포하고, may는 허가(permission)를 포함한다.

Student: **Can** I leave the room?

Teacher: You **can** leave the room if you have legs, but you **may** not leave the room until you
　　　　　receive permission.

그러나, 일상 생활 회화의 경우에는 허가(informal permission) 및 공손한 부탁(informal polite request) 을
표현하기 위하여 may와 can이 혼용되어 사용된다.

Can I use your telephone? = **May** I use your telephone?

➡ 집중조명 1

◆ 공손한 부탁(polite request): may, might, can, could, will, would

may는 주로 1인칭의 경우에만 사용되고, might은 너무나 격식이 있는 표현이기 때문에 흔하게
사용되지는 않으며, can은 informal한 표현법이다. please를 첨가하여 표현을 다양화시킬 수도
있다.

　　May I borrow your pen?

　　Would you (please) pass the salt? (will보다 격식있고 공손한 표현)

　　Please shut the door. Shut the door, **could** <u>you</u>? Shut the door, <u>**won't you**</u>?

2) 추측: ~일지 모른다(less than 50% certainty)

She **may** be at home now,

= She **might** be at home now,　⎤

= She **could** be at home now,　⎦　but it's very unlikely. (50% 이하의 확신)

◆ 확신에 대한 강도

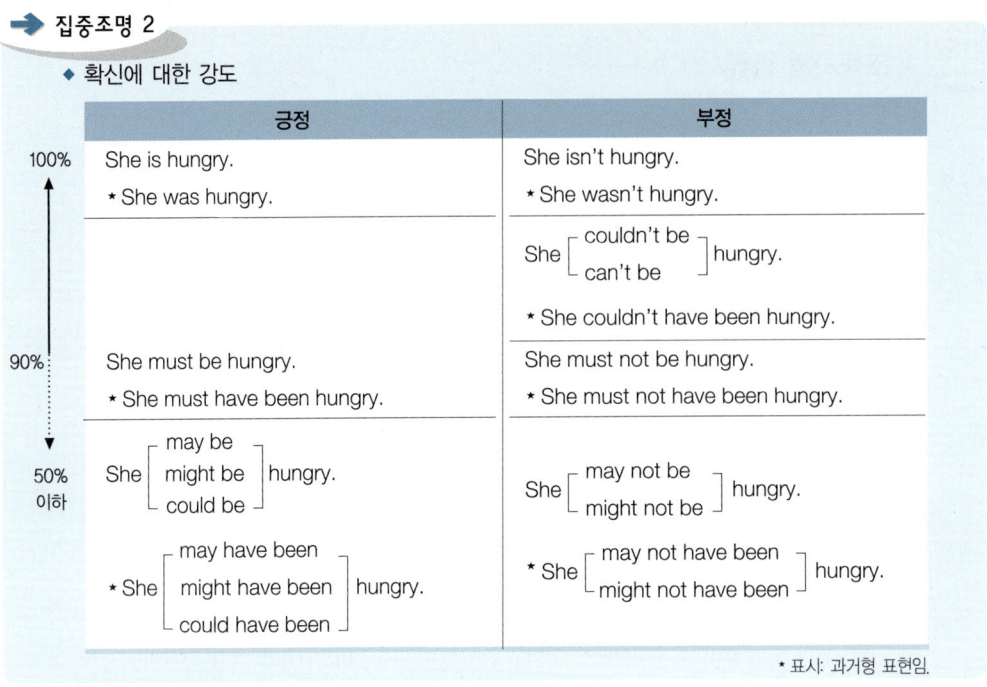

	긍정	부정
100%	She is hungry. * She was hungry.	She isn't hungry. * She wasn't hungry.
		She [couldn't be / can't be] hungry. * She couldn't have been hungry.
90%	She must be hungry. * She must have been hungry.	She must not be hungry. * She must not have been hungry.
50% 이하	She [may be / might be / could be] hungry. * She [may have been / might have been / could have been] hungry.	She [may not be / might not be] hungry. * She [may not have been / might not have been] hungry.

* 표시: 과거형 표현임.

- may (= might, could) have + pp   (~ 이었을지도 모른다)
  cannot (= could not) have + pp   (~ 이었을리가 없다)
  must have + pp   (~ 이었음에 틀림없다)

3   **MUST:** 필요, 금지, 확신(necessity, prohibition, 95% certainty)

1) 필요(= have to, have got to): ~해야 한다, ~를 꼭 해야 할 필요가 있다

I **must** go now. = I **have to** go now. = I **have got to** go now.

(must가 가장 강렬한 의미 전달. have got to는 informal 표현)

He **had to** do his homework last night. (must와 have got to의 과거형 표현)

She **has to** get up at 5 o'clock. = She **will have to** get up at five o'clock. (must의 미래형 표현)

※ must와 should의 차이점(necessity vs. advisability)

- must, have to, have got to는 필요(necessity)의 개념이며, should, ought to, had better ('d better)는 충고(advisability)의 개념으로 이해해야 한다.
  You**'d better** not be late. (~해야 한다, ~하는 편이 낫다)
  *should나 ought to보다 had better가 강력한 표현이다.

2) 확신 또는 논리적인 결론, 금지: ~임에 틀림없다. ~를 해서는 안된다

She **must** be sick. (현재시제, 95% 확신또는 논리적 결론)

You **must not** (= mustn't) call her again. (금지)

You **do not have to** call her again. (필요가 없음. = don't need to = need not)

4   **SHALL:** 제안(suggestion)의 의미(we와 I가 주어인 경우에 사용)

Shall I close the door? (문을 닫아도 될까요?, 문을 닫는게 어떨까요?)

Shall we go? (이제 그만 갈까요?)

Let's go, **shall we?** (청유문의 부가의문문에 사용, 제안의 의미 포함)

❋ SHOULD: 강력한 충고 (= ought to, had better)

You **should**n't leave your keys in the car.

• should의 과거형: should have + p.p: ~했어야 했는데 (실제로는 하지 않았음)

You **shouldn't have** start**ed** cheating.

5 WILL(부정: will not = won't)

1) 단순미래(= is going to)

My sister **will** meet us at the airport. (ch.5, p.100참조)

2) 말하는 순간의 미래 행동에 대한 의지: ~하겠다

Just a minute. I **will** try again.

3) 명령문의 부가 의문문

Show me the picture of your girlfriend, **will you?** (상대방의 의지에 대한 질문)

4) 권유, 부탁: ~할래요? (p.133 집중조명 1 참조)

❋ WOULD

• will의 과거형

He said that his brother **would** arrive soon.

• 권유, 부탁(will보다 공손한 표현, p.133 집중조명 1 참조)

Would you please open the door?

• 과거의 규칙적인 습관: ~하곤 했다(action 포함. would를 불규칙적인 습관의 의미를 나타내는 것으로 설명하는 교재들도 있기는 하지만 정확한 설명이라고 할 수는 없다. 참고: Cobuild English Usage p.801, Oxford Practical English Usage p.629)

When I was young, I **would**(= used to) listen to the radio.

* used to: 과거의 규칙적 습관 (action을 포함한 경우와 situation을 표현하는 경우에 모두 쓰임)

I **used to**(≠ would) have a BMW. (situation)

I **used to**(= would) listen to the radio before bed. (action 포함)

• **would rather**: preference, 선호의 의미(참고로 had better는 advisability의 의미)

What **would** you **rather** do than go to class?

B-1 알맞은 낱말에 동그라미를 치세요.

(1) Ms. Wilson must (is, be) over thirty.

(2) I (will, would) write letters when I was in my teens.

(3) He may (be, have been) at home last night.

(4) I'd like (eat, to eat) out this evening.

(5) (Will, Shall) I go and get him? No, you don't have to.

B-2 두 문장이 같은 뜻이 되도록 알맞은 말을 넣으세요.

(1) I should return this to the owner.

= I (　　) (　　) return this to the owner.

(2) You don't have to come to the meeting.

= You (　　) not come to the meeting.

(3) He could solve the problem.

= He was (　　) (　　) solve the problem.

(4) I want to talk with him.

= I (　　) (　　) to talk with him.

(5) Keep quiet during the exam.

= You (　　) keep quiet during the exam.

B-3 주어진 의미가 되도록 괄호 안에 알맞은 낱말을 넣으세요.

(1) You (　　) better get up earlier. 「너는 더 일찍 일어나는 게 좋겠어.」

(2) We (　　) to take a walk every evening. 「우리는 매일 저녁 산책을 하곤 했지.」

(3) There (　　) (　　) been an accident. 「사고가 일어났었음에 틀림없다.」

(4) He (　　) be a doctor. 「그 사람이 의사일 리가 없어.」

(5) This car (　　) be Mrs. Taylor's. 「이 차는 테일러 부인 차일지 몰라.」

B-4   문장을 지시대로 고쳐 쓰세요.

(1)   She must be happy to get the prize. (과거로)

→ _____ .

(2)   You may come home late. (부정의 의미로)

→ _____ .

(3)   Mr. Jones should pay the bill. (의문문으로)

→ _____ ?

(4)   We must finish the work by tomorrow morning. (부정의 의미로)

→ _____ .

(5)   Mark must do the work by himself. (미래로)

→ _____ .

B-5   다음을 영작하세요.

(1)   나는 춤추는 데 익숙하지 않다.

→ _____ .

(2)   로저(Roger)는 오늘 일찍 집에 가야 한다.

→ _____ .

(3)   우리는 내일 학교에 갈 필요가 없다.

→ _____ .

(4)   당신 방에 들어가도 돼요?

→ _____ ?

(5)   앤(Anne)은 어렸을 때는 피아노를 못 쳤었다.

→ _____ .

Chapter · 7

Power Up Test

1   우리말에 알맞은 조동사를 찾아 쓰세요.

(1) I learned how to play the piano, so I _____ play it. (~할 수 있다)

(2) I _____ like to listen to rock music now. (~하고 싶다)

(3) I have a test tomorrow. So, I _____ to study tonight. (~해야 한다)

(4) I _____ to tell a lie when I was a child. (~하곤 했다)

(5) He _____ be happy to see his mother. (~임에 틀림없다)

(6) You _____ have this book. I'll give it to you. (~해도 좋다/된다)

(7) You _____ better take a rest for a moment. (~하는 편이 낫다)

(8) You _____ not play with a lighter. (~해서는 안 된다)

(9) You _____ not give up your job. (~할 필요가 없다)

(10) You _____ be a Korean. You can't speak Korean at all. (~일리가 없다)

2   나머지 세 문장과 의미가 다른 한 문장을 찾으세요.

(A) You should do the job by 2 o'clock in the afternoon.

(B) You would do the job by 2 o'clock in the afternoon.

(C) You ought to do the job by 2 o'clock in the afternoon.

(D) You'd better do the job by 2 o'clock in the afternoon.

[3-5]   (   )에 가장 알맞은 조동사를 고르세요.

3   Let's study together tonight, (   ) we?

(A) will   (B) would

(C) shall   (D) should

4   He dances very well. He (   ) a professional dancer when young.

(A) cannot be   (B) cannot have been

(C) must be   (D) must have been

Vocabulary

□ **for a moment**: 잠시 동안

5   My house (   ) be here, but it burned down in a fire.

(A) used to   (B) would

(C) should   (D) might

6   짝지어진 두 문장의 의미가 서로 다른 것은 어느 것입니까?

(A) I can help you to clean the room. = I am able to help you to clean the room.

(B) I will drive to Los Angeles next week. = I am going to drive to Los Angeles next week.

(C) You don't have to work too hard. = You must not work too hard.

(D) You should keep the traffic rules. = You ought to keep the traffic rules.

7   어법상 가장 올바른 문장을 고르세요.

(A) You had not better eat something between meals.

(B) You ought to not make a noise here.

(C) I will must go to see a doctor an hour later.

(D) I would rather help my mother than read this book.

8   아래의 우리말에 맞게 주어진 영어 단어들을 배열하세요. (첫 단어는 반드시 대문자로 시작하세요.)

(1) 착한 학생은 수업을 빼먹어서는 안 된다. (a, not, should, any, good, miss, student, class)

→ _____ .

(2) 그 아기는 배가 고픈 것이 틀림없다. (baby, be, the, must, hungry)

→ _____ .

(3) 나는 여기에서 세라를 기다려야만 한다. (I, for, to, here, have, Sera, wait)

→ _____ .

Vocabulary

□ **traffic**: 교통

유형 31   조동사 뒤에 동사 원형을 쓰지 않은 경우

1 No one can <u>proves</u> that something really <u>happened</u> billions of years <u>ago</u>.
    A   B   C   D

2 <u>Animals</u> must <u>eating</u> <u>living</u> things, <u>including</u> plants and animals.
       A   B   C   D

Vocabulary

□ **prove**: 증명하다   □ **billion**: 10억   □ **include ~**: ~를 포함하다

140

Pattern Review

1   Because coffee can <u>helps</u> me <u>stay</u> <u>awake</u>, I usually drink <u>it</u> when I study.
                     A   B   C   D

2   Our world is mostly <u>water</u>, <u>as</u> you can <u>seeing</u> <u>from</u> the map of the world.
                     A   B   C   D

3   <u>An</u> invitation should <u>included</u> <u>your</u> name, the date and <u>the time</u>.
     A   B   C   D

4   We must <u>to learn</u> <u>from</u> the mistakes <u>which</u> our mothers and fathers <u>have made</u>.
              A   B   C   D

5   You used to <u>coming</u> at ten <u>o'clock</u>, <u>but</u> now you come <u>at noon</u>.
                 A   B   C   D

Vocabulary

□ **awake**: 깨어있는   □ **mostly**: 대부분, 주로   □ **invitation**: 초대, 초대장

1 Veterans are men <u>who</u> left the army when <u>they</u> became <u>too</u> old to <u>fighting</u>.
         A   B   C   D

2 American classes are <u>usually</u> <u>made up of</u> students <u>from</u> many different
                                   A   B   C

    <u>country</u>.
        D

3 Very little is known _____ the family life of most cat species.

    (A) because   (B) that

    (C) about   (D) and

4 The boy <u>in the red</u> jacket <u>he is</u> Jane's brother, and I <u>get along</u> with <u>him</u>.
                    A   B   C   D

5 _____ in space is thin and carries sound poorly.

    (A) The air   (B) The air is

    (C) If the air is   (D) The air which

6 <u>Bees</u> will <u>sting</u> animals and people <u>only</u> in <u>self-defensive</u>.
        A   B   C   D

7 Some animals move to warmer areas when _____ .

    (A) for winter to come   (B) winter comes

    (C) winter coming   (D) in winter comes

8 Gravity is <u>the pull</u> that <u>makes</u> things slide, fall or <u>rolling</u> <u>downward</u>.
                      A   B   C   D

9   A blue whale weighs over _____ as an average elephant.

      (A) 20 times as much   (B) 20 times as many

      (C) 20 times much   (D) much more 20 times

10   I don't have <u>many</u> homework, <u>so</u> I have <u>enough time</u> to go to the <u>movies</u>.
                          A   B   C   D

11   Certain male jumping spiders, which are covered with hairs of brilliant colors, _____ the most extraordinary antics before the females.

      (A) performing   (B) they perform

      (C) performance   (D) perform

12   Increased levels of ultraviolet radiation <u>are</u> expected <u>to cause</u> <u>markedly</u> increases in sunburn, skin cancer and <u>eye problems</u> such as cataracts.

Vocabulary

□ **veteran**: 퇴역 군인, 베테랑, 전문가	□ **be made up of ~**: ~로 구성되다, 이루어지다	□ **species**: 종(種)
□ **get along with**: 사이좋게 지내다	□ **thin**: 얇은, 희박한	□ **poorly**: 부족하게, 서툴게
□ **sting**: (벌이) 쏘다	□ **self-defensive**: 자기 방어적인	□ **gravity**: 중력
□ **pull**: 당기는 힘	□ **slide**: 미끄러지다	□ **roll**: 구르다
□ **downward**: 아래쪽으로	□ **weigh**: 무게가 ~ 나가다	□ **average**: 평균적인
□ **brilliant**: 찬란하게 빛나는	□ **extraordinary**: 대단한	□ **antic**: 익살맞은 행동
□ **ultraviolet**: 자외선의	□ **radiation**: 방사	□ **cataract**: 백내장

STRUCTURE

가정법

Grammar Up / Power Up Test / Pattern Drill / Pattern Review / Mini Test

법

1   **법이란:** 영어로 말을 하거나 글을 쓸 때 어떤 사실을 단정하거나 상상/가정하거나 하는 등의 마음의 태도가 동사의 형태로 나타나는 것.

1) **직설법:** 사실을 그대로 이야기함. (내용이 진실인지 거짓인지는 무관)

I will go to see a movie with him this weekend.

What did you buy for him?

2) **명령법:** 상대방에게 어떤 행동을 하도록 요청함.

Stand up. Don't look so sad.

3) **가정법:** 사실이 아닌 것을 가정하거나 상상함.

If I were a poet, I would write a beautiful poem for you.

2   **가정법과 직설법**

If I **had** money, I **could buy** you a delicious dinner. (가정법)

= I **can't buy** you a delicious dinner **because I don't have** money. (직설법)

If he **had come** to the party, he **would have met** her. (가정법)

= He **didn't meet** her **because he didn't come** to the party. (직설법)

3   **가정법과 직설법의 if 조건절**

1) **직설법의 조건절:** 어떤 행동을 하겠다는 의지가 나타남. <u>아쉬움은 없음</u>.

If I **have** time, I **will take** a trip.

→ 직설법의 문장처럼 동사의 시제에 특별한 변화 없음.

2) **가정법:** 사실이 아닌 것을 표현하거나, 어떤 행동을 못해 <u>아쉬워 함</u>.

If I **had** time, I **would[could] take** a trip.

(= I can't take a trip because I don't have time.)

→ 흔히 말하는 가정법으로 **if**절의 동사는 사실보다 한 단계 과거 시제가 되고, 주절에는 would, could, should, might 등 과거형의 조동사가 첨가됨.

Vocabulary

□ **look so sad:** 슬퍼 보이다, 슬픈 표정을 하다

Check-Up

A-1 다음을 해석하세요.

(1) If he were an honest man, he would not do such a thing.

→ _____ .

(2) If I were a man, I would marry a woman like you.

→ _____ .

(3) I wonder what you would have said if you had seen the sight.

→ _____ .

(4) If I were young, I would read a lot, travel a lot, and meet a lot of people.

→ _____ .

(5) If she had seen him, she would have fallen in love with him.

→ _____ .

A-2 직설법은 가정법으로, 가정법은 직설법으로 바꾸세요.

(1) If we had more money, we could eat a more expensive lunch.

→ _____ .

(2) Because it is raining, I don't go out.

→ _____ .

(3) If mother were at home, she would make us a delicious meal.

→ _____ .

(4) As she is short, she can't take part in the beauty contest.

→ _____ .

B 가정법의 종류

1 가정법 과거: 현재 사실의 반대를 가정, 상상함.

■ If ~ 과거, ~ would/should/could/might + 동사원형

If I **were** you, I **would forgive** him.

If I **had** enough money, I **could travel** to Europe.

❋ if it were not for ~: ~가 없다면 (= But for, Without)
If it were not for electricity, we would live inconveniently.

2 가정법 과거완료: 과거 사실의 반대를 가정, 상상함.

■ If ~ 과거완료, ~ would/should/could/might + have + 과거분사

If I **had taken** the bus, I **would not have been** late for work.

If I **had known** the situation, I **could have helped** you.

❋ if it had not been for ~: ~가 없었더라면 (= But for, Without)
If it had not been for your advice, I would have never carried it out.

3 가정법 현재: 현재나 미래의 일에 대한 단순한 가정, 상상.

■ If ~ 원형, ~ will/shall + 동사원형

If it **be** fine tomorrow, we **will go** on a picnic.

→ 최근에는 보통 직설법으로(if절의 동사가 현재형) 쓴다.

If it **is** fine tomorrow, we **will go** on a picnic.

4 가정법 미래

1) 의심을 갖고 가정함.

■ If ~ should, ~ will/shall/would/should + 동사원형

If it **should** snow on Christmas Eve, I **will give** you 100 dollars.

2) 있을 수 없는 일을 가정함.

■ If ~ were to, ~ would/should + 동사원형

If I **were to** live my life again, I **would become** a movie director.

Vocabulary

□ **director**: 감독

148

5 **if 생략:** 동사가 주어 앞으로 도치되어 나간다.

Were I you, I would leave her.

(= If I were you, I would leave her.)

Had I **known** the fact, I would not have said so.

(= If I had known the fact, I would not have said so.)

(?) **Did I know** her e-mail address, I would write to her.

= If I knew her e-mail address, I would write to her.

❋ if절의 동사가 일반동사인 경우, if를 생략하고 조동사 do를 사용하여 '**Did** I **know** her e-mail address, I would write to her.' 라고 쓸 수도 있으나 이는 매우 어색한(marginal) 표현이다. 따라서, 이런 경우는 if를 생략하지 않고 사용하는 것이 좋다.

단, 일반동사 have의 경우는 if를 생략하고 have를 문장 앞으로 도치시켜 사용해도 무방하다.
If I had ten dollars, I could buy the cake. = **Had** I ten dollars, I could buy the cake.

✳ 가정법(Subjunctive Mood)이 만들어지는 원리

가정법이란 (1) 사실과 반대 및 가능성이 없는 일에 대한, 또는 (2) 어떠한 행동을 이행하지 않으면 큰일이 일어날지도 모르는 것에 대한 <u>아쉬움 및 불안감</u>을 나타내는 어법이다.

우리말에서는 가정법에 대한 표현을 만들기 위하여 '~라면' 이라는 말을 사용한다.

예를 들어, "내가 새라면…"과 같다. 영어에서 가정법이 만들어지는 원리를 살펴보자.

영어에서는 ① <u>말하는 시점과 다른 시제를 사용</u>함으로써 사실이 아닌 내용을 말하거나, 무슨 일이 벌어질지 모르는 앞날에 대한 불안감을 표시할 수 있다. 말하는 시점과 다른 시제란 말하는 시점보다 과거의 시제를 사용하는 것을 뜻하는데, 이때 주절에 조동사를 첨가함으로써 감정의 변화를 격화시킬 수 있다. 즉, 말해지는 시제보다 과거의 동사를 사용하고 조동사를 첨가하면 감정이 더욱 격화되어 현실과 반대의 상황에서 아쉬워하는 감정의 표현인 가정법이 만들어진다. 그리고 ② <u>동사의 원형을 사용</u>하는 경우도 있다.

1) 말하는 시점보다 과거의 시제와 조동사를 이용하여 가정법이 만들어지는 과정

   We **won** the game. (사실의 내용: 말하는 시점의 시제는 과거)

   → 말하는 시점보다 과거인 대과거로 변경하면

   → We **had won** the game.

   → 조동사 will을 첨가하되, 변경된 대과거의 시제에 맞추면

   → We **would have won** the game. (가정법 과거 완료)

   우리가 그 경기를 이겼을 텐데…: 사실과 반대의 내용 (아쉬운 감정)

✳ 직설법의 조건절 문장을 가정법으로 바꾸어보자.

   • If I had much money, I bought the dictionary.

   (아쉬운 감정이 없음. 단지 사실 표현임: 직설법)

   → If I had had much money, I would have bought the dictionary. (아쉬운 감정이 있음: 가정법)

   • If she teaches this class, she won't give tests.

   (아쉬운 감정 없음: 직설법)

   → If she taught this class, she wouldn't give tests. (아쉬운 감정이 있음: 가정법)

2) 동사의 원형을 사용하는 경우

   He insisted that Mary **finished** her assignment by 10.

   (그는 메리가 10시까지 숙제를 끝냈다고 주장했다: 직설법)

   → He insisted that Mary **finish** her assignment by 10.

   (그는 메리가 10시까지 숙제를 끝내야 한다고 강요했다: 메리가 10시까지 숙제를 안 하면 무슨 일이 생길 것만 같은 불안감이 있음: 가정법)

Vocabulary

□ dictionary: 사전   □ assignment: 숙제

150

Check-Up

B-1 괄호 안의 동사를 알맞은 형태로 바꾸세요.

(1) I could go by bus if I (have) just 1 dollar.

(2) If I had not had to do that, I would (go) with you.

(3) What would you (do) if he asked you to marry him?

(4) If I had been in your place, I would (go) to the United States to study.

(5) She would do worse if she (be) in my place.

B-2 다음을 해석하세요.

(1) If she had been born to a better family, she might have succeeded as a pianist.

→ _____.

(2) If it were not for music, the world would be very dull and gloomy.

→ _____.

(3) What would you do if the earth were to be ruined tomorrow?

→ _____.

B-3 알맞은 낱말에 동그라미를 치세요.

(1) If he had not been killed in the war, he would (be, have been) forty years old now.

(2) (Were, Did) I you, I would not treat him so.

(3) If he (saved, had saved) money when young, he would be better off now.

(4) You would not be sick if you (didn't walk, hadn't walked) in the rain last night.

(5)   I would (be, have been) healthier now if I had not smoked for so long.

B-4 If를 생략하여 문장을 다시 쓰세요.

(1) If I were rich, I would buy her everything she wants.

→ _____.

(2) If she had a sister or a brother, she could depend on her or him.

→ _____.

(3) If he had gone there by bus, he would have arrived earlier.

→ _____.

(4) If it were not for air, there would be no living thing.

→ _____.

(5)   If it had not been for his wife's help, he would not have succeeded as a director.

→ _____.

Vocabulary

□ **gloomy:** 음울한   □ **be ruined:** 멸망하다 (ruin: 멸망, 파괴시키다)   □ **better off:** = richer

I wish 가정법, as if 가정법

1   **I wish** +
┌ **과거**: ~라면 좋을 텐데
└ **과거완료**: ~했더라면 좋았을 텐데

I **wish** I **were** prettier.

I **wish** we **had bought** it at the bargain sale.

---

 wish와 hope

1) wish

(a) wish + 가정법: 과거나 현재에 일어나지 않았거나, 미래에 일어날 가능성이 없는 일을 소망할 때
  (사실과 반대 및 불가능한 일에 대한 아쉬움의 감정 표현)

I **wish** (that) Phil **had** come. (In fact, Phil didn't come.)

I **wish** (that) I **lived** in Berkeley now. (In fact, I don't live in Berkeley now.)

Rarely is life easy. I **wish** that it **were**.

(b) wish + 직설법: want보다 간절한 감정이 포함될 때 (가능성 있는 일에 대한 기대감)

I **wish to go** home. I **wish** you **to go** home.

I **wish** you a merry Christmas.

2) hope + 직설법: 과거에 일어났을 수 있거나 현재나 미래에 일어날 가능성이 있는 일을 기대할 때
  (가능성 있는 일에 대한 기대감)

I **hope to see** you soon. I **hope** (that) I'll see you soon.

I **hope** that he **came** home yesterday.

I **hope** that he **will come** home tomorrow.

---

2   **as if** +
┌ **과거**: 마치~인 것처럼
└ **과거완료**: 마치 ~였던 것처럼

She talks **as if** she **were** his wife.

He looks **as if** he **had been** sick for a long time.

Check-Up

C-1 주어진 의미가 되도록 괄호 안에 알맞은 낱말을 넣으세요.

(1) She looks as (   ) she were a model.

「그녀는 마치 모델처럼 보인다.」

(2) I (   ) I had been born in the 19th century.

「19세기에 태어났더라면 좋았을걸.」

(3) The man talks as (   ) he (   ) (   ) it.

「그 남자는 마치 그것을 본 것처럼 말한다.」

(4) I wish I (   ) a little smarter.

「내가 좀 더 똑똑하다면 좋을 텐데.」

(5) He acts (   ) (   ) he (   ) our leader.

「그는 마치 우리의 지도자인양 행동한다.」

1   문장의 의미에 맞게 주어진 동사의 형태를 바꾸세요.

(1) I don't have enough time tonight. But if I (have) _____ enough time, I (write) _____ a letter to my cousin.

(2) My mother will give me enough money tonight. If I (have) _____ enough money, I (buy) _____ a ticket to the jazz concert.

(3) Mary didn't come to the party yesterday. She (meet) _____ my boyfriend if she (come) _____ to the party.

(4) Your mother doesn't allow you to meet him. If I (be) _____ your mother, I (allow) _____ you to have a date with him.

(5) Thank you for your help yesterday. If it (not + be) _____ for your help, I (not + solve) _____ the problem.

(6) If Willy (leave) _____ his house an hour earlier, he (be) _____ here now.

(7) I'm going to buy a car next month. If I (buy) _____ a car, I (drive) _____ to Busan to visit my friend.

(8) I'm happy because you love me. If it (not + be) _____ for your love, I (not + live) _____ .

2   주어진 표현을 사용하여 두 문장의 뜻이 같도록 쓰세요.

(1) It is a pity that you have to work tonight.

    → I wish _____ .

(2) My son treats me as his friend.

    → My son treats me as if _____ .

(3) If you had finished high school, you could get a better job.

    → As you _____ .

Vocabulary

□ **treat:** 대우하다

154

3 짝지어진 두 문장의 의미가 같지 않은 것을 고르세요.

(A) A true friend would not say such a thing.

= If he/she were a true friend, he/she would not say such a thing.

(B) I'm sorry I don't know her address.

= I wish I had known her address.

(C) Without water and air, we could not live.

= If it were not for water and air, we could not live.

(D) He talks like a doctor.

= He talks as if he were a doctor.

[4-6] 다음의 괄호 안에 들어갈 알맞은 단어를 보기 중에서 찾으세요.

4 If yesterday (　　　) Christmas, today would be my birthday.

(A) is (B) were (C) would be (D) had been

5 My younger sister always talks (　　　) she were my elder sister.

(A) if (B) that (C) as if (D) I wish

6 (　　　) for police officers, our society would become dangerous.

(A) Were it not (B) Were not

(C) Had not been (D) Had it not been

7 자신의 상황에 맞게, 다음에 이어질 말을 직접 완성하세요.

(1) If I were a girl/boy, _____.

(2) If it snowed now, _____.

(3) If I had a million won, _____.

(4) If the weather is nice tomorrow, _____.

(5) If I had had no class yesterday, _____.

Vocabulary

□ **police officer**: 경관　　　　　□ **million**: 백만의

유형 32 가정법 찾기

If the poet _____ herself, she would be sixty-seven now.

(A) kills

(B) is killed

(C) had not killed

(D) were not killed

유형 33 가정법을 잘못 쓴 경우

If it <u>is</u> not <u>for</u> the Internet, we <u>would</u> not be able to do many <u>things</u>.
   A   B   C   D

Vocabulary

□ poet: 시인

1 Alice smiled, <u>because</u> the rabbit looked <u>as if</u> he <u>is</u> about <u>to speak</u>.
                 A   B   C   D

2 Many parents _____ surprised if their children were caught by the police.

(A) are   (B) would be   (C) to be   (D) was

3 If it _____ tomorrow, there would be no baseball games.

(A) raining   (B) have rained   (C) will rain   (D) should rain

4 If <u>there were</u> not <u>for</u> flowers and trees, <u>the world</u> would be very <u>unhappy</u>.
         A   B   C   D

5 I wish that I _____ my mother once again, who passed away last year.

(A) had seen   (B) will see   (C) could see   (D) am seeing

6 <u>If</u> you <u>would have</u> told the secret <u>to me</u>, I could have <u>helped</u> you.
  A   B   C   D

7 If I had received your letter then, I _____ in love with you now.

(A) would be   (B) would have been

(C) have been   (D) had been

8 If I had had <u>a college</u> student <u>as</u> a friend, she / he <u>can have</u> helped me <u>much</u>.
               A   B   C   D

9 The sun goes on shining after your death as if nothing _____.

(A) happens   (B) had happened

(C) would happen   (D) happen

10 _____ for good friends, I would have given up.

(A) If it is not   (B) If it has not

(C) Were not   (D) Had it not been

1   <u>In</u> the <u>eighteen</u> century, <u>millions of</u> people <u>died of</u> smallpox.
     A   B   C   D

2   <u>To connect</u> two <u>sentence</u>, we <u>usually</u> put a comma <u>before</u> the conjunction.
        A   B   C   D

3   In America, there aren't any lions _____ an African lion.

    (A) exactly like   (B) like exactly

    (C) exact like   (D) like exact

4   Biographies <u>help</u> us <u>understand</u> <u>other</u> people <u>as well</u> ourselves.
                A   B   C   D

5   In the Ice Age, the oceans were lower, and _____ was attached to Asia.

    (A) which Alaska   (B) because Alaska

    (C) Alaska   (D) in Alaska

6   <u>Body</u> temperature is <u>usually</u> highest <u>into</u> the afternoon or <u>evening</u>.
     A   B   C   D

7   Hay _____ too much moisture will spoil.

    (A) contains   (B) containing

    (C) that contains it   (D) to contain it

8 _____ under the microscope, a fresh snowflake has a delicate six-pointed shape.

(A) If seeing　　　　　　　　　(B) Seen

(C) When we see　　　　　　　　(D) If we see

9 I read a <u>shocked</u> report yesterday <u>that</u> <u>too</u> many children <u>are starving</u> in the
　　　　　　A　　　　　　　　　　B　　C　　　　　　　　　D
world.

10 <u>There</u> are two students in my class who <u>speaks</u> Spanish, and <u>they</u> can
　　A　　　　　　　　　　　　　　　　B　　　　　　　　C
speak English, <u>too</u>.
　　　　　　　　D

11 There are many different minerals in North Carolina, but only about 40 occur
_____ of economic value.

(A) to be sufficient quantity in　　　(B) in quantity to be sufficient

(C) sufficient quantity to be in　　　(D) in sufficient quantity to be

12 Modern canoes <u>still</u> look <u>like</u> the <u>one</u> the Indians made <u>long ago</u>.
　　　　　　　　　　A　　　　B　　　C　　　　　　　　　　D

Vocabulary

□ **smallpox**: 천연두	□ **connect**: 연결하다	□ **sentence**: 문장
□ **comma**: 쉼표	□ **conjunction**: 접속사	□ **exactly**: 정확하게
□ **biography**: 전기(문)	□ **Ice Age**: 빙하기	□ **attached to ~**: ~에 붙은
□ **body temperature**: 체온	□ **hay**: 건초	□ **contain**: 포함하다
□ **moisture**: 습기	□ **spoil**: 부패하다	□ **microscope**: 현미경
□ **delicate**: 정교한	□ **six-pointed shape**: 육각형	□ **starve**: 굶주리다, 굶어 죽다
□ **Spanish**: 스페인어	□ **mineral**: 광물	□ **sufficient**: 충분한

STRUCTURE

CHAPTER 9

일치, 병렬, 어순(도치), 강조, 동격

Grammar Up / Power Up Test / Pattern Drill / Pattern Review / Mini Test

일치

1 주어와 동사의 일치

문장의 동사는 문장의 주어와 수가 일치해야 한다.
단수주어 ― 단수동사, 복수주어 ― 복수동사

My dog and my cat **are** best friends.

A Christmas tree **is** shining in front of the church.

✳ 주의해야 할 주어 – 동사 일치

1) 복합 주어 – 단수 취급: 형식상 복합이지만 내용상 한 단위

The mirror and frame **looks** pretty. (틀에 끼워진 거울. 하나의 관사가 사용되었음)

The musician and teacher **is** my father. (음악가이자 선생님: 동일인. 하나의 관사)

cf) The musician and the teacher **are** my friends. (음악가와 선생님. 두개의 관사)

2) 집합 명사 – 단수 취급, 군집 명사 – 복수 취급

The committee **meets** at 5. (위원회)

The committee **are** attending the meeting. (위원들)

3) –s형태이지만 단수 취급하는 명사

Physics **is** my favorite subject. → –s로 끝나는 학문 이름

The United States **has** many different cultures. → 연방국 이름

The first news in the morning **is** at 5 a.m. → 관습적으로 단수 취급

4) 복수형으로 쓰이는 명사

My gloves **are** made in Korea. → 짝(pair)의 개념이 들어있는 명사

Korean manners **are** very polite. → 관습적으로 쓰이는 복수형

5) 시간, 거리, 무게, 돈의 표현 – 단수 취급

Two hours **isn't** so long a time for a baseball game.

→ 'Two hours' 전체를 하나의 단위로 취급

6) all / most / a lot / some / half / 분수 + of the + ⌈ 단수명사 + 단수동사
  ⌊ 복수명사 + 복수동사

Most of the **movie was** a lot of fun.

Most of the married **women** in the country **are** housewives.

Vocabulary

□ **frame:** 틀   □ **committee:** 위원회   □ **physics:** 물리학   □ **manners:** 예의범절

7) one / a variety / either / neither + of + 복수명사 + 단수동사

A variety of **vitamins is** necessary to the human body.

Neither of the **two compositions was** satisfying.

8) a number of + 복수명사 + 복수동사: 많은 수의~ (복수명사가 주어)

the number of + 단수/복수명사 + 단수동사: ~의 수 (the number가 주어)

A number of **people were** swimming in the pool. (a lot of와 같은 용법으로 사용되었음.)

The number of **people** who want to go to the concert **keeps** increasing.

9) each, every, -body (+ 단수 명사) – 단수 취급

Each **student** in my class **has** her or his own talent.

Nobody **has** to call the police.

10) 상관 접속사의 주어 – 동사 일치

	동사의 일치	
both A and B	복수로 받음	**Both** Mike **and** Judy **attend** Mr. Hart's class.
either A or B	B에 일치	**Either** you **or Paul has** to work tomorrow.
neither A nor B	B에 일치	**Neither** Paul **nor I have** to work tomorrow.
not only A but also B	B에 일치	**Not only** my parents **but also my uncle is** a teacher.
A as well as B	A에 일치	**My uncle as well as** my parents **is** a teacher.
such A as B	A에 일치	**Such able workers as** Miss Kelly **are** not common.

2   명사와 대명사의 일치

대명사는 자신이 받는 명사와 인칭과 성, 수가 일치해야 한다.

수의 일치	단수 명사 → 단수 대명사	Did you see my **doll**? **It** is red-haired.
	복수 명사 → 복수 대명사	**My wife and I** will build **our** house.
	each / every → 단수 대명사	**Every parent** loves **her or his** children.
성의 일치	여성 명사 → 여성 대명사	The **queen** of this country lives in **her** palace.
	남성 명사 → 남성 대명사	This is my **brother**, and those toys are **his**.
	사물 명사 → 중성 대명사	I like **money**, so I work hard to make **it**.

※ 사람 명사 중에서 성을 구별할 수 없는 일부 명사는 중성대명사 it으로 받는다.

The **baby** in the cradle resembles **its** mother.

Vocabulary

□ **talent**: 재능   □ **red-haired**: 빨간 머리의   □ **palace**: 궁전

□ **make money**: 돈을 벌다   □ **cradle**: 요람   □ **resemble**: 닮다

A-1   괄호 안에 알맞은 동사를 고르세요.

(1)   Every boy and girl (like, likes) TV stars.

(2)   Economics (is, are) a difficult subject to study.

(3)   My pants (has, have) big pockets on them.

(4)   Some of the apples in the basket (is, are) rotten.

(5)   Neither Mary's brothers nor Mary (is, are) going to come tonight.

(6)   Five hundred miles (is, are) a long distance to drive in one day.

(7)   David's daughter as well as her friends (was, were) at the concert last night.

(8)   The book and the CD on the desk (is, are) mine.

(9)   Both Jane and I (am, are) high school students.

(10)   Slow and steady (win, wins) the race.

(11)   My family (is, are) a large one.

(12)   The news last night (was, were) surprising.

(13)   Two-thirds of his homework (was, were) done by his mother.

(14)   (Is, Are) there anybody who can speak English?

(15)   The poet and novelist always (eat, eats) in this restaurant.

A-2   빈칸에 들어갈 알맞은 대명사를 쓰세요.

(1)   Every student has _____ locker at school.

(2)   My son doesn't finish _____ homework.

(3)   The dog hurt _____ leg.

(4)   Ms. Ostrow has to sign _____ name on the letter.

(5)   One of the boys didn't take an umbrella with _____.

Vocabulary

□ economics: 경제학   □ rotten: 썩은   □ distance: 거리

□ steady: 꾸준한   □ novelist: 소설가   □ locker: 사물함

□ hurt: 다치다

 **병렬**

접속사로 서로 연결되는 둘 이상의 단어 혹은 구, 절이나 비교 구문에 의해 서로 비교되는 단어, 구, 절은 반드시 문법적 형태가 같아야 한다. (예, 명사 – 명사, 형용사 – 형용사, 부정사 – 부정사, 분사 – 분사, 전치사구 – 전치사구, 절 – 절 등)

1 열거구문

Apples, **bananas**, <u>and</u> **oranges** are my favorite fruits. → 명사

You can **buy** something, **go** somewhere, <u>or</u> **help** someone with this money. → 동사

2 등위접속사 구문

It is **hard** <u>but</u> **exciting** to climb mountains. → 형용사

My dream is to **be** a doctor <u>or</u> **to be** a nurse. → to 부정사

I know **that you love her** <u>and</u> **that she also loves you.** → 절

3 상관접속사 구문

not A but B, both A and B, either/neither A or/nor B, A as well as B

not only A but also B

I lost weight <u>not</u> **by diet** <u>but</u> **by exercise.** → 전치사구

(나는 식이요법에 의해서가 아니라 운동으로 살을 뺐다.)

His job is <u>not only</u> **writing** <u>but also</u> **teaching.** → 동명사

(그의 직업은 글 쓰는 일 뿐 아니라 가르치는 일이다.)

4 비교 구문

I made this box more **strong** <u>than</u> **pretty.** → 형용사

(나는 이 상자를 예쁘기보다는 튼튼하게 만들었다.)

The window of my room is larger <u>than</u> **that of your room**. → 명사구

(내 방의 창은 네 방(의 창)보다 크다.) (that = the window)

B-1 틀린 문장을 골라 옳게 고치세요.

(1) We were singing and to dance at the Christmas party.

(2) The ears of a rabbit are longer than a dog.

(3) My husband is good at not only eating but also cook.

(4) To do or not do it is your choice.

(5) I bought some apples, oranges, and strawberries at the market.

(6) Either desk or chair have been sold.

(7) Lucy is more cute than beauty.

(8) Neither you nor him is going to buy the house.

(9) He could play golf as well soccer.

(10) She studied not history but also English.

B-2 괄호에 알맞은 접속사를 넣으세요.

(1) He is both brave (   ) handsome.

(2) Roger saw neither a bird (   ) a flower for two hours.

(3) She became not only a famous singer (   ) also a great painter.

(4) Either Mary (   ) John will come to our party.

(5) She became not a teacher (   ) a writer.

(6) I grow tomatoes as well (   ) potatoes in my garden.

(7) The chairs in my classroom are bigger (   ) those in your classroom.

(8) John, Mike, (   ) Nancy drive a car to work each morning.

(9) The river is more long (   ) wide.

(10) The book is expensive (   ) interesting.

Vocabulary

□ choice: 선택 □ strawberry: 딸기 □ brave: 용감한

166

 **어순(도치)**

1 주의해야 할 수식어의 위치, 어순

1) 후위 수식하는 형용사 (명사 + 형용사)

- -thing, -body, -one을 수식하는 형용사

  There is <u>something</u> **strange** in your story.

  This water is for <u>someone</u> **thirsty**.

- 〈주격관계대명사 + be 동사〉가 생략된 경우

  Look at <u>that house</u> (which is) **built** of wood.

  I know <u>the girl</u> (who is) **crying** over there.

2) 위치가 정해진 부사

- 빈도 부사: be 동사 및 조동사 뒤, 일반동사 앞 (always, often, rarely, frequently, occasionally, ever, seldom, usually, sometimes, never 등)

  I <u>can</u> **sometimes** <u>look</u> after your baby.

  He <u>is</u> **never** on time.

- 수식하는 단어 바로 옆에: only, just, nearly, almost 등

  I have only ten dollars. (only는 ten을 수식)

  I only have ten dollars. (X)

- 문장의 의미는 부사가 수식하는 어구에 따라 바뀌게 된다.

  Happily, he didn't die in the accident. (문장 전체 수식)

  (다행히도, 그는 그 사고로 죽지 않았다.)

  cf) He didn't die **happily** in the accident. (동사 die 수식)

  (그는 그 사고로 행복하게 죽지 못했다.)

2 도치의 기본 (Inverting the normal word order)

표현의 다양성 및 강조를 위하여 문장의 중간 및 뒤에 위치한 단어 또는 어구들이 문장 앞으로 이동함으로써 발생하는 어순의 변화를 말한다. 앞으로 이동하는 단어의 품사 종류 및 문장 형식(또는 동사의 종류)에 따라 동사가 주어 앞쪽으로 이동하기도 한다. 특히, 앞으로 나간 것이 부사(구)일 때 그 부사(구)는 자신이 수식하던 동사를 계속 가까이에 두려 한다. 따라서 동사가 부사(구)를 따라 주어 앞으로 나가게 된다.

현대의 영어에서는 도치의 문장이 단독으로 쓰이는 것은 바람직하지 않으며, 계속(successive)되는 문장에서 의미적으로 연결, 확대되는 경우에 사용된다. 계속되는 문장은 마침표에 의하여 독립되어 있어도 무방하다.

She wasn't angry, and neither was I.

He would love to go, and so would she.

Her face was stony, and even stonier was the tone of her voice.

※ 부정어구, so, neither, 장소에 관한 전치사구의 도치가 가장 흔하며 중요하다.

1) 부사(구) 및 부정 어휘가 앞으로 이동하는 경우

① 1형식의 경우

My father stood <u>in the doorway</u>.

→ <u>In the doorway</u> stood my father. (동사가 주어 앞으로 이동한다.)

We <u>rarely</u> go to a movie.

→ <u>Rarely</u> do we go to a movie.*

⇏ <u>Rarely</u> go to a movie we.

② 타동사의 경우

I would <u>seldom</u> visit her house.

→ <u>Seldom</u> would I visit her house. (조동사가 있는 경우는 조동사 앞으로 이동)

She gave <u>nothing</u> on my birthday.

→ <u>Nothing</u> did she give on my birthday. (명사안에 부정형 부사 not의 의미 포함)

  cf) That piano I want to buy. (목적어인 명사가 도치된 경우. 부정의미 없음.)

❋ She *did* **not** *come* until it started raining.

→ **Not until it started raining** *did she come*. (Not until 구문: ~해서야 비로소 ~하다)

The bell had **no sooner** *rung* than the telephone also rang.

→ **No sooner** *had the bell rung* than the telephone also rang. (No sooner ~than 구문)

2) 목적어 / 보어가 앞으로 이동하는 경우

① 2형식의 경우 (보어가 앞으로 이동)

She is great. → <u>Great</u> is she. (be동사가 주어 앞으로 이동)

② 타동사의 경우 (목적어가 앞으로 이동)

Now Harry detests <u>all dogs, especially barking dogs</u>.

→ Now <u>all dogs, especially barking dogs</u>, Harry detests. (주어, 동사 어순 무변화)

---

*rarely가 이동하면 rarely의 수식을 받는 go도 위의 예문 "In the doorway stood ~"같이 함께 이동해야 하는데, go는 to a movie의 수식도 받고 있으므로 go to a movie가 함께 이동해야 하는데, 그것은 너무 어색하므로 대동사 do를 사용. 도치의 기본 원칙은 수식하는 것 또는 수식 받는 것과 함께 이동하는 것이다.

Check-Up

C-1a 밑줄 친 단어의 위치가 올바르지 않은 것을 골라 고치세요.

(1) She smiles <u>always</u> like an angel.

(2) I have <u>special</u> nothing to say.

(3) You <u>often</u> should check up your computer.

(4) I saw <u>singing</u> him in the rain.

(5) Tara looks at her <u>sleeping</u> baby peacefully in the bed.

(6) We visited Megan's home <u>full</u> of toys and dolls.

C-1b 부사에 주의하여, 두 문장의 우리말 뜻을 비교해 보세요.

(1) Clearly, he didn't draw the picture.

(2) He didn't draw the picture clearly.

C-2a 다음 문장의 주어에 밑줄을 치세요. (복문인 경우, 주절과 종속절의 주어를 구분해서 표시하세요.)

(1) There are many fish in the pond.

(2) All I want is to sleep right now.

(3) Not until Jane heard the news, did she start to cry.

(4) Such was my surprise at his loud voice.

(5) High in the sky fly birds.

(6) Little did I dream you would be a doctor!

C-2b 주어진 문장을 고쳐 쓰세요.

(1) He had no sooner seen me than he ran into me.

→ No sooner _____ than he ran into me.

(2) He never writes to her!

→ Never _____ !

Vocabulary

□ **peacefully**: 평화롭게   □ **such**: 대단한

 **강조**

1 It (is) ~ that 강조 구문: 명사(구), 부사(구) 강조

In America, people sell things in their front yard.

→ **It is** in America **that**(= **where**) people sell things in their front yard.

I saw Sera and her boyfriend on the street.

→ **It was** Sera and her boy friend **that**(= **who**) I saw on the street.

    cf) It is **certain** that it will be fine tomorrow.

       → It ~ that 가주어, 진주어 구문 (certain은 형용사이므로 강조구문이 아니다.)

2 일반 동사의 강조: do 이용

My mother **does** ask me everything.

I **did** forget the appointment yesterday.

3 비교급, 최상급의 강조: much, still, a lot, by far 이용

My mother is **much** older than your mother.

I have a **still** bigger car than a Volkswagen.

Your idea is **by far** the best one.

4 부정문, 의문문의 강조: at all, ever, on earth, in the world 이용

I can't remember your name **at all**. (전혀)

Who **on earth** are you? (도대체)

5 그 밖의 강조어구

He is **the very** man I'm looking for. → 명사 수식, 강조 (바로 그)

The only person in the room is Toby. → 명사 수식, 강조 (유일한)

I **only**(= **just**) see that picture. → 동사 수식, 강조 ('보기만 했다')

I prepared this dinner **myself**. → 강조의 재귀대명사 (직접)

I want to see you **over and over again**. → 동일 어구 반복, 강조

Vocabulary

□ **front yard:** 앞마당   □ **over and over again:** 준비하다

 **동격**

명사(구, 절)를 보충 설명하는 또 다른 명사(구, 절).
주로 명사의 뒤에 위치하며 두 개의 쉼표로 구분되는 경우가 많다.

1 동격어구

Mr. Hwang, **my old friend**, now lives in London.
I liked that special event, **the party on the ship**, very much.
My summer plan is this, **to rest at home**.

2 동격절

I heard the news **that there had been a fire in Seoul.**
The mystery, **why he went there**, is still in my mind.

Vocabulary

□ fire: 화재

171

D-1   다음 문장에서 밑줄 친 어구를 강조하세요.

(1)   This question is <u>more difficult</u> than that one.

(2)   You <u>pay</u> your debt.

(3)   <u>What</u> are you doing now? (in the world를 이용)

(4)   You are the <u>woman</u> who can do that work. (the very를 이용)

(5)   <u>Thomas</u> built the house. (It ~ that 강조 구문 이용)

E-1   동격을 이루는 말을 찾아서 표시하세요.

(1)   Mr. Jones, a writer and critic, will join us.

(2)   His suggestion is this, to have a coffee break.

(3)   I know the fact that he can't visit his mother.

(4)   Seoul, the largest city in Korea, is my hometown.

Vocabulary

□ **debt**: 빚   □ **critic**: 비평가   □ **suggestion**: 제안   □ **break**: 휴식

1 빈칸에 들어갈 말이 바르게 연결된 것을 고르세요.

> 보기
> This calendar has a beautiful picture on _____ cover.
> I'm waiting for my guests. _____ will come soon.

(A) his - They   (B) its- Them

(C) his - Them   (D) its - They

2 다음 중에서 밑줄 친 형용사나 부사의 위치가 잘못된 문장을 고르세요.

(A) <u>Luckily</u>, our team won the championship.

(B) You are <u>such</u> a pretty and nice girl.

(C) Please, give me <u>hot</u> something to drink.

(D) He <u>always</u> gets up at the same hour.

[3-4] 다음 중 동사가 바르게 쓰이지 않은 문장을 고르세요.

3 (A) My family are all Koreans.

(B) The scissors cut well.

(C) Politics teaches us many things.

(D) Ten kilograms are too heavy for me.

4 (A) Half of the apple is eaten.

(B) My dog as well as I am 12 years old.

(C) One of these girls has your purse.

(D) Every student does a good job.

[5-6] 다음 빈칸에 들어갈 말을 고르세요.

5 We enjoy swimming in summer and _____ in winter on the pond.

(A) to skate   (B) skating

(C) skated   (D) skates

Vocabulary

□ guest: 손님   □ championship: 우승   □ scissors: 가위

□ politics: 정치학   □ purse: 지갑   □ do a good job: 잘하다

6 Both you and _____ want to be teachers.

(A) I   (B) my

(C) me   (D) mine

7 밑줄 친 부분을 강조하여 다음 문장을 다시 쓸 때, 빈 칸에 들어갈 말을 쓰세요.

(1) We cannot start the meeting until our teacher comes.

→ _____ _____our teacher comes _____ _____ start the meeting.

(2) I have long wanted this book.

→ _____ is this book _____ I have long wanted.

(3) My wife buys things only in the department store.

→ Only in the department store_____ _____ _____ _____things.

(4) I haven't thought that you would fail.

→ I haven't thought that you would fail _____ _____.

8 밑줄 친 부분이 강조된 문장이 아닌 것을 고르세요.

(A) Mr. Chung does work for the poor.

(B) Daegu is much hotter than Kwangju in summer.

(C) It is certain that your father will recover.

(D) This is the very flower that Lily likes best.

9 밑줄 친 단어의 동격어구나 동격절에 괄호를 치세요.

(1) Your mother, a doctor, takes care of the sick.

(2) I know the fact that Mr. Bak told a lie.

(3) I think her job, delivering newspapers, is difficult.

10 주어진 문장을 우리말로 해석하세요.

(1) If you live in a dormitory, you should wash your clothes yourself.

(2) To succeed, you have to not only work hard but also be honest.

(3) No sooner had my hat blown off than people laughed at my bald head.

Vocabulary

□ **the poor**: 가난한 사람들   □ **recover**: (병에서) 회복하다   □ **the sick**: 아픈 사람들

□ **deliver**: 배달하다   □ **dormitory**: 기숙사   □ **blow off**: 바람에 날리다

□ **bald head**: 대머리

유형 34 주어와 동사의 수 일치

1 The tallest animal in the world are the giraffe.
    A   B   C   D

2 Doing something over and over make you good at it.
          A   B   C   D

유형 17 명사와 대명사의 일치

1 Amelia Earhart was a famous woman in its time.
          A   B   C D

유형 35 병렬 – 열거 구문

1 When I feel sad, I would like to listen to music, to sleep in bed, or crying loudly.
          A   B   C   D

2 Football players, who are very popular in the US, carry, to throw, or kick a ball.
    A   B   C   D

유형 36 병렬 – 등위 접속사로 연결된 구문

1 Driving a car through the heavy rain is exciting but danger.
    A   B   C   D

유형 37 병렬 – 상관 접속사로 연결된 구문

1 Penguins use their wings not in flying, but helping them swim.
       A   B   C   D

유형 38 병렬 – 비교구문

1 When you catch a cold, it is better to rest at home than play outside.
    A   B   C   D

Chapter • 9

1 The sky is <u>of full</u> fish <u>and</u> animals, <u>which</u> are <u>kites</u>.
         A   B   C   D

2 People used _____ hats and coats.

(A) make to the beaver fur   (B) to make fur the beaver

(C) to the beaver fur make   (D) the beaver fur to make

1 Reindeer <u>are</u> <u>animals strong</u>, and <u>they</u> are <u>fast-moving</u>.
            A   B   C   D

2 _____ fly to this lake in winter.

(A) Several birds million   (B) Birds million several

(C) Several million birds   (D) Million several birds

1 Long ago in Scandinavia, Germany, and Iceland, _____.

(A) lived the Norsemen   (B) the Norsemen living

(C) the Norsemen live   (D) lived with the Norsemen

2 Not only _____, but I also received a scholarship.

(A) passed the exam   (B) the exam passed

(C) the exam I passed   (D) did I pass the exam

Vocabulary

□ scholarship: 장학금

유형 42   동격어 찾기

1 In Legoland, _____, the houses are much smaller than the real ones.

(A) is a model town in Denmark

(B) a model town in Denmark

(C) where a model town in Denmark

(D) and a model town in Denmark

2 The *Mona Lisa* was painted by an Italian painter, _____.

(A) who Leonardo da Vinci

(B) was Leonardo da Vinci

(C) Leonardo da Vinci

(D) Leonardo da Vinci had

1   The hummingbirds are <u>such</u> tiny and <u>light</u> birds that <u>it</u> can sit on <u>a flower</u>.
                                       A   B   C   D

2   One of the people who made jazz famous was Louis Armstrong, _____ .

     (A) an Afro-American man

     (B) who an Afro-American man

     (C) he was Afro-American man

     (D) a man is Afro-American

3   We must <u>clean</u> our teeth, hands, and <u>on foot</u> when <u>we</u> come <u>home</u>.
                    A   B   C   D

4   Four <u>main</u> directions, east, <u>west</u>, north, and south, <u>tells</u> you <u>where</u> things are.
              A   B   C   D

5   In Britain, breakfast is _____ if they have time for eating.

     (A) big a meal   (B) a big meal

     (C) a meal big   (D) meal a big

6   <u>Pigeons</u> can remember <u>where</u> they live and <u>find</u> their <u>home way</u>.
          A   B   C   D

7   <u>A written</u> sentence begins with a capital <u>letter</u>, and <u>they</u> usually ends <u>with</u> a period.
          A   B   C   D

Vocabulary

□ **hummingbird**: 벌새   □ **tiny**: 조그마한   □ **pigeon**: 비둘기

8 For all the <u>times</u> of the day <u>from</u> 12 midnight <u>noon until</u>, we use a.m.
    A   B   C   D

9 Animals <u>and</u> plants are <u>things living</u>, and human <u>beings</u> belong <u>to</u> animals.
           A   B   C   D

10 Not a word _____ while she is studying.

    (A) does she usually say

    (B) says usually that she

    (C) which she usually says

    (D) she says usually

11 I don't know <u>whether</u> <u>the</u> weather will be clear, <u>cloud</u>, or windy <u>tomorrow</u>.
               A   B   C   D

12 In the old days painters made portraits, _____, like photos today.

    (A) pictures of people

    (B) people who in pictures

    (C) pictures and people

    (D) pictures of people which

13 Chewing gum <u>comes</u> from <u>a kind</u> of juice of the tree, which <u>grow</u> in hot <u>countries</u>.
                  A   B   C   D

14 When I was <u>at table</u>, a <u>bee small</u> flew <u>in through</u> the <u>open</u> window.
               A   B   C   D

15 <u>Too</u> many cars cause not only <u>heavy</u> traffic <u>but</u> also air <u>pollute</u>.
    A   B   C   D

Vocabulary

□ **belong to ~**: ~에 속하다　　□ **portrait**: 초상화　　□ **chewing gum**: 껌　　□ **pollute**: 오염시키다

1   Chopin <u>was</u> not only a <u>talented</u> pianist <u>and also</u> a great <u>composer</u>.
               A   B   C   D

2   Harriet Tubman, herself a runaway slave, helped _____ to get their freedom back.

(A) many black slaves

(B) many slaves black

(C) black many slaves

(D) slaves many black

3   <u>About</u> 300 A.D. the American Indians <u>in the</u> Ohio River region developed
       A   B

a <u>high level</u> of <u>civilized</u>.
   C   D

4   The beagle, a <u>favorite</u> dog in America, <u>is</u> one of the <u>best dog</u> for <u>hunting</u> rabbits.
               A   B   C   D

5   London is the _____ and still has many traditional characteristics.

(A) capital of England is

(B) England whose capital

(C) England is the capital

(D) capital of England

6   Folk songs <u>have</u> been <u>pass down</u> from parents to <u>their</u> children <u>for</u> many years.
              A   B   C   D

7   In America, <u>travel</u> by <u>automobile</u> is <u>by far</u> the most <u>commonest</u>.
               A   B   C   D

8   An autobiography is the story of your own life, _____ by yourself.

(A) written   (B) that it writes

(C) which writes   (D) to write

9   Trees <u>make</u> one ring for <u>every year</u>, and <u>wide</u> tree rings tell the story of
                A   B   C

<u>years wet</u>.
   D

10   When a tortoise is afraid, _____ pull its head in, under its hard, round shell.

(A) its   (B) and it   (C) it can   (D) can

11   <u>For over</u> three centuries the United States <u>has been</u> a destination for the
       A   B

oppressed and the <u>hunger</u> of Europe and of <u>other parts</u> of the world.
                 C   D

12   Most present-day cameras have a lens mounted over the light-admitting holes, _____ it possible to take pictures with less light.

(A) makes   (B) making

(C) that they make   (D) they makes

Vocabulary

□ talented: 재능있는	□ composer: 작곡가	□ runaway: 도망 친
□ slave: 노예	□ get back: 되찾다	□ freedom: 자유
□ develop: 발전시키다	□ civilized: 문명화된	□ beagle: 비글(토끼사냥에 쓰이는 사냥개)
□ capital: 수도	□ traditional: 전통적인	□ characteristic: 특징
□ pass down: 전수하다	□ automobile: 자동차	□ common: 흔한
□ autobiography: 자서전	□ ring: 나이테	□ wet: 습한
□ tortoise: 거북이	□ shell: 껍데기	□ oppress: 압박하다
□ mount: 장치하다		

STRUCTURE

부정사, 동명사, 분사

Grammar Up / Power Up Test / Pattern Drill / Pattern Review / Mini Test

✳ 구

두 개 이상의 단어가 하나의 무리를 이루어 명사, 형용사, 부사 중 한 가지 품사 구실을 하되 주어와 동사가 들어있지 않은 어군. 구는 하나의 사고 단위(thought unit)이므로 연결해서 읽도록 한다. (p. 194 참조)

❋ 구가 만들어지는 2가지 방법과 구의 쓰임 3가지

구분	형태	명사구 (명사 역할)	형용사구 (형용사 역할)	부사구 (부사 역할)
전치사구	전치사+(형용사)+명사	×	①	②
준동사구	to + 동사원형 + α -ing + α -ed + α	③ 명사적 용법 ⑥ 동명사 ×	④ 형용사적 용법 ⑦ 현재분사 ⑨ 과거분사	⑤ 부사적 용법 ⑧ 현재분사구문 ⑩ 과거분사구문

① This robot will be of use.
② Princess Diana had dinner in this French restaurant.
③ My wish is to live happily.
④ I want a newspaper to read on a bus.
⑤ I went there to eat nang-myeon.
⑥ Being on time is very important.
⑦ Look at the mosquito flying in the room.
⑧ Having finished the work, I went to bed.
⑨ Love is a feeling experienced by many.
⑩ Compared with New York, Seattle is not so big a city.

❋ 문장에서의 역할
- 명사 – 주어, 목적어, 보어, 전치사의 목적어
- 형용사 – 보어, 명사 수식
- 부사 – 동사/형용사/부사/구/절/문장 수식

 **A** **to 부정사**

준동사(verbals)의 하나로써 「to+ 동사원형 + α」을 이루어 하나의 사고 단위(thought unit)를 형성하며, 그 단위가 하나의 명사, 형용사 및 부사의 역할을 하는 것을 말한다.
• '준동사' 의 전반에 대한 내용은 chapter 11참조

to 부정사구	동사의 기본 성격 유지	
to + 동사원형 + α	① 의미상의 주어 ③ 부사 수식을 받을 수 있고	② 목적어, 보어를 갖거나 ④ 시제를 갖는다

She ran **to win.**

to 부정사구	win의 동사적 성격	문장에서의 역할
to win	① 의미상의 주어(She) ② 시제(ran과 같은 과거)	부사(ran수식)

※ win은 완전자동사로 쓰였으므로 보어나 목적어가 필요없다.

The second role of TV is **to educate people.**

to 부정사구	educate의 동사적 성격	문장에서의 역할
to educate people	① 의미상의 주어(The second role of TV) ② 목적어(people) ③ 시제(is와 같은 현재)	명사(보어)

To exercise regularly is good for health.

to 부정사구	educate의 동사적 성격	문장에서의 역할
to exercise regularly	① 의미상의 주어(일반인) ② 부사수식(regularly) ③ 시제(is와 같은 현재)	명사(주어)

Vocabulary

□ **role**: 역할   □ **educate**: (사람을) 교육하다

185

1 to 부정사의 용법

1) 명사적 용법: 명사처럼 ①주어 ②목적어 ③보어로 사용된다.

To live without air is impossible.

He arranged **to meet his friend Anne for lunch.**

My plan is **to travel around the world.**

　✻ 「의문사 + to 부정사」의 to 부정사도 명사적 용법이다.

　　I don't know **how to play the guitar.**

　　= I don't know **how I should play the guitar.**

　✻ to 부정사가 주어로 쓰일 경우 주어의 자리에 it을 쓰고, to 부정사를 문장의 뒤에 놓는 경우가 흔하다.
　　이 때 it을 가주어, to 부정사를 진주어라 한다.

　　To see you is a great pleasure.

　　= It is a great pleasure **to see you.**

2) 형용사적 용법: 형용사처럼 ①보어로 사용되거나 ②명사를 수식한다.

He is **to leave Seoul tomorrow.**

She always has energy **to use.**

　✻ be to 용법 (서술용법)

　　be 동사 뒤에 to 부정사가 와서 보어로 쓰이기는 하지만, 명사적 용법에서처럼 '주어 = to 부정사' 의 관계가
　　성립되지 않고 형용사와 같이 주어의 상황을 나타내는 경우가 있다. 즉, to 부정사가 to 동사 다음에 위치하여
　　형용사적 용법으로 사용되는 경우를 'be to 용법' 이라한다. 'be to 용법' 은 to 부정사 안에 조동사의 의미가
　　포함되어 있으며, 상황에 따라 예정, 의무, 의도, 가능 등 알맞은 것으로 해석한다.

　　The new manager **is to work from tomorrow.** → 예정

　　Students **are to keep many rules.** → 의무

　　The moon **is to be seen tonight.** → 가능

　　If you **are to have a girlfriend**, you should be kind to girls. → 의도

　　The rich man **was to lose most of his money.** → 운명

　✻ 수식을 받는 말이 전치사의 목적어가 되는 경우 전치사의 쓰임에 주의한다.

　　I have no <u>pen</u> **to write with.**

　　I have no <u>paper</u> **to write on.**

Vocabulary

□ **impossible**: 불가능한　　　□ **arrange**: ~의 준비를 하다　　　□ **pleasure**: 기쁨　　　□ **manager**: 지배인

3) **부사적 용법**: to 부정사구가 부사의 역할을 하는 경우를 말하며, 목적 · 감정의 원인 · 이유 및 판단의 근거 · 조건 · 결과 등의 의미를 갖는다. 부사적 용법의 의미에 대한 분류는 암기할 필요 없이 문맥을 통하여 자연스럽게 해석하면 된다.

He stopped at a shopping mall **to buy a jacket.**

She was glad **to hear the news.**

He was wrong **to do such a thing.**

You will be surprised **to see the wounded soldier.**

Edison grew up **to be a great scientist.**

Check-Up

A-1 to 부정사의 용법을 구체적으로 말해 보세요.

(1) I went to his house, never to meet him.

(2) My holiday plan is to play tennis.

(3) I need a pencil to write with.

(4) It is possible to be there on time.

(5) He didn't know where to go.

(6) Our team is to start for Busan tomorrow.

(7) If you are to be a singer, you should listen to much music.

(8) The question is hard to answer.

(9) I would be sad to see you cry.

(10) To get up early, you'd better set the alarm clock.

A-2 괄호 안에 필요한 의문사나 전치사를 넣으세요. (불필요한 곳에는 X표 하세요.)

(1) I need a piece of paper to write ( ).

(2) Kelly knows ( ) to swim.

(3) She has no house to live ( ).

(4) I have no books to read ( ).

※ 문법 학습에 있어서 암기란 절대적으로 효과적이지 못하다. 그리고 암기란 언젠가는 잊게 된다. 명사는 주어, 보어, 목적어 및 전치사의 목적어의 역할을, 그리고 부사는 수식어의 역할을 한다는 등의 품사의 기본 역할에 대한 내용 등 몇가지의 기본 사항에 대한 암기 이외에는 원리 연구와 이해를 통하여 모든 문법 사항을 해결 할 수 있도록 하여야 한다. 올바른 방법을 통하여 문법은 한번 학습으로 영원히 기억되어야 한다.

Vocabulary

☐ **mall**: 쇼핑 센터   ☐ **wounded**: 부상당한   ☐ **holiday**: 휴일   ☐ **had better**: ~하는 편이 더 낫다

2 to 부정사의 의미상의 주어

to 부정사는 동사의 성격을 지니기 때문에 동작의 주체를 갖게 되는데, 이를 'to 부정사의 의미상의 주어' 라 한다.

1) 의미상의 주어를 따로 쓰지 않는 경우

의미상의 주어가 일반인일 때	It is a good habit to get up early.
의미상의 주어 = 문장의 주어	**He** was sad to see the movie end.
의미상의 주어 = 문장의 목적어	I want **you** to have dinner with me.

2) 의미상의 주어를 따로 쓰는 경우 : 1)이외의 경우에는 의미상의 주어를 따로 써야하며 의미상의 주어는 to 부정사 앞에 위치한다.

① 「for + 목적격」

There remain many questions **for you** to answer.

② 「of + 목적격」: 사람의 성격을 나타내는 형용사(kind, good, nice, polite, careful, wise, bad, silly, foolish, stupid, rude, cruel 등)가 있을 경우

It is kind **of you** to take good care of my baby.

Check-Up

A-3   틀린 문장을 골라 옳게 고치세요.

(1) It is difficult to me to find the right answer.

(2) How kind for you to help me!

(3) I want for you to work hard.

(4) It's important students to do their homework.

3 완료 부정사 (to have + 과거분사)

단순부정사(to + 동사원형)는 to 부정사의 시제가 주절 동사와 같거나 더 나중의 일임을, 완료부정사(to have + 과거분사)는 주절 동사보다 먼저 일어난 일임을 의미한다.

He seems **to be rich**. (= It seems that he is rich.)

He seems **to have been rich**. (= It seems that he was rich.)

She was said **to make a mistake**. (= It was said that she made a mistake.)

She was said **to have made a mistake**.

(= It was said that she had made a mistake.)

4 to 부정사의 부정

to 부정사 바로 앞에 부정어를 두어 「not/never + to 부정사」의 형태가 된다.

They decided **not** to attend the meeting.

5 원형부정사

to 부정사의 「to + 동사원형」 형태에서 to가 생략된 부정사를 말한다.

1) 지각동사(see, watch, hear, listen to, smell, feel 등)나 사역동사(have, make, let)의 목적격보어로 쓰인다.

I **heard** her cry out with pain last night.

Mom **had** me clean the room.

※ 사역동사의 의미 차이

X makes Y do ~	"X" forces "Y" to do ~ (억지로 시키다)
X has Y do ~	"X" requests "Y" to do ~ (요청하다)
X gets Y do ~	"X" persuades "Y" to do ~ (가까스로 설득하다)
X lets Y do ~	"X" gives permission "Y" to do ~ (허락하다)
X helps Y do ~	"X" assists "Y" to do ~ (도와주다)

- The doctor **made** me stay in bed.
  (I had no choice. The doctor insisted that I stay in bed.)
- Phil **had** the plumber repair the leak.
  (The plumber repaired the leak because Phil asked him to.)
- I **got** him to translate a letter for me. (I managed to persuade him to translate a letter.)
  cf) get이 회화체적 표현으로 사용되며, 사역의 의미를 띄기는 하지만, 문법적으로는 사역동사가 아니다. 따라서, 원형부정사가 아닌 to 부정사와 함께 쓰인다.
- My father **let** me drive his car. (My father gave me permission to drive his car.)
- She **helped** me (to) clean my room. (She assisted me to clean my room.)

2) 관용적 표현

① had better~ (='d better): ~하는 게 낫다

(advisability를 나타내고, 주어는 주로 1인칭 이외의 인칭인 경우가 많다)

You'd better go home now.

   cf) You had better not waste time.(부정형)

② would rather~ (='d rather): 차라리 ~하겠다

(preference를 나타내고, 주어는 주로 1인칭인 경우가 많다)

I'd rather marry him.

③ Mr. Nonaka cannot but **sing**. → ~하지 않을 수 없다 (= cannot help ~ing)

④ He may well **think** so. → ~하는게 당연하다.

⑤ You may as well **stay** here. → ~하는 편이 낫다.

6 독립 부정사

관용적으로 쓰여서 문장 전체를 수식하는 부정사구

To tell the truth, he is not really Santa Claus. → 사실을 말하면
Needless to say, you are my daughter. → 말할 것도 없이

❊ to begin with (우선), to be frank with you (솔직히 말하면)
  so to speak (말하자면), to say nothing of ~ (~은 말할 것도 없고)

Check-Up

A-4 주어진 문장을 고쳐 쓸 때 괄호 안에 들어갈 말을 쓰세요.

(1) It seems that he is happy.

  → He seems (   ) happy.

(2) It is said that she answered the phone.

  → She is said (   ) the phone.

(3) She seems to have lost her watch.

  → It seems that she (   ) her watch.

(4) It appeared that he exercised hard.

  → He appeared (   ) hard.

(5) He was said to have bought a car.

  → It was said that he (   ) a car.

A-5 틀린 문장을 골라 옳게 고치세요.

(1) I saw him to enter the store on the corner.   **(2)** I cannot but to choose her suggestion.

(3) Let the dog to come into the house.   **(4)** She wanted me wait for her.

(5) You had not better stay here.   **(6)** Cold wind made me stayed inside.

(7) They felt the wind blow on their faces.

A-6 밑줄 친 독립 부정사를 해석하세요.

(1) She is, <u>so to speak</u>, a walking dictionary.

(2) <u>To begin with</u>, Molly didn't agree with you.

(3) He is able to speak Japanese, <u>to say nothing of</u> English.

(4) <u>To be frank with you</u>, she is not beautiful.

7 to 부정사를 포함한 주요 구문

1) ··· enough to ~ : ~할 만큼 충분히 ···하다

She is old **enough to** stay home alone.

= She is **so** old **that** she **can** stay home alone.

2) too ··· to ~ : 너무 ···해서 ~하지 못하다.

I was **too** sleepy **to** finish my homework last night.

= I was **so** sleepy **that** I **could not** finish my homework last night.

3) in order to~ : ~하기 위해서

I went to the post office **in order to** mail a letter.

= I went to the post office **so that** I **might** mail a letter.

= I went to the post office **in order that** I **might** mail a letter.

4) seem to, appear to: ~처럼 보이다, ~인 것 같다

My baby **seems to** be sick. = It **seems that** my baby is sick.

This summer **appears to** be very hot. = It **appears that** this summer is very hot.

5) want / ask / tell / expect + 목적격 + to~

목적어가 ~하기를 원하다 / 요청하다 / 말하다 / 기대하다

I **want** you **to** dance with me.

He **asked** her **to** meet him again.

He **told** me **to** go on.

She **expects** me **to** pass my courses.

Check-Up

A-7 괄호 안에 알맞은 말을 넣으세요.

(1) She is ( ) strong as to lift the box.

(2) Larry is ( ) tired to go.

(3) Tom is old ( ) to go to school.

(4) Maria seems ( ) be late for the movie.

(5) I went to the post office ( ) to post the letter.

Vocabulary

□ lift: 들어올리다

 **동명사**

준동사(verbals)의 하나로써 「동사 + -ing + α」을 이루어 하나의 사고 단위(thought unit)를 형성하며, 그 단위는 하나의 명사의 역할(주어, 보어, 목적어, 전치사의 목적어)을 한다.

I enjoy **working in the garden.**

동명사구	work의 동사적 성격	문장에서의 역할
working in the garden	① 의미상의 주어(I) ② 부사수식(in the garden) ③ 시제(enjoy와 같은 현재)	명사(목적어)

Riding horses is fun.

동명사구	ride의 동사적 성격	문장에서의 역할
Riding horses	① 의미상의 주어(일반인) ② 부사수식(horse) ③ 시제(is와 같은 현재)	명사(주어)

1 동명사의 의미상의 주어

동명사는 명사의 역할로 사용되지만 동사의 성격을 지니기 때문에 동작의 주체를 갖게 되며, 이를 '동명사의 의미상의 주어' 라 한다.

1) 의미상의 주어를 따로 쓰지 않는 경우
   ① 의미상의 주어가 일반인일 때
      Making a decision is difficult.
   ② 의미상의 주어 = 문장의 주어
      I like walking in the snow.

2) 의미상의 주어를 따로 쓰는 경우: 1)이외의 경우에는 의미상의 주어를 (대)명사의 '소유격' 형태로 하여 동명사 앞에 표시한다.

   He hates **her** coming home late at night.

   ※ 명사가 동명사의 의미상의 주어가 될 때는 소유격으로 표시하지 않는 것이 일반적이다.
   He hates **his daughter** coming home late at night.

Vocabulary

□ **make a decision**: 결정하다

Check-Up

B-1   동명사의 의미상 주어에 해당하는 부분에 표시하세요.

   (1)   John seeing her did not surprise us.

   (2)   I object to her punishing him.

   (3)   It is said that seeing is believing.

   (4)   I am sorry for hurting your feelings.

2   완료형 동명사

단순형 (-ing)은 동명사의 시제가 주절 동사와 같거나 더 나중의 일임을, 완료형 (having -ed)은 주절 동사보다 먼저 일어난 일임을 의미한다.

I am sure of my father **recovering**. (= I am sure that my father will recover.)

He is ashamed of **being** short. (= He is ashamed that he is short.)

I regret **having missed** the train. (= I regret that I missed the train.)

3   동명사의 부정: not + -ing

You can help me by **not** helping me.

I heard the news about his **not** leaving us.

4   주요 동명사 구문

1) go ~ing ~: ~하러 가다

   They **went** swimm**ing**. =They went (out) for a swim.

2) on ~ing: ~하자마자.

   On see**ing** me, the cat ran away.

   = **As soon as** the cat saw me, it ran away.

3) be busy ~ing: ~하느라 바쁘다

   Every evening my mom **is busy** cook**ing**.

4) feel like ~ing: ~하고 싶다

   I **feel like** hav**ing** a cup of mocha.

5) cannot help ~ing: ~하지 않을 수 없다

   People **could not help** scream**ing** at the fire.

   = People **could not but** scream at the fire.

   = People **had no choice but to** scream at the fire.

6) (be) far from ~ing: 전혀 ~하지 않다

This news is **far from** be**ing** true. (= This news is never true.)

7) never without ~ing: …하면 반드시 ~하다

I **never** listen to this song **without** cry**ing**.

(= Whenever I listen to this song, I always cry.)

8) of one's own ~ing: 스스로 / 직접 ~한

I'll show you the film **of my own** mak**ing**.

(= I'll show you the film **made by myself**.)

9) prevent A from B: A가 B하는 것을 막다, 방해하다

A cold **prevented** me **from** enjoy**ing** the holiday.

(= I could not enjoy the holiday because of a cold.)

10) (be) worth ~ing: ~할 가치가 있다

This book **is worth** read**ing**. (= It **is worthwhile to** read this book.)

11) Would you mind ~ing?: ~해 주시겠습니까?, ~해도 됩니까?

Would you mind my smok**ing**?

❋ 'Would you mind~?'에 대한 대답

수락 : Of course <u>not</u>. 또는 Cetainly <u>not</u>.   거절 : I'm sorry, but + 변명, 이유

12) 전치사 to로 끝나는 동사구 뒤 (to부정사가 아님에 유의!)

be accustomed to ~ing (~에 익숙해지다)   be used to ~ing (~하는 데 익숙하다)

look forward to ~ing (~를 고대하다)   object to ~ing (~에 반대하다)

I **am** not **accustomed to** eat**ing** in a restaurant by myself.

They **object to** chang**ing** the plans.

The children are **looking forward to** having a Christmas party.

❋ 끊어 읽기와 붙여 읽기의 중요성

전치사 앞과 준동사 앞에서는 항상 끊어 읽는 연습을 해야한다. 전치사구와 준동사구는 하나의 의미(사고 단위)를 형성하기 때문이다. 청취 학습에 있어서 핵심이며, 문장의 구조를 쉽게 파악하는 연습에도 절대적으로 효과가 있다. 숙어라 하여 붙여 읽는 것은 잘못된 생각이다. 따라서 look forward / to -ing으로 끊어 읽어야 한다. 또한, 끊어 읽는다는 것은 붙여 읽는 부분이 있다는 말을 내포한다. 예를 들어 This is / a book의 문장은 This is와 a book을 각각 붙여 읽어야 하며 I live / in Seoul의 문장에서는 I live 와 in Seoul을 각각 붙여 읽어야 한다. 끊어 읽고 붙여 읽는 연습은 올바른 연음 학습과 Intonation 학습에 절대적인 요소이다.

Vocabulary

□ **accustom**: 익숙케 하다

Check-Up

B-2 괄호 안에 알맞은 말을 넣으세요.

(1) It is impossible to tell where he is now.

→ (　　　　) is no telling where he is now.

(2) We could not play soccer because of the heavy snow.

→ The heavy snow (　　　　) us from playing soccer.

(3) It is worthwhile to read a newspaper every day.

→ A newspaper is worth (　　　　) every day.

(4) Whenever I see your face, I always smile.

→ I never see your face (　　　　) smiling.

(5) Nancy could not but have breakfast.

→ Nancy could not (　　　　) having breakfast.

B-3 아래 문장을 우리말로 해석하세요.

(1) It goes without saying that airplanes are faster than cars.

(2) On hearing the news, she turned pale.

(3) I am looking forward to seeing you next Sunday.

(4) I feel like flying to the moon.

(5) It is of no use regretting your mistakes.

(6) Would you mind my using your phone?

(7) I'm proud of the picture of my own painting.

(8) I make a point of jogging every morning.

(9) I never enter this room without feeling at home.

(10) The question is far from being easy.

 **분사**

준동사의 하나로써 현재분사「동사 –ing + α」와 과거분사「동사의 과거분사 + α」가 있으며, 이들은 하나의 사고 단위(thought unit)를 형성하고 그 단위가 하나의 구로서 형용사 역할을 한다.

현재분사 (능동 : ~하고 있는)	명사수식	The **sleeping** baby is so cute, isn't it?
	주격보어	The game was **exciting**.
	목적격보어	He heard someone **singing** on the street.
	진행시제	The sun **is falling** below the horizon.
과거분사 (수동 : ~된)	명사수식	We have to find the **hidden** treasure.
	주격보어	I was **excited** at the game.
	목적격보어	She didn't hear her name **called**.
	완료시제	They **haven't seen** him for one week.
	수동태	This cake **is made** from cheese.

❉ 분사의 위치

A sleeping baby is pretty. (sleeping은 자동사로 명사 앞에서 수식)

The baby sleeping in the garden is my son. (자동사 sleeping이 sleeping을 수식하는 in the garden과 함께 분사구를 만들어 명사 뒤에서 수식)

The girl singing a song is my sister. (sing이 타동사로 사용된 경우로서 목적어 a song과 함께 분사구를 만들어 명사 뒤에서 수식)

It is an interesting piece of news.*

❉ 현재분사와 과거분사의 의미적 차이

현재분사는 능동적, 과거분사는 수동적 의미를 갖는다. 특히, excite, please, satisfy와 같은 "감정유발 타동사"의 능동, 수동에 대한 의미 구별에 주의.

This watch is made in Korea. Look at the man making watches in the room.

1 분사의 용법

1) 한정용법: 명사수식

It was a very **surprising** piece of news to me.

The woman **running there** is my English teacher.

2) 서술용법: 주격보어, 목적격보어로 쓰인다

He stood **drinking cold water**.

I found my glasses **broken**.

---

*interest는 타동사이므로 분사로 사용된다고 하더라고 목적어가 수반되어야 하지만(Ch. 11, p. 216 준동사의 "동사로서의 성격" 참조), 이 문장 에서의 interesting은 동사의 기본 성격을 잃어 버리고 완전히 형용사로 변화된 경우이다. 따라서 형용사와 같이 명사의 앞에서 수식이 가능하다. 이와 같이 분사가 완전히 형용사화 되어 사용되는 경우를 "전성 형용사"라고 칭한다.

2 주의할 분사

1) bore, excite, interest, please, satisfy 등의 '감정유발 타동사' 의 현재분사는 사물을 수식, 설명하는 데 사용되고, 과거분사는 사람이나 생물을 수식, 설명하는 데 사용된다.

'감정유발 타동사' 의 현재, 과거 분사 의미를 암기하지 말고 논리적으로 이해할 것!

The cartoon is **interesting**.　　　　　　　I am **interested** in the cartoon.

2) 지각 / 사역동사 + 목적어 + 목적보어

목적어와 목적격보어가 능동의 관계: 목적격보어로 동사원형을 쓰고,
목적어와 목적격보어가 수동의 관계: 목적격보어로 과거분사를 쓴다.

I <u>heard</u> the baby **cry/crying** at night.　　　He <u>heard</u> his name **called** in the crowd.

※ 지각동사의 경우는 동사원형 대신에 -ing를 쓸 수 있다.

Check-Up

C-1   주어진 동사를 현재분사형이나 과거분사형으로 고쳐 쓰세요.

(1) The program was _____. (bore)

(2) Young-hee is _____ in that book. (interest)

(3) I had my hair _____. (cut)

(4) Stay away from the _____ window. (break)

(5) I saw Ms. Lee _____ with her husband. (quarrel)

(6) The dog _____ there is mine. (run)

(7) I like the music _____ in this studio. (record)

(8) It is really a money- _____ idea. (make)

C-2   밑줄 친 부분이 틀린 문장을 골라 옳게 고치세요.

(1) I have <u>be</u> to New York.

(2) The teacher sat <u>surrounding</u> by his students.

(3) He saw her <u>to run</u> along the street.

(4) I didn't hear my name <u>calling</u>.

(5) The man <u>stand</u> at the door is my teacher.

(6) He is <u>did</u> his homework right now.

(7) I like <u>boiling</u> eggs.

(8) Barbara has <u>buying</u> a new car.

 **분사구문**

부사절을 축약하여 부사구(phrase)의 형태로 바꿀 수 있는데, 이러한 구를 분사구문이라 한다.

1 단순 분사구문(-ing)

When Ann saw Phil, she ran to him.

→ When **seeing** Phil, Ann ran to him.

→ **Seeing** Phil, Ann ran to him.

- 분사구문을 만드는 방법
  ① 부사절의 주어가 주절의 주어와 같으면, 부사절의 주어를 지운다.
  ② 부사절의 동사를 현재분사(-ing) 형태로 고친다.
  ③ 접속사의 명확한 의미가 문맥을 이해하는데 중요한 경우에는 접속사를 생략하지 않는다.
    접속사의 의미가 불명료하게 해석되어도 상관없는 경우에는 접속사를 생략할 수 있다. (단, 접속사 because는 반드시 생략한다)

※ 분사구문의 축약과 되돌림

Because Phil didn't feel too well, he left work early.

→ Not feeling too well, Phil left work early.

→ Phil, not feeling too well, left work early.

→ Phil, who didn't feel too well, left work early.

위 축약된 문장들의 구조는 다르지만, 부사절 또는 부사구의 구조를 지닌 문장으로 해석한 "Phil은 몸이 좋지 않아서 일찍 회사를 떠났다."와 형용사절 또는 형용사구의 구조를 지닌 문장으로 해석한 "몸이 좋지 않았던 Phil은 일찍 회사를 떠났다."는 의미적으로 차이점이 없다. 따라서 미국의 영문법서는 위의 축약된 문장들을 동일한 구조로 취급하여 분사구문을 형용사구로 분류하는 경우도 있다. 즉, 부사절이 축약되어 분사구문이 만들어졌다 하더라도 일단 분사구문이 만들어 진 후에는 분사구문으로 축약되기 이전의 원래 형태가 형용사절이었는지 부사절이었는지, 또는 부사절이었다면 어떠한 접속사가 생략되었는지 100% 확신할 수 없다. 그러므로 부사절을 분사구문으로 전환하는 연습도 필요하고, 축약된 분사구문을 부사구로 인식하는 것도 좋지만, 분사구문을 부사절로 되돌리는 시험문제는 좋다고 할 수 없다.

Check-Up

D-1 다음 문장을 분사구문으로 고치세요.

(1) Though she is 30 years old, she looks like a high school student.

→ _____, she looks like a high school student.

(2) When I walked along the street, I met my sister.

→ _____, I met my sister.

(3)　If you turn to the right, you will find the building.

→ _____, you will find the building.

(4)　She told me a story and gazed at my eyes.

→ She told me a story, _____.

2　수동 분사구문(-ed)

부사절이 수동태일 경우, 이를 분사구로 바꾸면 being+p.p.의 형태가 되는데, 이때 being은 생략할 수 있다.

- When ice is melted, it becomes water again.

→ **(Being) Melted**, ice becomes water again.

- As the piano is covered with dust, it looks awful.

→ **(Being) Covered** with dust, the piano looks awful.

cf)　As my sister is crazy about rock music, she wants to be a singer.

→ **(Being) Crazy** about rock music, my sister wants to be a singer.

3　완료 분사구문(having -ed)

분사구문의 시제가 주절 동사보다 앞설 때 쓰는 분사구문

- As Jun-hee failed the final exam, he is in the 2nd grade again.

→ **Having failed** the final exam, Jun-hee is in the 2nd grade again.

- Because I had not finished the homework before, I did it last night.

→ **Not having finished** the homework before, I did it last night.

- As I was born in winter, I like winter very much.

→ **(Having been) Born** in winter, I like winter very much.

4　독립 분사구문(주어 + -ing/ed)

분사구문의 주어가 주절과 달라서 주어를 따로 쓴 분사구문

- As there are many umbrellas, you can have one.

→ **There being** many umbrellas, you can have one.

- When the film was shown, everybody gave it applause.

→ **The film shown**, everybody gave it applause.

❋ with 독립분사구문 / 부대상황 (with + 목적어 + -ing / ed)
부대상황을 나타내는 독립분사구문에 with를 붙여서 동시적인 동작을 강조한다.
With the dog following, I walked to the park. (~한 채로)
→ I walked to the park, and the dog followed.
I was listening to music **with my eyes closed**.

Vocabulary

□ **melt**: 녹다　　　　　　　□ **awful**: 두려운　　　　　　　□ **grade**: (초, 중, 고등학교의) 학년

5 무인칭 독립 분사구문

독립분사구문의 주어가 일반인일 때 주어를 생략하고 관용적으로 쓰는 분사구문

Considering your age, you did a good job. (~을 고려하면)

Frankly/Strictly speaking, I can't do this. (솔직히/엄밀히 말하면)

Judging from his accent, he is not an American. (~으로 판단하자면)

❄ generally speaking(일반적으로 말하면), granting that(~을 고려하더라도), talking of(~에 대해 말하자면), taking A into consideration(A를 고려하면)

Check-Up

D-2   다음 문장을 분사구문으로 고치세요.

(1) As he was so surprised at the news, he couldn't say anything.

→ _____, he couldn't say anything.

(2) When she was left alone, she was scared.

→ _____, she was scared.

(3) After Tom had written a letter, he went out for a walk.

→ _____, Tom went out for a walk.

(4) When night came on, we started for home.

→ _____, we started for home.

(5) As it was very cold, we made a fire.

→ _____, we made a fire.

D-3   틀린 문장을 골라 옳게 고치세요.

(1) Seeing from a distance, the house seems beautiful.

(2) Generally speak, parents love their children.

(3) Being a rainy day, we couldn't go swimming.

(4) He was sitting with his legs crossing.

(5) Writing in English, the book is hard to understand.

Vocabulary

□ scare: 위협하다   □ cross: (손, 발 따위를) 엇걸다

1 to 부정사의 쓰임이 같은 세 쌍의 문장을 찾아 연결하세요.

(1) It is easy to read this book.   (   )

(2) We must walk fast to take the first bus.   (   )

(3) I was surprised to meet him.   (   )

(4) There is nothing to eat in my house.   (   )

(a) I go to the store to buy milk every day.

(b) To say such a thing is wrong.

(c) My mother gave me money to buy the guitar.

(d) This computer program is easy to learn.

2 밑줄에 들어갈 말을 보기에서 찾아 쓰세요.

> 보기 When I heard the news, I didn't know _____ to say.

(A) what   (B) how

(C) where   (D) when

3 밑줄 친 부분이 잘못된 문장을 고르세요.

(A) There is a glass of water to drink.

(B) I need a chair to sit on.

(C) Please, give me a pen to write.

(D) This is a matter to talk about.

4 다음 문장의 뜻에 가장 가까운 것을 고르세요.

> 보기 I started early, only to miss the train.

(A) I started early never to miss the train.

(B) I started early, but I missed the train.

(C) I started early in order to miss the train.

(D) I started so early as to miss the train.

5 다음 문장을 고쳐 쓸 때 밑줄에 알맞은 말을 쓰세요.

It seems that In-su saw the movie before.

→ In-su seems to _____ the movie before.

6 다음 문장을 to 부정사 구문으로 고쳐 쓸 때 밑줄에 알맞은 말을 쓰세요.

(1) My brother was so sick that he couldn't go to school.

→ My brother was _____ sick _____ go to school.

(2) It is impossible that Mr. Kim will come back by midnight.

→ It is impossible _____ Mr. Kim _____ come back by midnight.

7 to 부정사나 원형 부정사의 쓰임이 잘못된 것을 고르세요.

(A) You had better to turn off the TV.

(B) I asked him not to smoke.

(C) They cannot but stop working.

(D) My mother always makes me wash my feet.

8 독립부정사의 의미가 잘못 풀이된 것을 고르세요.

(A) I was late. To make matters worse, I had a flat tire. → 설상가상으로

(B) To tell the truth, I stole your shoes. → 사실을 말하면

(C) Frankly speaking, we drank beer. → 엄밀히 말하면

(D) You are, so to speak, my best friend. → 말하자면

9 아래의 우리말에 맞게 주어진 영어 단어들을 배열하세요.
(첫 단어는 반드시 대문자로 시작하세요.)

(1) 나를 도와주다니 넌 매우 친절하구나. (to, you, very, of, help, kind, me)

→ It is _____ .

(2) 그녀는 방에서 개가 짖는 소리를 들었다. (the dog, she, in the, heard, bark, room)

→ _____ .

10 밑줄에 주어진 동사를 알맞게 고쳐 쓰세요.

(1) He is used to _____ a car. (drive)

(2) I am ashamed of _____ at you. (laugh)

(3) I felt like _____ an ice cream. (eat)

(4) He is proud of _____ in the Olympics. (participate)

(5) I am sure of Tom's _____ in time. (come)

11 밑줄에 들어갈 알맞은 단어를 고르세요.

> 보기 My father objected to _____ majoring in music.

(A) I　　　　　　　　　(B) myself

(C) mine　　　　　　　(D) my

12 다음 문장을 고쳐 쓸 때 밑줄에 알맞은 말을 쓰세요.

(1) I had met him before, but I forgot it.

→ I forgot _____ him before.

(2) I remembered that I must stop by the store.

→ I remembered _____ by the store.

13 다음 질문에 대한 대답으로 옳지 않은 것을 고르세요.

> 보기 Would you mind my using this pen?

(A) Certainly not.　　　　(B) Of course not.

(C) Yes, I would.　　　　(D) I'm sorry, but it's not mine.

14 밑줄 친 부분의 쓰임이 잘못된 것을 고르세요.

(A) She began to read the poem loudly.

(B) Ally avoided touching his hands.

(C) Greg likes to drink some wine.

(D) We gave up to open the door by force.

15 괄호 안에 들어갈 알맞은 단어를 고르세요.

> (보기) It is impossible to finish the work until tomorrow.
> = There is (   ) finishing the work until tomorrow.

(A) no   (B) not

(C) nothing   (D) never

16 다음 문장을 동명사 구문으로 고쳐 쓰세요.

I regret that I lent him my car.

→ I regret ＿＿＿＿＿＿＿＿ him my car.

17 괄호 안에 알맞은 단어를 선택하세요.

(1) A (rolling, rolled) stone gathers no moss.

(2) People (living, lived) in the country generally live long.

(3) Today a (hiding, hidden) camera becomes a serious problem.

(4) They stood (looking, looked) at the (exciting, excited) game.

(5) I like the chocolate cake (making, made) by my mother.

18 다음 문장을 분사구문으로 고칠 때, 밑줄 친 곳에 들어갈 말을 고르세요.

> (보기) As she was given much money, she can buy some pencils.
> → ＿＿＿＿＿＿＿＿ much money, she can buy some pencils.

(A) Giving   (B) Given

(C) Having given   (D) As

19 다음 분사구문을 절로, 절을 분사구문으로 고치세요.

(1) If we judge from his appearance, he seems to be a thief.

　　→ ＿＿＿＿＿＿＿＿＿＿＿＿＿＿, he seems to be a thief.

(2) As it is made of glass, the cup is easily broken.

　　→ ＿＿＿＿＿＿＿＿＿＿＿＿＿＿, the cup is easily broken.

(3) He ate his breakfast reading a newspaper.

　　→ He ate his breakfast ＿＿＿＿＿＿＿＿＿＿＿＿＿.

[20-21] 괄호 안에 들어갈 알맞은 말을 고르세요.

20 My mother watched TV (   ) the baby crying.

(A) and   (B) to

(C) by   (D) with

21 (   ) no one in the room, I went out of the room.

(A) Being   (B) There being

(C) There been   (D) Been

22 주어진 의미에 알맞은 관용적인 독립분사구문을 쓰세요.

(1) (그의 나이를 고려하면), this work is too much for him.

(2) (솔직히 말하면), he seems to be a great teacher.

유형 6   주어 찾기

1 It is important for him _____ this.

(A) understand   (B) to understand

(C) understanding   (D) who understands

2 _____ on this bench is very pleasant.

(A) Lie   (B) Laying

(C) Lying   (D) I lie

유형 9   보어 찾기

1 You seem _____ this area very well.

(A) to know   (B) knowing

(C) knowledge   (D) have known

유형 10   목적어와 목적보어 찾기

1 I want her _____ Spanish.

(A) and learn   (B) learning

(C) learn   (D) to learn

유형 43   to 부정사 찾기

1 You can use a magnet _____ another magnet.

(A) made   (B) to make

(C) to make it   (D) is made

유형 44 to 부정사 자리에 동사를 쓴 경우

1 I <u>sometimes</u> use <u>an alarm clock</u> <u>get</u> up <u>in the</u> morning.
         A   B   C   D

2 Children <u>must</u> learn <u>what do</u> in <u>case</u> a fire <u>breaks</u> out.
            A   B   C   D

유형 46 원형부정사 자리에 다른 형태를 잘못 쓴 경우

1 <u>You</u> would rather <u>waiting</u> a moment <u>than</u> leave <u>immediately</u>.
    A   B   C   D

2 <u>Rules</u> of <u>boxing</u> matches have <u>each</u> player <u>to wear</u> a mouthpiece.
    A   B   C   D

유형 47 to 부정사의 형태가 잘못된 경우

1 <u>Long ago</u>, people happened <u>to seeing</u> <u>their</u> faces <u>in ponds</u> and lakes.
    A   B   C   D

2 In winter, it is <u>exciting</u> to <u>having</u> a snowball <u>fight</u> with <u>friends</u>.
                   A   B   C   D

유형 48 동명사 찾기

1 _____ can help us understand the earth.

(A) Geography learned that

(B) Learn geography

(C) It is geography that we learn

(D) Learning geography

2 We walked in the rain without _____ umbrellas.

(A) to carry   (B) carrying

(C) carried   (D) and carry

1 It was so lucky, your not be hurt in that bad traffic accident.
          A   B   C   D

2 Schweitzer is famous for help the sick in the poor African country.
             A   B   C   D

유형 **50** 분사(구문) 찾기

1 He rode his bike along the street, _____.

(A) smiled to wave

(B) smiling and waving

(C) he smiled and waved

(D) smile but wave

2 _____ by its master, the dog wagged its tail.

(A) To forgive   (B) As it forgave

(C) Forgiving of   (D) Forgiven

3 _____ cold, my mother built a fire.

(A) Being   (B) Having been

(C) It being   (D) To be

유형 **51** 현재분사와 과거분사를 혼동하여 쓴 경우

1 The snake is a very surprised animal: it sleeps with its eyes open.
                       A   B   C   D

2 Someone interesting in books may go to a library or a bookstore.
                A   B   C   D

유형 **52** 분사 자리에 동사나 다른 준동사를 쓴 경우

1 It is dangerous to get on or off the moves train.
  A   B   C   D

2 Today's computer is very different from the one first invent.
     A   B   C   D

1 _____ a message, people used electricity.

(A) They carry   (B) Carry that

(C) To carry   (D) It carries

2 There is no sure way _____ when an earthquake is coming.

(A) to know   (B) knows

(C) known   (D) know that

3 <u>Mr. Andropov</u> invited Samantha and <u>her</u> family <u>visit</u> him <u>in Russia</u>.
         A   B   C   D

4 When we <u>are in</u> a foreign country, we <u>had</u> better <u>to try</u> to understand <u>its</u> customs.
                  A   B   C   D

5 It <u>is</u> fun to <u>watching</u> fireflies glow <u>in</u> the dark <u>at night</u>.
        A   B   C   D

6 It was Nathan Stubblefield <u>who</u> was <u>the</u> first person <u>send</u> his voice <u>over</u> radio.
                                         A   B   C   D

7 We need <u>wood</u> for <u>cook</u> and heat, <u>so</u> we cut <u>down</u> trees.
                   A   B   C   D

8 For most people, _____ their work means going home to rest.

(A) finish   (B) they finish

(C) finishing   (D) who finishes

9 Children <u>usually</u> mind <u>turn off</u> the light before <u>they</u> fall <u>asleep</u>.
                   A   B   C   D

10 When the opossum is afraid, it tries to hide by _____.

(A) and play dead   (B) play and be dead

(C) play dead   (D) playing dead

11 Besides <u>work</u> eight <u>hours</u> every day, she <u>works</u> two hours <u>at night</u>.
               A   B   C   D

12 My father entered <u>the</u> army, <u>finished</u> school <u>when</u> he <u>was</u> twenty.
                        A   B   C   D

13 <u>A</u> computer <u>name</u> Big Blue beat <u>the</u> best chess <u>player</u> in the world.
 A   B   C   D

14 Becky, _____ , waved good-bye to her friends.

(A) crying softly   (B) and cried softly

(C) soft crying   (D) she cried softly

15 Hinduism is <u>a</u> religion <u>believing</u> in by <u>millions</u> of people <u>in</u> India.
                    A   B   C   D

16 Exams have <u>an effect</u> on the blood <u>pressure</u> of <u>the</u> students <u>took</u> them.
               A   B   C   D

17 _____ beneath its snout, the shark's mouth has between four and six rows of teeth.

(A) It located   (B) Located

(C) Its locating   (D) Because it located

18 John F. Kennedy was the <u>first</u> Catholic President <u>elects</u> in <u>the</u> U.S.
            A   B   C   D

19 <u>Being</u> no <u>bus</u> service, she had to <u>go</u> to school <u>on foot</u>.
      A   B   C   D

20 The list shows all the people's names _____ in this company.

(A) work   (B) worked

(C) working   (D) works at

1 The Pilgrims left they home in England in search of religious freedom.
           A   B   C   D

2 This engine is very practical; it works well without waste fuel.
                            A   B   C   D

3 From the nation's early days, _____ used in trade with the Far East.

(A) American's sailing vessels

(B) American vessels were sailing

(C) American sailing vessels were

(D) American vessels to sail

4 _____ wood plentiful, early Americans built clapboard houses.

(A) Which   (B) With   (C) Because   (D) Though

5 Jesse Owens was born in Alabama in 1913 to a poverty and black family.
                        A   B   C   D

6 One reason Mozart was so good at music_____ his father's job was teaching music.

(A) being that   (B) to be   (C) was that   (D) that was

7 Millions of years ago, horses were no big than cats, and they lived in the forest.
                        A   B   C   D

Chapter • 10

8   Tree frogs have <u>stick</u> pads at the ends of <u>their</u> toes, <u>which</u> keep the tree frogs
                                A   B   C

from <u>falling</u>.
     D

9   When people came to know _____, they could stay in one place
and grow it.

(A) food grows   (B) how to grow food

(C) that grow food   (D) food which grow

10   Mexico City is <u>such</u> crowded that <u>it</u> doesn't have <u>enough</u> houses <u>and</u> jobs.
                              A   B   C   D

11   The goal of science <u>is to</u> discover facts about the <u>natural</u> world and the
                           A   B

principles <u>that</u> explain <u>this</u> facts.
         C   D

12   The average pH of normal rainfall is about 5.6, _____ of the
combination of carbon dioxide with water vapor to produce carbonic acid.

(A) resulting in   (B) that results

(C) a result   (D) in a result

Vocabulary

□ **religious**: 종교적인	□ **freedom**: 자유	□ **practical**: 실용적인
□ **work**: 작동하다	□ **fuel**: 연료	□ **vessel**: 배
□ **trade**: 무역	□ **poverty**: 빈곤	□ **stick**: 달라붙다
□ **toe**: 발가락	□ **keep A from B**: A가 B하는 것을 막다	□ **crowded**: 혼잡한, 가득 찬
□ **principle**: 원리, 원칙	□ **normal**: 정상의	□ **carbon dioxide**: 이산화탄소

STRUCTURE

준동사

Grammar Up / Power Up Test / Pattern Drill / Pattern Review / Mini Test

준동사

　준동사란 움직임의 감정 및 복합적인 내용을 포함한 명사, 형용사, 부사의 역할을 할 수 있도록 동사에 to–, –ing, –ed가 첨가되어 변형된 것이다. 준동사는 명사, 형용사, 부사 역할을 하더라도 "동사로서의 기본 성격"은 여전히 갖고 있다.

　to 부정사(to-infinitive): to + 동사원형
　동명사(gerund)　　　　: –ing
　분사(participle)　　　 : 현재분사(present participle): –ing
　　　　　　　　　　　 : 과거분사(past participle): –ed

1　문장에서의 역할

명사적 역할(주어, 목적어, 보어, 전치사의 목적어)	to 부정사, 동명사
형용사적 역할(보어, 명사 수식)	to 부정사, 분사
부사적 역할(동사/형용사/부사/구/절 수식)	to 부정사, 분사구문

• 참고: 부정사는 전치사의 목적어로 사용되지 못한다

2　동사로서의 성격

　1) 의미상의 주어를 갖는다.

　　She ran **to win**.　　　　I enjoy **working in the kitchen**.

　　The baby **sleeping in the room** is my daughter.

　2) 동사의 종류에 따라 목적어 또는 보어를 취한다.

　　She was glad **to be** a May Queen.　　　　Everyone hates **feeling** alone.

　　The man **wearing** sunglasses is Tom Cruise.

　3) 부사(구)의 수식을 받을 수 있다.

　　To exercise regularly is good for health.　　　　Her problem is **eating** too much.

　　I heard someone **closing the window** loudly.

　4) 시제를 갖는다.

　　He stopped at a shopping mall **to buy his shirt**. (stopped와 같은 과거 시제)

　　My favorite activity is **reading poetry**. (is와 같은 현재 시제)

❊ 동사로서의 성격을 잃어버린 동명사와 분사

　동명사와 분사가 동사로서의 성격을 잃어 버리고 완전히 명사나 형용사화 되어 버린 경우를 말한다. 이러한 경우를 "전성 명사", "전성 형용사"라 칭한다. 예를 들어, 전성 명사는 완전히 명사화 되어 버린 것이므로 관사가 붙을 수 있으며 형용사의 수식을 받을 수 있다. (Ch. 10, p. 196 참조)

to 부정사와 동명사

> ✳ **to 부정사와 동명사의 기본적인 의미의 차이**
>
> **to 부정사:** 기대, 소망, 의도 등의 감정을 표현(조동사의 의미가 포함되어 있음).
> **동명사:** 행위나 사실 자체를 말함.
>   I like to **watch** a movie. (현재의 감정: 나는 지금 영화가 보고 싶다)
>   I like **watching** movies. (일반적인 사실: 나는 영화 보는 것을 원래 좋아한다)
> 따라서 기대, 소망, 예정, 의도 등을 나타내는 동사들(want, hope, wish, intend, expect, try, promise 등)은 보통 to 부정사를 목적어로 취한다.

1 동명사와 to 부정사를 모두 목적어로 갖고 의미에도 차이가 거의 없는 동사

begin, start, continue 등

She **continued** play**ing** the computer game for ten hours!
= She **continued to** play the computer game for ten hours!

2 동명사와 to 부정사를 모두 목적어로 갖지만 의미에 차이가 있는 동사

remember, forget, try, stop 등

1) remember / forget + 동명사: 이미 한 일을 기억하다/잊다
   remember / forget + to 부정사: 앞으로 해야 할 일을 기억하다/잊다
   I **remember** mail**ing** the letter. (편지를 부친 것 자체를 기억하다)
   I **remember to** mail the letter. (편지를 부칠 것을 기억하다)

2) try + 동명사: 시험삼아 해 보다
   try + to 부정사: ~하려고 노력하다
   The girl **tried** diet**ing**. (시험삼아 식이요법을 해 보다)
   The girl **tried to** diet. (식이요법을 하려고 노력하다)

3) stop + 동명사: ~하는 것을 멈추다
   stop + to 부정사: ~하기 위해 멈추다
   He **stopped** drink**ing** from yesterday. (술 마시기를 멈추다)
   He **stopped to** drink at the bar. (술을 마시기 위해 멈추다. to 부정사는 부사적 용법)

3 동명사만을 목적어로 갖는 동사

avoid, complete, enjoy, finish, give up, mind, stop, understand 등
I **gave up** gambling. (up은 부사)

4 to 부정사만을 목적어로 갖는 동사

agree, ask, choose, decide, expect, hope, promise, want, wish 등
He **promised to** be with her.

✳ **목적의 의미 : to 부정사만 되고 + -ing는 안 된다**

Susan left her hometown for New York to get a good job. (○)
Susan left her hometown for New York for getting a good job. (×)
Susan left her hometown for New York for a good job. (○)

Check-Up

B-1   괄호 안에 주어진 동사를 문장에 알맞은 형태로 고치세요.

(1)   Can you consider (live) in such a dirty place?

(2)   Why don't you stop (smoke)?

(3)   She enjoyed (play) the piano.

(4)   Let's stop for a while (take) a picture.

(5)   He continued (run) for two hours.

(6)   I forgot (make) an appointment with you tomorrow.

(7)   I have to admit (lose) the game.

(8)   She remembered (see) the picture a few years ago.

C 동명사와 현재분사

1) It is fun **making** a dish. → 동명사(진주어)
   This is a machine **making** a dish. → 현재분사(명사 수식)

2) A <u>sleeping</u> baby was in the <u>sleeping</u> car.
   　　현재분사　　　　　　　　　동명사

   a sleeping baby = a baby (who is) sleeping: 현재분사 – 형용사절의 의미
   the sleeping car = the car for sleeping: 동명사 – 목적, 도구
   ⇒ 〈현재분사 + 명사〉의 경우 강세가 꾸밈을 받는 명사에 있고(sleeping baby),
   　〈동명사 + 명사〉의 경우 강세는 동명사에 있다(sleeping car).

■ 현재분사의 예

   a **dancing** girl (a girl who is dancing)
   boiling water (water which is boiling)

■ 동명사의 예

   a **dining** room (a room for dining)
   a **working** day (a day for working)
   a **waiting** room (a room for waiting)
   a **smoking** room (a room for smoking)
   a **washing** machine (a machine for washing)

Check-Up

C-1　밑줄 친 부분이 동명사인지 현재분사인지 말해 보세요.

(1) Don't wake up the <u>sleeping</u> baby.
(2) Boys like <u>playing</u> basketball.
(3) She is in the <u>dressing</u> room.
(4) Min-young called her son <u>playing</u> the violin.
(5) <u>Walking</u> slowly is good for health.

1   짝지은 두 문장이 어색한 것을 고르세요.

(A) I wanted a lot to receive your letter.

     = I looked forward to receive your letter.

(B) It is worthwhile to visit Korea.

     = Korea is worth visiting.

(C) She has no choice but to clean the kitchen.

     = She cannot help cleaning the kitchen.

(D) We could not enjoy the concert because of noise.

     = Noise prevented us from enjoying the concert.

2   두 문장의 의미를 비교하세요.

(1) She stopped drinking from yesterday.

(2) She stopped to drink at the bar.

3   괄호 안에 들어갈 동사가 올바르게 짝지어진 것을 고르세요.

> (보기) Mr. James yelled at me with his son (   ).
> He fell down with his arms (   ).

(A) to sing - broken   (B) singing - breaking

(C) singing - broken   (D) to sing - breaking

4   어법상 올바르지 않은 문장을 고르세요.

(A) Eating too much, he couldn't sit on the chair.

(B) Having not much information, he couldn't solve the problem easily.

(C) Having finished with his homework, he played with his friends.

(D) Tired with his work, he went to bed.

Vocabulary

□ **bar**: 술집   □ **yell at**: 고함치다

유형 43   to 부정사 찾기

1 Water and food are too valuable _____ .

    (A) throw away

    (B) throwing away

    (C) to throw away

    (D) that throw away

유형 45   to 부정사와 동명사를 혼동하여 쓴 경우

1 In some parts in the world, there isn't enough food eating.
         A   B   C   D

2 Some of old tradition is not worth to follow in this computerized age.
        A   B   C   D

3 We should go to the dentist regularly checking our teeth.
         A   B   C   D

Chapter • 11

Vocabulary

□ **throw away**: 내버리다

1   <u>Thousands</u> of years <u>ago</u>, people began to <u>taming</u> the <u>wild</u> dogs.
        A   B   C   D

2   Airplanes enable us <u>traveling</u> such <u>a long</u> distance <u>in</u> a short <u>time</u>.
                 A   B   C   D

3   Magicians use some tricks _____ who are watching the show.

    (A) the people amused   (B) the people amusing

    (C) to the amused people   (D) to amuse the people

4   We go to the museum <u>seeing</u> some <u>art</u> works which <u>are</u> produced by <u>famous</u>
                       A   B   C   D
    artists.

5   Some disc jockeys in New York City were found to have lost some of

    _____ .

    (A) their hearing   (B) to hear them

    (C) for them to hear   (D) they hear

6   I know that it is <u>no</u> use <u>crying</u> over <u>spilt</u> milk, but I cannot help <u>to cry</u>.
                 A   B   C   D

7   There <u>is</u> a way <u>to fill</u> a balloon <u>with</u> air without <u>blow</u> it up.
          A   B   C   D

8   People sometimes have difficulty _____ someone's name.

    (A) remember   (B) remembering

    (C) remembered   (D) remember that

9   Inuit, <u>called</u> Eskimos, are used <u>to live</u> in <u>extremely</u> cold <u>areas</u>.
         A   B   C   D

10   Ali Baba was leading his donkey through the forest, _____
    firewood.

    (A) gathered   (B) which gathering

    (C) gathering   (D) and to gather

1 <u>Peace</u> is one of the <u>principle</u> of the Quakers, and <u>they</u> oppose <u>war</u>.
  A   B   C   D

2 The Cliff Palace is the huge building _____ back almost a thousand years.

(A) which dating   (B) dates

(C) as to date   (D) dating

3 Before the Civil War, a <u>secretly</u> operation, <u>called</u> the Underground Railroad, <u>was</u>
                              A   B   C
carried on to <u>free</u> slaves.
              D

4 The middle of the world is hot, but at the very top and bottom of the world _____ very cold.

(A) it is   (B) being   (C) there is   (D) is that

5 <u>Traditionally</u>, <u>the</u> American farmer has <u>always</u> be independent and <u>hard-working</u>.
        A   B   C   D

6 You can <u>vote for</u> the people <u>what</u> run our country <u>when</u> you become a <u>certain</u> age.
                A   B   C   D

7 From the fossils, scientists can learn _____ grew long ago.

(A) of what kind trees

(B) what kind of trees

(C) kind trees of what

(D) tree of what kind

8 People do not <u>talk to</u> one <u>another</u> in Latin today, but <u>they</u> still use <u>much</u> Latin
                       A   B   C   D
words.

9 <u>At</u> first, there <u>were</u> a word for one, for two, for three, and more <u>than</u> three
     A   B   C
were <u>many</u>.
       D

10 Soil is made when ground-up rocks _____ other things.

(A) mix with   (B) to mix with

(C) with mixing   (D) which mixed with

11 Genealogy <u>was once</u> closely <u>link</u> with heraldry, the use of coats of arms
                    A   B
<u>to identify</u> the members of <u>noble families</u>.
     C   D

12 When liquid water <u>cools</u>, the molecules not only move more slowly, <u>and they</u>
                        A   B
also pack more closely together and <u>take up less space</u>.
                                        C   D

Vocabulary

□ oppose: 반대하다	□ date back: ~로 거슬러 올라가다	□ the Civil War: 미국 남북전쟁
□ secretly: 몰래	□ free: 자유롭게 하다	□ slave: 노예
□ bottom: 바닥	□ traditionally: 전통적으로	□ independent: 독립적인
□ hard-working: 근면한	□ vote for: 찬성 투표하다	□ run: 운영하다
□ fossil: 화석	□ one another: 서로	□ soil: 흙, 토양
□ ground: grind(가루로 만들다)의 과거, 과거분사	□ genealogy: 가계, 혈통	□ heraldry: 문장
□ molecule: 분자	□ pack: 묶다	

STRUCTURE

전치사

Grammar Up / Power Up Test / Pattern Drill / Pattern Review / Mini Test

전치사구의 역할

전치사구는 문장에서 형용사구 혹은 부사구로 쓰인다.

Please get *in*. (in은 부사. in 뒤에 명사가 없음)
Please get <u>in</u> this room. (in은 전치사. this room은 전치사 in의 목적어)

Your old stereo is **of no use** now. → 형용사구: 주격보어
I want to buy the flowers **in that basket**. → 형용사구: 명사수식
She lives **in Dallas**. → 부사구: 동사 수식
To my surprise, she gave up schooling. → 부사구: 문장 수식(놀랍게도)

 전치사의 목적어와 위치

1   전치사의 목적어

전치사는 명사(전치사의 목적어)와 함께 구를 이루어 형용사구 혹은 부사구로 쓰인다.
전치사의 목적어로는 명사, 대명사, 동명사, 명사절이 쓰인다.

He stood <u>against</u> the **wall**. → 명사

When your father speaks, you have to listen <u>to</u> **him**. → 목적격 대명사

She improved her Spanish <u>by</u> **practicing**. → 동명사

I am interested <u>in</u> **why Charles left for Africa**. → 명사절(의문사절)

❊ 주의해야 할 경우
   He does nothing <u>but</u> **sleep** on Sundays. → 원형 부정사
   I'm <u>afraid of</u> snakes.
   I'm <u>afraid</u> **that you will be sick**. (that절은 전치사 of의 목적어로 사용되지 못한다)

228

2 전치사의 위치

전치사는 원칙적으로 그 목적어 앞에 위치한다.

The new semester will begin **in** March.

❊ 주의해야 할 경우

What are you looking **at**? → 의문사가 목적어일 때

It isn't a problem to worry **about**. → 부정사 구문의 목적어일 때

This is a company I work **for**. → 목적격 관계대명사가 생략된 구문일 때

Gold has been searched **for**. → 수동태 구문일 때 (= We have searched **for** gold.)

Vocabulary

□ **against ~**: ~에 기대어   □ **improve**: 향상시키다   □ **do nothing but ~**: ~만 하다   □ **search for**: 찾다

A-1   다음 문장에서 밑줄 친 전치사구의 쓰임을 말해 보세요.

(1)   This village is in need of rain.

(2)   She wore a hat with a flower on it.

(3)   She felt uneasy at first.

(4)   I have worked there for three years.

(5)   To his disappointment, he failed the exam.

B-1   괄호 안에 주어진 단어를 알맞은 형태로 고쳐 쓰세요.

(1)   She isn't familiar with (study) this subject.

(2)   His father is very proud of (he).

(3)   For the purpose of (succeed), he studied day and night.

(4)   He repaired the bicycle for (I).

(5)   Don't talk about (my father).

B-2   틀린 문장을 골라 옳게 고치세요.

(1)   He was good at speak French.

(2)   She spent two days alone without he.

(3)   I found my CD the desk on in your room.

(4)   I look forward to see you tomorrow.

(5)   This is the about question to think.

(6)   She cannot but to choose him.

(7)   You can get some information about policemen by see this movie.

(8)   Everyone has gone home except Mary and I.

(9)   Amy talked about why she had decided to get a job.

(10)   She was ashamed of that she didn't pay her debt.

Vocabulary

□ in need of ~: ~이 필요한   □ uneasy: 불편한   □ to one's disappointment: 실망스럽게도

□ be familiar with ~: ~에 익숙하다   □ for the purpose of ~: ~할 목적으로   □ be good at ~: ~에 능숙하다

□ be ashamed of: 부끄러워하다

C 전치사의 종류

1 단일 전치사

after, at, beside, by, for, from, in, of, on, over, to, under, with 등

2 구 전치사

전치사가 다른 단어와 함께 쓰여서 하나의 전치사 역할을 하는 것.

because of(~ 때문에), by means of(~으로), for fear of(~이 두려워서)

for the sake of(~을 위해서), in addition to(~과 더불어), in case of(~할 경우에),

in front of(~ 앞에), instead of(~ 대신에)

In spite of the heavy rain, I have to go to pick him up. (~에도 불구하고, despite)

I could not study here **on account of** the noise. (~ 때문에)

※ 구 전치사는 아니지만 두 개의 전치사가 함께 쓰이는 경우
The little puppy came out **from behind** the cabinet. (~ 뒤에서)

Check-Up

C-1 괄호 안에 알맞은 말을 쓰세요.

(1) She painted this picture ( ) means of oil colors.

(2) He went there instead ( ) his boss.

(3) The tree was ( ) front of the house.

(4) In addition ( ) a ring, he gave me a necklace.

(5) Please, be quiet for the ( ) of my baby.

(6) ( ) fear of ghosts, Kelly couldn't enter the house.

(7) Kate couldn't go to the hospital on ( ) of much work.

Vocabulary

□ **puppy**: 강아지   □ **cabinet**: 케비넷   □ **oil colors**: 유화 물감

□ **necklace**: 목걸이   □ **ghost**: 유령

D 전치사의 쓰임

1 시간의 전치사

1) 정해진 시간

at	시간, 정오, 자정, 밤, 식사, 짧은 휴가 (시간의 한 지점 혹은 그렇게 여겨지는 기간을 나타낸다)
on	요일, 날짜, (특정한) 날
in	하루의 일부분, 달, 계절, 연도, 연대, 세기 (다소 길다고 여겨지는 기간을 나타낸다)

at 8 a.m. / noon / midnight / night / breakfast / Christmas

on Monday / June 26 / any other day that you may prefer

in the afternoon / July / the fall / 2002 / the 1990s / the 17th century

2) 지속되는 시간

for	시간의 길이 ('How long something continues?'에 대한 대답 으로 쓰이며, 보통 '숫자'가 온다)
during	기간 ('When something takes place?' 대한 대답으로 쓰인다)
from ~ to …	~ 부터 …까지

I was in Seattle **for** three days.

I was in Seattle **during** the vacation.

I work **from** 9 a.m. **to** 6 p.m.

3) 시작점이나 끝점만을 나타내는 지속되는 시간

before	~ 전에
within	~ 이내에
in	~ 지나면, ~후에 ('특정한 시간이 지난 후'를 나타낸다)
since	~ 이래로
by	~ 까지 (특정한 시간 이전에, 혹은 늦어도 그 시간까지 일어남을 나타낸다)
until	~ 까지 (특정한 시간까지 계속됨을 나타낸다)

He will not be there **before** Saturday night.

The ambulance arrived **within** two minutes.

It's one o'clock; I'll come **in** two hours.

He has been sleeping **since** ten o'clock.

Can you finish the work **by** five o'clock?

I have to be at the stadium **until** 2 o'clock.

- 회화체에서는 until 대신 till을 사용하기도 한다.
- I slept till midnight. (자정이 될 때까지 잤었다.)
  I didn't sleep till midnight. (자정이 될 때까지 자지 않았다.)

2　장소의 전치사

1) 위치와 방향

at	좁은 장소, 주소 (하나의 지점이라 생각되는 장소에 쓰인다)
on	평면, 거리(street, road, avenue), 강, 층 (평면에 닿은 위치나 길(road) 또는 강과 같이 선(line)의 개념을 지닌 장소에 쓰인다)
in	넓은 장소(도시, 주, 나라, 대륙)
for	목적지
to	목적지 (목적지에 실제로 도착했음을 나타낸다)
toward	(대체적인) 방향

at my house / 20 Main Street

on the ceiling / King's Road / the Han River / the third floor

in L.A. / Ohio / Korea / Africa

Columbus sailed **for** India.

I drove **to** Seoul. ('그래서 서울에 도착했다'는 의미가 내포되어 있다)

I drove **toward** Seoul. (서울이 목적지가 아닐 수 있다)

2) 상대적 위치

above ↔ below	(어떤 것으로부터 멀리 떨어져서 그 위/아래에 높이/낮게 있는 경우를 나타낸다)
over ↔ under	(바로 위나 바로 아래를 나타낸다)
in front of ↔ behind	~의 앞에 ↔ ~의 뒤에
close to / near (to)	(일반적으로 실제적인 접촉은 없지만, 멀리 떨어져 있지 않음을 나타낸다)
beside / by / next to	~의 곁에

Look at the moon **above** the clouds. / The sun set **below** the horizon.

He held an umbrella **over** her. / The cat was sleeping **under** the table.

A child ran out **in front of** the car. / He ran out from **behind** a tree.

Please move this table **close(r) to** / **near(er) (to)** the wall.

- close와 near는 형용사적 성격을 띠는 전치사이므로 비교급이 가능하다.

She sat **beside** / **by** / **next to** me with her legs crossed.

3) 통과

across	~을 가로질러서 (평평한 면이라고 생각하는 것이나 나라, 바다 등과 함께 쓰인다)
through	~을 통하여 (사방이 둘러싸인 3차원에서의 움직임을 나타낼 때 쓴다)
up ↔ down	~ 위로 ↔ ~ 아래로 (수직적 이동을 나타낸다)
along	~을 따라 ('길, 강, 해변과 같은 선(line)을 따라' 라는 의미가 포함되어 있다)
between	~ 사이에 (개별적이거나 분리되어 있다고 여겨지는 두 개의 사람, 사물 또는 집단에 쓰인다)
among	~ 사이에 (두 개의 사람이나 사물에 대해서는 사용하지 못한다)

She walked **across** the garden. / The program was broadcast **across** Korea.

My husband loves walking **through** woods in spring.

The cat ran **up** the tree when he heard the dog. / They ran **down** the hill.

We walked **along** the river until we came to a small bridge.

There must be space to walk **between** the chairs and the door.

I left the card **among** her birthday presents.

3 수단, 도구의 전치사

by	뒤에 명사나 동명사가 따라오며, 어떠한 것을 하기 위해 취한 행동 즉, 수단(means)을 나타낸다
with ↔ without	뒤에 명사가 따라오며, 어떠한 것을 하기 위해 사용한 사물 즉, 도구(instrument)를 나타낸다

We can make the bread taste better **by** adding sugar.

He told me that I couldn't hope to catch a big fish **with** a small rod like that.

4 재료(원료)의 전치사

결과물 + be made of + 재료	재료가 물리적 변화만을 일으킬 때 사용한다
결과물 + be made from + 재료	재료가 물리적, 화학적 변화를 일으킬 때 사용한다

This case is made **of** wood.   Bread is made **from** flour.

• 재료 + be made **into** + 결과물

I'm going to make this material **into** a shirt.

234

5 찬성, 반대의 전치사

with / for	~에 찬성하여
against	~에 반대하여

Are you **with / for** your father?　　　He is **against** the plan.

6 주요 전치사 구문

1) 동사+전치사

agree on + 의견: ~에 동의하다　　　compare with: ~과 비교하다

agree with + 사람: ~에게 동의하다　　depend on: ~에 의존하다

believe in: ~을 믿다　　　　　　　insist on: ~을 고집하다

belong to: ~에 속하다　　　　　　laugh at: ~을 비웃다

compare to: ~에 비유하다　　　　　look forward to: ~을 기대하다

2) 형용사/분사 + 전치사

absent from: ~에 결석한　　　　　fond of: ~을 좋아하는

afraid of: ~을 두려워하는　　　　interested in: ~에 흥미가 있는

certain of: ~을 확신하는　　　　prepared for: ~할 준비가 된

crowded with: ~로 붐비는　　　　proud of: ~을 자랑스럽게 여기는

dependent on: ~에 의존하는　　　responsible for: ~에 책임이 있는

different from: ~과 다른　　　　satisfied with: ~에 만족하는

famous for: ~로 유명한　　　　　surprised at/by: ~에 놀란

filled with: ~로 채워진

3) 명사 + 전치사

example of: ~의 예　　　　　　use of: ~의 사용

price of: ~의 가격

4) 그 외

according to: ~에 따르면　　　by land/sea/air: 육로로/바닷길로/항공편으로

along with: ~와 함께　　　　　by chance: 우연히

at first/last: 처음에는/마침내　in front of: ~의 앞에

at times: 때때로　　　　　　　in spite of: ~에도 불구하고

as a result of: ~의 결과로　　instead of: ~대신에

because of: ~때문에

D-1   괄호 안에 알맞은 전치사를 고르세요.

(1) She arrived (at, in) four o'clock.

(2) He has waited for her (for, during) 10 years.

(3) (Until, By) tomorrow, it should be done.

(4) He has been studying English (since, from) noon.

(5) She will arrive (in, on) Sunday.

(6) He came back (after, in) two weeks.

(7) My brother threw the ball (in, into) the pond.

(8) (During, For) the summer vacation, he has been to New York.

(9) He worked (from, at) 8 a.m. to 6 p.m.

(10) He studied history (on, in) 1955.

D-2   틀린 문장을 골라 옳게 고치세요.

(1) He is at Paris right now.

(2) The sun rose on the horizon.

(3) I saw him go in the office.

(4) This elevator goes over to the 10th floor.

(5) He traveled from Asia in Europe.

(6) I was standing between two trees.

(7) The bridge lies on the narrow river.

(8) The books are in the shelf.

D-3   두 문장을 비교하여 해석하세요.

(1) He said the problem was between them.

He said the problem was among them.

(2) I'll finish my homework by 5 o'clock.

I'll be doing my homework until 5 o'clock.

Vocabulary

□ **threw**: 던지다 (throw-threw-thrown)   □ **shelf**: 선반

D-4 괄호 안에 알맞은 전치사를 고르세요.

(1) The leaves turn (into, of) red in fall. → The leaves turn red in fall.

(2) He took the knife (from, of) the child.

(3) Mr. Brown went to Paris (to, on) business.

(4) A thief robbed a woman (from, of) her purse.

(5) Wine is made (of, from) grapes.

(6) She went to the hospital (in, by) subway.

(7) We went to the theater (with, by) our friends.

(8) He died (of, with) cholera.

(9) She went to the store (for, to) some cigarettes.

(10) Monica was surprised (about, at) the news.

(11) I was starving (at, to) death.

(12) We laughed (at, for) his jokes.

(13) Thank you (for, to) your kindness.

(14) He who runs (after, to) two hares will catch neither.

(15) My teacher was satisfied (with, to) my homework.

✳ 혼동하기 쉬운 전치사

1) beside, besides

My teacher sat **beside** me. → ~ 옆에

Besides you, I have many friends. → ~ 외에도

2) instead of, instead

I'll buy this skirt **instead of** that one. → ~ 대신에

Instead, I took a taxi. → 대신 (부사)

3) despite, in spite of

Despite the cold weather, we ate ice cream. → ~ 에도 불구하고

I succeeded **in spite of** lack of experience. → ~ 에도 불구하고

Vocabulary

□ **cholera**: 콜레라   □ **cigarette**: 담배   □ **hare**: 산토끼

□ **lack**: 부족   □ **experience**: 경험

[1-3] 다음 밑줄에 들어갈 전치사를 고르세요.

1 The book is written _____ English.

(A) by   (B) to

(C) of   (D) in

2 _____ account of heavy snow, there is a traffic jam on the road.

(A) For   (B) On

(C) By   (D) With

3 People didn't know the difference _____ two pictures.

(A) among   (B) for

(C) between   (D) in

4 밑줄에 들어갈 말을 보기에서 찾아 쓰세요.

> 보기   from   during   of   into   to

(1) Children were afraid _____ losing their way in the woods.

(2) He was frozen _____ death.

(3) Nancy has studied German _____ this semester.

(4) She painted the picture _____ morning till night.

(5) Milk is made _____ cheese.

5 밑줄에 들어갈 말이 올바르게 연결된 것을 고르세요.

> 보기   He stood _____ the wall.
> _____ my disappointment, she didn't come to the meeting.

(A) on – By   (B) in – For

(C) against – To   (D) from – At

Vocabulary

□ **lose one's way**: 길을 잃다   □ **frozen**: 얼다(freeze-froze-frozen)

6 다음 밑줄에 공통으로 들어갈 전치사를 고르세요.

> 보기
> I have lived in Seoul _____ 16 years.
> I bought some flowers _____ you.

(A) for   (B) in

(C) to   (D) on

7 보기의 밑줄 친 of와 같은 용법으로 쓰인 것을 고르세요.

> 보기   She cleaned her pants <u>of</u> a spot.

(A) The legs of the table were made <u>of</u> steel.

(B) Only one <u>of</u> them will win the prize.

(C) He robbed me <u>of</u> my heart.

(D) It's kind <u>of</u> you to say so.

[8-9] 틀린 문장을 고르세요.

8 (A) She was angry at he.

(B) He will do her homework instead of her.

(C) I'm afraid of being late.

(D) I'm looking for an interesting book.

9 (A) He has lived in Washington, D.C. since 1995.

(B) There is no school in Sunday.

(C) The weather is getting warm in spring.

(D) He was born in 1953.

Vocabulary

□ **spot**: 얼룩   □ **win a prize**: 상을 타다

유형 53   전치사(구) 찾기

1 _____ their old age, my grandparents succeeded in climbing up Hallasan.

(A) Despite   (B) Because

(C) By   (D) Though

2 Gesturing is one _____ by which human beings communicate.

(A) are the ways   (B) of the ways

(C) that is the way   (D) its ways

유형 54   전치사를 잘못 쓴 경우

1 Many Jews <u>were</u> killed, <u>hurt</u>, or imprisoned <u>for</u> World War Ⅱ .
               A   B   C   D

2 Swimming <u>in</u> a lake is <u>very</u> different <u>than</u> swimming in <u>the sea</u>.
                A   B   C   D

유형 55   필요한 전치사가 빠진 경우

1 The Smiths called <u>off</u> <u>their</u> fishing trip <u>because</u> rain.
         A   B C   D

2 We see <u>or</u> <u>listen</u> many <u>ads</u> in the newspapers and <u>on TV</u>.
            A B   C   D

유형 56   불필요한 전치사가 있는 경우

1 My mother <u>married to</u> my father <u>when</u> she <u>was</u> nineteen <u>years</u> old.
                    A   B   C   D

1   He told me <u>that</u> you were not <u>for</u> the <u>best</u> of <u>terms</u> with his family.
               A   B   C   D

2   <u>The</u> idea of one god <u>spread</u> from the Christians <u>to</u> many <u>parts the</u> world.
   A   B   C   D

3   _____ , cars cause many social problems, such as traffic accidents.

(A) Besides air pollution   (B) In polluted air

(C) Air polluted besides   (D) It pollutes air

4   This machine will work _____ electricity.

(A) unless   (B) if

(C) without   (D) as

5   People in this company <u>usually</u> work for nine <u>hours</u> a day, <u>at nine</u> in the
                             A   B   C
morning to six <u>in</u> the evening.
             D

6   Men must <u>learn</u> to live <u>into</u> the <u>limitations</u> of <u>their</u> environment.
          A   B   C   D

7   <u>In spite</u> his <u>physical</u> handicap, <u>Beethoven</u> composed <u>many</u> great symphonies.
   A   B   C   D

8   Many Tibetans left <u>their</u> home country <u>to find</u> a better <u>place which</u> they would
                      A   B   C
live more <u>freely</u>.
         D

9   Mr. Lee is known _____ a teacher but also as an artist.

(A) not only   (B) he not only

(C) not only as   (D) as not only

10   <u>Owing</u> to <u>with her</u> advice, I came <u>to know</u> what I <u>have</u> to do.
     A   B   C   D

Chapter • 12

1   Most people living in high mountains are used to the thinness air.
         A   B   C   D

2   In pioneer days in America, _____ turns living with each child's
         family.

(A) teachers took   (B) taking teachers

(C) teachers to take   (D) taken as teachers

3   _____ it does not rain for weeks and weeks, plants and animals
         can still live in the desert.

(A) That   (B) Why

(C) Though   (D) There

4   You can trade in a torn bill at a bank a whole bill.
                  A   B   C   D

5   Too many dreaming can be harmful because the mind is hard at work when we
             A   B   C   D
         dream.

6   Huskies work for the Inuit, _____ sleds over snow and ice.

(A) they pulled   (B) pulling their

(C) who pulled them   (D) pulled by them

7   Long ago, both the settlers or the Native Americans used strings of shells as
                  A   B   C   D
         money.

8   <u>Once</u>, this seashell <u>by the</u> sea was <u>covering</u> of a <u>living</u> animal.
           A   B   C   D

9   A marathon is a _____ race, and it is very hard to run it.

(A) very long running   (B) running very long

(C) very running long   (D)long running very

10   By <u>killing</u> the old and <u>weakness</u>, wolves help many animal <u>herds</u> stay <u>strong</u>.
            A   B   C   D

11   Sign languages use hand, face or other body movements in a three-dimensional

space _____ physical means of communication.

(A) the   (B) as the

(C) such as   (D) where

12   New Hampshire was <u>first settled</u> in 1623, <u>only</u> three years <u>after</u> the Pilgrims <u>land</u>
                                A   B   C   D

at Plymouth, Mass.

Chapter • 12

Vocabulary

□ **thinness**: 희박

□ **desert**: 사막

□ **bill**: 지폐

□ **sled**: 썰매

□ **seashell**: 조개

□ **herd**: 가축의 떼

□ **pioneer**: 개척

□ **trade in**: 교환하다

□ **harmful**: 해로운

□ **settler**: 이주민

□ **covering**: 외피

□ **dimensional**: ~차(원)의

□ **take turns**: 교대로 하다

□ **torn**: 찢어진

□ **husky**: 에스키모 종의 개

□ **string**: 줄

□ **weakness**: 연약함

STRUCTURE

접속사

Grammar Up / Power Up Test / Pattern Drill / Pattern Review / Mini Test

A   등위접속사

접속사의 역할에 따른 분류: 등위접속사, 종속접속사

   a. 등위접속사로 서로 연결되는 말은 문법적으로 대등한 관계이다.

   b. 등위접속사로 연결된 문장은 중문이 된다.

1   등위접속사의 역할

We can sometimes see **the sun** <u>and</u> **rain** together. → 단어와 단어 연결

You may have your lunch **at home** <u>or</u> **at school**. → 구와 구 연결

I **called Jessy**, <u>but</u> **no one answered**. → 문장 연결   cf) I like <u>this picture</u> **and** <u>to go fishing</u>. → 틀린 문장

2   등위접속사의 종류

The brushes **and** the paints were kept in a cabinet. → 순접

   • **Buy** this ticket, **and** you can see the movie. → 〈명령문 + and: 그러면〉

Mary opened the door **but** she didn't come in. → 역접

I will go there by bus **or** by train. → 선택

   • The ninth month of the year, **or** September, is so beautiful. → '즉'

   • **Stop** there, **or** I'll call the police. → 〈명령문 + or: 그렇지 않으면〉

It will be raining, for the sky is full of clouds. → 이유

등위접속사는 '등위' 라는 용어 자체가 나타내는 바와 같이 (1) 같은 품사의 역할을 하며 (2) 같은 형태를 유지하고 (3) 동등한 자격의 것을 연결한다. (4) 수식어로 하나의 명사를 한정할 때는 논리적으로 그 의미가 상반된 것을 연결할 수 없다.

Check-Up

A-1   괄호 안에 알맞은 접속사를 쓰세요.

(1) Linda likes baseball, (   ) she can't play it well.

(2) Hurry up, (   ) your dad and I will depart without you.

(3) Last night, I washed my hair, (   ) I wrote a letter to my mother.

(4) It's summer, (   ) the weather is getting hot.

(5) Rain (   ) shine, I will go.

Vocabulary

□ **brush**: 붓   □ **paint**: 물감

 종속접속사

a. 종속접속사는 종속절을 주절에 연결해서 복문을 만든다.
b. 종속절은 명사절, 부사절 및 형용사절(관계사절)로 쓰인다.

1 명사절 접속사

1) It isn't important **that** you didn't finish high school. → 주어

My problem is **that** I like both boys. → 보어

I heard (**that**) Mr. Smith would be president. → 목적어

The news was reported **that** the war had come to an end. → 동격

※ She suggested **that** he (**should**) go to meet us.
  → ask, insist, recommend, require, suggest, urge 등의 〈제안, 명령, 요구, 주장 동사〉
    뒤에 따라나오는 목적절(that 절)에서는 "주어 + 원형동사"를 쓴다.

2) Please tell me **whether**(= **if**) this cake is made of wheat. → 목적어('~인지 아닌지')

It isn't certain **whether** she is an Italian **or not**. → 주어

I asked her **if** the news was true. → 목적어

  → if 가 명사절을 이끌 때, 뒤에 **or not**을 쓰지 않는다.

2 부사절 접속사

1) 때의 접속사: when, as, before, after, while, until, since, once, as soon as

cf) the moment, every time → 접속사 역할을 하는 명사구

When he returned to Korea, it had changed a lot.

Kevin has been working **since** he graduated.

While he was drawing a curtain, she watched the window.

Once you meet her, you cannot help liking her.

As soon as the comedian arrived, the show started.

The moment the movie started, he fell asleep.

Every time it rains, the dog makes a strange sound.

※ **When** spring **comes**, I will go to the zoo. (will come을 쓰지 않는다.)
  → 시간이나 조건의 부사절에서는 현재시제가 미래시제를 대신한다.

Vocabulary

□ **president**: 의장

□ **come to an end**: 끝나다

□ **suggest**: 제안하다

□ **require**: 요구하다

□ **urge**: 주장하다

□ **wheat**: 밀

□ **draw**: 끌어당기다

□ **the moment**: ~하자마자

2) 원인, 이유의 접속사: because, as, since

Since he knows the way to City Hall, let's just follow him.

We are using an electric fan **because** it is too hot.

❋ I **didn't** go there **because** I was busy

→ 두 가지 해석: ① '나는 바빠서 거기에 가지 않았다.', ② '내가 바빠서 거기에 간 것은 아니다.'

3) 목적, 결과의 접속사

I stepped aside (**so**) **that** the car **might** pass through. → ~하기 위해서 (목적)

Susan ran fast **lest** she **should** be caught. → ~하지 않도록 (목적)

= Susan ran fast (**so**) **that** she **might not** be caught.

The pen is **so** expensive **that** I cannot buy it. → 너무 …해서 ~하다 (결과)

4) 조건의 접속사: if, unless, in case, as long as, suppose, provided

If my son **comes** back, please hand this key to him.

→ 시간이나 조건의 부사절에서는 현재시제가 미래시제를 대신한다.

I won't go to the market <u>**unless** you go</u>. (= **if** you **don't** go)

As long as he breathes, there is hope of his recovery. → '~하는 한'

5) 양보의 접속사: though, although, as, even if, even though, while

Although she is young, she supports her family.

Poor **as** Brown is, he never asks help from others. → 〈형 / 부 / 명 + as + S + V〉

She likes quiet jazz music, **while** I like rock music. → '~이지만'

6) 기타

As it got dark, I became sleepy. → '~함에 따라'

The child walks **as** his father walks. → '~처럼'

Vocabulary

□ **electric fan**: 선풍기   □ **step aside**: 옆으로 비키다   □ **hand**: 건네다

□ **breathe**: 숨을 쉬다   □ **recovery**: 회복   □ **support**: 부양하다

Check-Up

B-1 틀린 문장을 골라 옳게 고치세요.

(1) He asked her if she liked to dance or not.

(2) It is impossible whether I will meet him again.

(3) When school will be over, I am going to play tennis.

(4) He required that he went back to the dormitory.

(5) He is a Korean is known to everyone.

(6) The doctor knew her patient would die in a year.

(7) If he will succeed, he must thank his mom.

B-2 괄호 안에 알맞은 접속사를 고르세요.

(1) He gets up early (lest, unless) he should be late.

(2) (Although, Since) she had little experience, she didn't do well.

(3) You will fail the exam (unless, if) you pay attention to what teachers say.

(4) (But, As) he was ill, he didn't do his homework.

(5) He can play basketball well, (as, while) I don't know even the rules of the sport.

(6) She bought a bag so (as, that) she might put her books in it.

(7) (As long as, Unless) I am alive, I will follow you.

(8) Young (as, because) he is, he can understand his parents.

(9) I don't believe him (and, because) he sometimes tells a lie.

(10) The chair is so big (that, as) I can't move it by myself.

(11) He has studied English (when, since) he came back home.

(12) (In case, While) it rains, take this umbrella.

(13) (If, Whether) it rains, you should dry clothes indoors.

(14) Please tell me (after, before) you go home.

(15) (When, As) she grew older, she looked like her mother.

Vocabulary

□ **be over**: 끝나다　　　　　　□ **patient**: 환자　　　　　　□ **even**: 심지어

□ **pay attention**: 주의를 기울이다　　□ **indoors**: 실내에서

C 상관접속사

서로 떨어져서 짝으로 쓰이는 접속사

both A and B, not only A but also B, either A or B, neither A nor B,
not A but B, whether A or B, no sooner A than B

The glass is **not only** beautiful **but also** strong.
= The glass is strong <u>as well as</u> beautiful.
I like **neither** summer **nor** winter. → 'A, B 둘다 ~이 아닌'
No sooner <u>had</u> the music <u>started</u> **than** we began to dance. → '~하자마자': 과거완료 시제로 쓰인다.
= **Hardly/Scarcely** had the music started **when/before** we began to dance.
= <u>As soon as</u> the music started, we began to dance.

 접속사

문장과 문장을 연결하는 부사: besides, in addition, then, however, yet, otherwise, therefore

He was late. **Besides**, he left his homework at home. → '게다가'

She doesn't like me. **Yet**, she is still kind to me. → '그렇지만'

Check-Up

C-1 틀린 문장을 골라 옳게 고치세요.

(1) No sooner had he entered the room before he opened the window.

(2) He gave me not a watch and a book.

(3) I forgot not only his face also his voice.

(4) Neither Mary or her brother is going to come tonight.

D-1 괄호 안에 알맞은 접속부사를 골라서 쓰세요.

> 보기   Otherwise, However, Therefore, Besides

(1) Peter didn't like the shirt. (   ), he gave it to me.

(2) Go to see a doctor. (   ), your headache must get worse.

(3) He sings and dances very well. (   ), he can play the piano.

(4) She read the book. (   ), she didn't understand it.

Vocabulary

□ **in addition**: 게다가   □ **otherwise**: 그렇지 않으면   □ **therefore**: 그래서

1 밑줄에 들어갈 말을 보기에서 찾아 쓰세요.

> 보기
>
> I like the boy, _____ he is very kind.
>
> The computer is so expensive _____ mom won't buy it for me.

(A) that - that

(B) because - although

(C) because - that

(D) for - when

2 두 문장의 의미가 같지 않은 것을 고르세요.

(A) Hardly had the movie started before he got out of the room.

→ As soon as the movie started, he got out of the room.

(B) I will give up hiking unless it is fine tomorrow.

→ I will give up hiking if it is not fine tomorrow.

(C) Rich as she is, she is unhappy.

→ Though she is rich, she is unhappy.

(D) She baked a lemon pie as well as an apple pie.

→ She baked not only a lemon pie but also an apple pie.

[3-4] 밑줄에 들어갈 알맞은 말을 고르세요

3 He didn't know the meaning of the word. _____, he looked it up.

(A) In addition

(B) Therefore

(C) Yet

(D) Otherwise

4 He is not a teacher _____ a writer.

(A) but

(B) that

(C) and

(D) so

Vocabulary

□ **expensive**: 비싼

□ **get out of**: 나가다

□ **bake**: 빵을 굽다

□ **lemon pie**: 레몬 파이

□ **look up**: 찾아보다

□ **writer**: 작가

[5-6] 다음 중 틀린 문장을 고르세요.

5
(A) Did you hear the news that James would be our boss?

(B) He said a fire engine would arrive quickly.

(C) She suggested that we send her two tickets for a musical.

(D) I wondered if he kicked the door or not.

6
(A) Last night, I wanted to see a movie and singing a song.

(B) He thought about the question, but he couldn't find the answer.

(C) You must be Mr. Baker, for I heard you would visit our store.

(D) Which color do you like, red or blue?

7 밑줄 친 접속사의 쓰임이 틀린 것을 고르세요.

(A) He ordered <u>either</u> a pizza <u>or</u> a piece of cake.

(B) <u>Sooner</u> had I come into the cafe <u>than</u> Susan called me.

(C) I like <u>neither</u> math <u>nor</u> English.

(D) You <u>as well as</u> I are wrong.

8 괄호 안에 알맞은 말을 고르세요.

(1) If he (comes, will come), we will know everything.

(2) Both Young-su (and, or) Mi-ra can speak French well.

(3) I don't know (if, whether) I can remember her name or not.

(4) Tom insisted that we (take, took) care of grandmother.

(5) I held the paper softly (lest, if) I should tear it.

9 밑줄에 들어갈 수 없는 말을 고르세요.

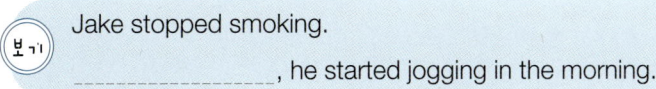

보기 Jake stopped smoking.
_____, he started jogging in the morning.

(A) Also   (B) Besides

(C) However   (D) In addition

Vocabulary

☐ **fire engine**: 소방차   ☐ **kick**: 차다   ☐ **softly**: 살며시   ☐ **tear**: 찢다

유형 57 접속사 찾기

1 _____ astronomers know a lot about Venus, the clouds are still a mystery.

    (A) If   (B) Although

    (C) There are   (D) By

2 The baby slept soundly _____ the music was playing.

    (A) with   (B) in

    (C) whether   (D) while

유형 58 부사절 찾기

1 _____, people all run for shelter.

    (A) If it rains   (B) Raining

    (C) It rains   (D) Is it raining

2 The sun appears to rise in the east _____ rotates.

    (A) because of the earth

    (B) because the earth is

    (C) because the earth

    (D) the earth because

유형 59 축약된 부사절 찾기

1 When _____, steel doesn't cool easily.

    (A) it heats   (B) they heated

    (C) heating   (D) heated

유형 60 접속사를 잘못 쓴 경우

1 The driver could not avoid the accident, though the brake could not stop
　　　A　　　　　　　　　　　　B　　　　　　C　　　　　　　　　　　D
the car.

2 Malls are popular because people like to both shop or do things all in one
　　　　　　　　　　　　A　　　　　　　　B　　　　C　　　　　D
place.

유형 61 필요한 접속사가 빠진 경우

1 A dog's nose tells it more its eyes do.
　　　A　　　　　B　　　C　　　D

유형 62 불필요한 접속사가 쓰인 경우

1 Because no one came to save him, so he began to explore the island.
　　　A　　　　　　B　　　　　　　　　　C　　　　　D

1 It was not long Nancy saw the little girl in the red-checked dress.
       A   B   C   D

2 _____ you have found where the sun rises, you can find all
       the directions.

       (A) So   (B) That   (C) Once   (D) Then

3 When cowboys burned a mark into the cattle, which were branded.
        A   B   C   D

4 _____ acorns in fall, it hides them in the ground.

       (A) When does the squirrel find

       (B) The squirrel which finds

       (C) When the squirrel is found

       (D) When the squirrel finds

5 Stop your bike, but wait for the traffic light to change.
            A   B   C   D

6 His English teacher recommends _____ he begin an easier
       program.

       (A) why   (B) what   (C) that   (D) it is

7 _____ damaged the road, no one was injured.

       (A) There was the rock slide   (B) Although the rock slide

       (C) The rock which was sliding   (D) The rock slide which

8   Not only the American government <u>also</u> the <u>American</u> people are <u>trying</u> to
                                            A   B   C

protect <u>the bald</u> eagle.
            D

9   The soccer game will not be put off, _____ it is raining or
snowing.

(A) which   (B) when   (C) neither   (D) whether

10   _____ with her family, Elizabeth studied at Oxford
University.

(A) While in England   (B) England where she is

(C) Her being in England   (D) In England, while she

1　Many blind people have guide dogs _____ them.

(A) that help

(B) helped

(C) that helping

(D) that they help

2　Abebe Bikila was the first man black from Africa to win the marathon.
　　　　　　　　　　　A　　　　B　　　　　　　　　C　　　　　D

3　When birds fly, they move their wings down very slow, then up fast.
　　　　　　　　A　　　　　　　　　　B　　　　　　C　　　　　D

4　_____ a grasshopper fly, but it also has two pairs of wings.

(A) Not only

(B) Only does not

(C) Does not only

(D) Not only does

5　Hard rocks worn away by strong waves, rain, and wind turns into soft sand.
　　　　　　　　　　　A　　　　　　　　　　B　　　　　　C　　　D

6　_____ in the early 1960s in the U.S. was a medium for social
criticism.

(A) As folk music

(B) It was folk music

(C) Folk music was

(D) Folk music

7　Changing flat tire is really not a very complicated process.
　　　　　　　A　　　B　　C　　　　　D

8   <u>Many</u> years ago gold <u>found</u> in California, <u>where</u> people went to find gold
          A   B   C

and get <u>rich</u>.
          D

9   There are many efforts, such as reforestation, _____ the desert.

(A) to push back   (B) which is pushed back

(C) they push back   (D) push back

10   When you are <u>in</u> the <u>woods</u>, you should <u>be sure</u> your <u>cook</u> fire is out.
                       A   B   C   D

11   _____, a fossil is any trace or impression of an organism of past

geologic time that has been preserved in the earth's crust.

(A) It is defined   (B) Broad definition

(C) Broadly defined   (D) Defined as

12   Morphine, heroin, and <u>other</u> exogenous opiates <u>combine with</u> the endorphin
                                  A   B

<u>receptors</u>, relieving stress, <u>elevate</u> mood, and soothing pain.
          C   D

Vocabulary

□ **blind people**: 시각 장애인	□ **grasshopper**: 메뚜기	□ **pair**: 한 쌍
□ **wear away**: 마멸시키다	□ **wave**: 파도	□ **turn into**: ~로 변하다
□ **medium**: 수단	□ **social**: 사회적인	□ **criticism**: 비평
□ **flat**: 공기 빠진	□ **complicated**: 복잡한	□ **process**: 과정
□ **effort**: 노력	□ **reforestation**: 나무심기	□ **impression**: 자국 흔적
□ **exogenous**: 외래의	□ **opiate**: 아편제	□ **receptor**: 감각기관
□ **soothe**: 진정시키다, 완화하다		

STRUCTURE

CHAPTER 14

관계사

Grammar Up / Power Up Test / Pattern Drill / Pattern Review / Mini Test

 **관계대명사**

관계대명사: 문장에서 대명사와 접속사의 역할을 동시에 수행
관계대명사절: 관계대명사에 의해 이끌려 선행하는 명사를 수식하는 형용사절
선행사: 관계대명사절 앞에 위치하여 관계대명사절의 수식을 받는 명사

I have a friend. + She is a famous movie star. (a friend = She)

→ I have **a friend who** is a famous movie star. (who = and she)

　　　　　선행사　　관계대명사
　　　　　　　└── 관계사절(형용사의 역할) ──┘

1 관계대명사의 종류

선행사	격		
	주격	소유격	목적격
사람	who	whose	whom(who)
동물, 사물	which	whose / of which	which
사람, 동물, 사물	that	•	that
선행사 없음	what	•	what

1) 격에 따른 분류(관계대명사의 관계대명사절 안에서의 역할)

❋ 주격 관계대명사

Take care of this puppy. + It seems to be lost. (this puppy = It)
= Take care of this puppy **that(which)** seems to be lost. (that = and **it**)

❋ 소유격 관계대명사

There is the book. + *The cover* of the book is yellow.
→ There is the book **whose** *cover* is yellow. (whose = and **its**)
= There is the book, *the cover* **of which** is yellow.
= There is the book, **of which** *the cover* is yellow.

❋ 목적격 관계대명사

Do you know the boy? + Joan met him. (the boy = him)
→ Do you know the boy **whom(who)** Joan met? (whom = and him)

Check-Up

A-1a 관계대명사를 이용하여 두 문장을 연결하세요.

(1) I know the boy. He likes sports.

(2) I like the girl. Her hair is long.

(3) I saw the expensive watch. The chain of it was made of gold.

(4) This is the boy. I saw him there.

(5) This is the letter. It arrived yesterday.

(6) My brother is a student. He lives in Busan.

(7) This is the dog. I like it.

(8) Bob is the young man. She interviewed him.

(9) She put away the book. The cover of it was missing.

(10) The farmer burnt out the tree. Its fruits had poison.

2) 선행사에 따른 분류

❋ who, whose, whom: 선행사가 사람일 때

I saw the old man **who** was sweeping the snow.
I called the teacher **whose** class I attended.
Mr. Pak, **whom** I had helped before, visited me.

Ms. Baker is the lady **whom** you are looking **for**.
= Ms. Baker is the lady **for whom** you are looking.
→ 〈전치사 + 관계대명사〉: 전치사는 문장의 끝이나 관계대명사 앞에 놓는다.

❋ which, whose, of which: 선행사가 사물일 때

Ms. Shin wants to buy the tree **which** is growing here.
The bear **whose** hair is gray runs fast.
I have a question **which** you must answer.
I'll give you this pen **which** I wrote the novel **with**.
(= I'll give you this pen **with which** I wrote the novel.)

I want to go to Jeju-do, **which** is also my father's wish.
Tom spoke rudely, **which** made his mother angry.
→ which의 특별용법: which는 명사 외에 앞 절 내용의 일부나 전체를 선행사로 받는다.

Vocabulary

□ **interview**: 인터뷰하다   □ **burn out**: 다 태워버리다   □ **sweep**: 쓸다   □ **attend**: 출석하다

✳ that: 선행사가 사람 혹은 사물일 때

You should find <u>someone</u> **that[who]** will live with you.
<u>This orange</u> **that**[or **which**] I bought in the market tastes good.

This is <u>the beautiful lake</u> (**that**) the city is famous **for**.
= This is <u>the beautiful lake</u> (**which**) the city is famous **for**.
= This is <u>the beautiful lake</u> **for which** the city is famous.
= This is <u>the beautiful lake</u> **for that** the city is famous. (X)
→ 전치사를 that 앞에 두지 않는 것에 주의한다.

The report is about <u>Melville and his works</u> **that** I like very much.
Please, tell me <u>something</u> **that** you know.
→ **that**을 써야하는 경우:
  • 선행사에 the only, the very, 최상급, 서수 등이 들어있을 때
  • 선행사가 사람 + 동물/사물이거나
  • something과 같이 -thing으로 끝나는 말일 때

✳ what: 선행사를 포함(the thing which)

선행사를 포함하고 있으므로 명사절의 역할을 하게된다.

What he did was to watch TV all day. (주어)
I cannot believe **what** I saw and heard. (목적어)

✳ what의 관용어구

I love **what you are**, not **what you used to be**. → 현재의 너 / 과거의 너
Bret is **what is called** a walking dictionary. (소위, 말하자면)
The house is pretty, and **what is better**, very cheap. (더욱 좋은 것은)
Music **is to** me **what** water **is to** a fish.
→ A is to B what C is to D: A와 B의 관계는 C와 D의 관계와 같다.

Vocabulary

□ **taste**: 맛이 나다   □ **walking dictionary**: 박식한 사람

Check-Up

A-1b 괄호 안에 알맞은 관계대명사를 쓰세요.

(1) This is the first train (   ) will start today.

(2) Don't put off till tomorrow (   ) can be done today.

(3) He said that he had been ill, (   ) was a lie.

(4) This is the house in (   ) he lives.

(5) The man is my teacher (   ) teaches me music.

(6) Tom met the man (   ) I already had met.

(7) I am not (   ) I used to be.

(8) This is the magazine (   ) I've talked about.

(9) My brother is (   ) is called a genius.

(10) I don't know (   ) has happened.

(11) Please hand me the book of (   ) the size is as big as the newspaper.

(12) Do you know the girl (   ) eyes are brown?

(13) A book is to a human's mind (   ) food is to a human's body.

(14) She looked at the child and the tree (   ) were in front of her.

(15) He failed the exam, and (   ) was worse, he lost all the money.

A-1c 틀린 문장을 골라 옳게 고치세요.

(1) Ara is the person won the prize.

(2) I have the book in that George is interested.

(3) I saw the boy and the dog which were running together.

(4) I thought her unfriendly, that was not true.

(5) She has a son who is a painter.

(6) I know the man whom uncle is a famous architect.

(7) He shook the tree what she was climbing.

(8) It will be the first chance who you can beat him.

Vocabulary

□ **as … as ~**: ~만큼 …한(동등비교) □ **prize**: 상 □ **architect**: 건축가

□ **shook**: 흔들다 □ **beat**: 이기다

  (shake-shook-shaken)

2 관계대명사의 계속 용법

1) 제한 용법 vs. 계속 용법

- 한정적 용법(제한 용법)은 문장 내의 관계사절이 제공하는 정보가 없으면 문장을 이해하지 못하는 경우(essential)이며,
- 계속적인 용법이란 부가적인 정보를 관계사절을 이용하여 보충하는 것(non-essential)을 말한다.

Mr. Kim who teaches English 501 is a good professor. (관계사 절이 없으면 대화를 나누고 있는 사람들이 김교수가 누구인지를 모른다. essential)

Mr. Kim, who teaches English 501, is a good professor. (관계사 절이 없더라도 김교수가 누구인지를 알고 있다. non-essential)

There are **two rooms which** you can sleep in.

『네가 잘 수 있는 방이 두 개 있다.』: 또 다른 방이 있을 수 있다.

There are **two rooms, which** you can sleep in.

『방이 두 개 있는데, 네가 거기서 잘 수 있다.』: 방이 모두 두 개이다.

→ 계속적 용법은 관계사절 앞에 쉼표를 쓰며, that과 what을 제외한 관계대명사(who, whose, whom, which)와 관계부사(when, where)에서 가능하다. 계속적 용법이 사용되는 원칙적인 경우는 (1) non-essential 부가적 정보를 제공하는 경우와 (2) 문맥의 흐름을 명확하게 전달하고자 하는 경우이다. 목적격 관계대명사라 하더라도 계속적 용법일 경우는 생략할 수 없다.

3 관계대명사의 생략

1) 목적격 관계대명사의 생략

That is the man (**whom**) I love. → 목적격(타동사)

This is the business (**which**) they engage in. → 목적격(전치사)

전치사의 목적어인 관계대명사가 생략되면 전치사는 문장의 끝에 위치한다.

전치사가 앞에 있으면 관계대명사를 생략할 수 없다.

Peace is the subject I want to talk **about**. (○)

Peace is the subject **about** I want to talk. (×)

2) 〈주격 관계대명사 + be 동사〉의 생략

Did you see my sister (**who was**) playing here?

He denied the facts (**which were**) announced in the article.

Vocabulary

□ **business**: 일, 사업   □ **engage in ~**: ~에 종사하다   □ **subject**: 주제

□ **deny**: 부인하다   □ **announce**: 발표하다   □ **article**: 기사

 **관계형용사**

관계대명사가 바로 뒤의 명사를 수식하여 형용사와 접속사의 역할을 할 때

I need **what help** you can give me. → ~ 만큼의
(= I need <u>all help that</u> you can give me.)

Check-Up

A-2 다음 관계대명사를 올바르게 해석하세요.

(1) She had three sons who became doctors.

(2) She had three sons, who became doctors.

(3) Susan wanted to go abroad, who was too young.

(4) She decided to buy the house, which was not expensive.

(5) He found the woman, whom he fell in love with.

A-3 다음 관계대명사 문장에서 생략될 수 있는 부분에 괄호를 치세요.

(1) This is the city which George Washington was born in.

(2) I'm looking for the book which was published last year.

(3) It was Susan who designed this house.

(4) She'll introduce her husband who is a pilot.

(5) The dictionary that I bought last week is very useful.

(6) He walked over to his friend who was sitting at the table.

(7) I can't give you the money for which you ask.

(8) My mother buys me everything that I want.

(9) The woman whom she spoke to is her teacher.

(10) She doesn't understand what I said.

B-1 밑줄 친 부분을 한 단어의 관계대명사로 고쳐서 문장을 다시 쓰세요.

(1) Let him have <u>all</u> comfort <u>that</u> he can.

→ _____ .

(2) Give me <u>all</u> money <u>that</u> you have.

→ _____ .

(3) You misunderstood <u>the thing which</u> I meant.

→ _____ .

C 관계부사

관계부사는 접속사와 부사의 역할을 하며 형용사절을 이끈다.

Snow White went into the <u>house</u>. + She saw the seven small beds <u>in the house</u>.

= Snow White went into the house **which** she saw the seven small beds **in**.

= Snow White went into the house **in which** she saw the seven small beds.

= Snow White went into the house **where** she saw the seven small beds.

1 관계부사의 종류(선행사에 따라)

I remember <u>the moment</u> **when**(at which) you were born. → 시간

<u>The school</u> **where**(from which) we graduated is closed. → 장소

This is <u>the reason</u> **why**(for which) I missed the class. → 이유

I don't know **how**(the way in which) you came in. → 방법

= I don't know <u>the way</u> **that** you came in. (the way how는 쓰지 않는다.)

→ 관계부사 that은 when, where, why, how 모두를 대신할 수 있다.

2 관계부사의 계속 용법

It is the spring season, **when** I can see many kinds of flowers. (= **and then**)

I walked on the road, **where** I saw a truck hit the waste box. (= **and there**)

3 선행사와 관계부사의 생략

1) 선행사 생략: 선행사가 생략될 경우 관계부사절은 구조적으로 명사절로 취급된다.

Tell me (**the time**) <u>when the summer vacation will start</u>. → 목적어

This church is (**the place**) <u>where we married</u>. → 보어

This is (**the reason**) <u>why I have to go early</u>. → 보어

It's <u>how I could pass the exam</u>. → 보어

(It's the way <u>in which I could pass the exam</u>.)

2) 관계부사 생략

There is <u>no reason</u> (**why**) Susan will refuse the offer.

That is <u>the way</u> (**that**) the criminal escaped from prison.

Vocabulary

□ **Snow White**: 백설공주   □ **close**: 폐교하다   □ **refuse**: 거절하다

□ **offer**: 제안   □ **criminal**: 범죄자   □ **escape from**: 탈출하다

□ **prison**: 감옥

Check-Up

C-1 다음 두 문장을 관계부사를 써서 연결하세요.

(1) I remember the day. He left on the day.

(2) I don't know the reason. You like her for the reason.

(3) He explained the way. He opened the door in the way.

(4) He met Jane on Friday. He went to the hospital on the day.

(5) She likes the company. She works for the company.

C-2 틀린 문장을 골라 옳게 고치세요.

(1) This is the country which Gloria lived.

(2) He can't tell the time how she left the house.

(3) There is no reason for I should go.

(4) This is the way which I feel about the problem.

(5) I'll meet him on Tuesday, when is my birthday.

(6) She cried at the corner at where people didn't look.

(7) I don't like the way how she treats me.

(8) I need the chair on which your books are put.

(9) I waited for him at the room where he used.

(10) He told me the way that I can write a good composition.

(11) I went to the park for which they grew many flowers.

(12) Let me know which you will come back.

(13) She goes to the city, when there is a large lake.

(14) I don't understand the reason he got angry.

(15) I don't know the city from where he came.

Vocabulary

□ **explain:** 설명하다   □ **treat:** 대하다   □ **composition:** 작문

D 복합관계사

관계대명사 / 부사 + –ever: 선행사를 포함한다.

1 복합관계대명사: whoever, whomever, whichever, whatever

1) 명사절을 이끌 때

Whichever you buy is a waste. (= Anything that)
『네가 사는 것은 어느 것이나 쓰레기이다.』 → 주어
Please tell me **whatever** you know. (= anything that: 무엇이나) → 목적어
I'll invite **whoever** wants to come. (= anyone who: 누구나) → 목적어
I'll invite **whomever** I like. (= anyone whom: 누구나) → 목적어

2) 부사절을 이끌 때

Whoever hits my child, I can't excuse him or her. (= No matter who)
『누가 내 아이를 때리더라도, ~』
Whatever you give me, I will be very happy. (= No matter what)
『네가 무엇을 내게 주더라도, ~』

2 복합 관계형용사: whatever, whichever
명사절, 부사절을 이끈다.

You can cheer **whichever team** you like. (= any team that)
『너는 네가 좋아하는 어느 팀이나 응원할 수 있다.』 → 명사절(목적어)
Whatever clothes you wear, you look good. (= No matter what clothes)
『네가 무슨 옷을 입던지, ~』 → 부사절

3 복합 관계부사: wherever, whenever, however
부사절을 이끈다.

Wherever you may hide my book, I'll find it. (= No matter where)
『네가 내 책을 어디에 숨기더라도, ~』 → 양보
I'll follow you **wherever** you go. (= to any place where)
『네가 가는 곳 어디라도 나는 너를 따라갈 테야.』 → 장소
Whenever you may finish your work, I'll wait for you here. (= No matter when)
However busy you may be, it's time to rest. (= No matter how busy)
→ however + 형용사 / 부사: 아무리 ~할지라도

Vocabulary

□ **excuse**: 용서하다   □ **cheer**: 응원하다

Check-Up

D-1 괄호 안에 알맞은 관계대명사나 복합 관계대명사를 고르세요.

(1) Look at the cat the legs of (which, whose) are broken.

(2) I'll tell you (whatever, which) you want to know.

(3) I want you to meet my mother (whoever, who) wants to see you.

(4) She showed me the letter (which, whom) he wrote to her.

(5) (Whatever, What) you give me, I cannot forgive you.

(6) He is a good husband, and (what, which) is better, a good father.

(7) You can bring (whomever, whom) you want to be together with.

(8) He doesn't like (what, whoever) she is.

(9) She tried to hide the fact, (which, that) was impossible.

(10) (Whatever, Whoever) wants to be a scholar has to read many books.

(11) The man (whomever, whom) you are blaming is my teacher.

(12) Choose (whichever, whomever) color you like.

(13) (Whoever, Whomever) comes late should pay for our dinner.

(14) I'll do (whatever, whoever) can make money.

(15) (Whoever, Who) calls me tonight, I'll not answer the phone.

D-2 복합 관계부사절을 양보의 부사절로 고쳐쓰세요.

(1) Wherever you may go, I'll find you.

(2) However smart you may be, you should study hard.

(3) Whenever I may get up, dad prepares my breakfast.

(4) However late you may come, the door of my house will be kept unlocked.

(5) Wherever you may be, the place is a home.

Vocabulary

□ **scholar**: 학자   □ **blame**: 비난하다   □ **answer**: 전화를 받다   □ **unlocked**: 잠기지 않은

1 두 문장을 합칠 때 빈칸에 들어갈 알맞은 말을 고르세요.

> 보기
> I know the novelist. Her novel is very interesting.
> → I know the novelist _____ novel is very interesting.

(A) that   (B) whose

(C) of which   (D) whom

2 다음의 두 문장을 한 문장으로 고치세요.

(1) Is this the pie? It was made by Su-mi.

→ _____ .

(2) She has a son. He will be a dancer.

→ _____ .

(3) I'll visit the house. The artist worked and died at the house.

→ _____ .

3 빈칸에 들어갈 알맞은 말을 찾으세요.

> 보기
> I don't like him, who tells a lie.
> → I don't like him, _____ he tells a lie.

(A) and   (B) but

(C) for   (D) so

4 빈칸에 공통으로 들어갈 말을 찾으세요.

> 보기
> He doesn't remember _____ he did to me yesterday.
> Wheels are to cars _____ legs are to horses.

(A) which   (B) who

(C) what   (D) that

[5-6]   다음 밑줄에 들어갈 관계대명사를 고르세요.

5   He is _____ is called a bookworm.

(A) which   (B) who

(C) whom   (D) what

6   She is the first woman _____ climbed Mt. Everest.

(A) that   (B) whom

(C) which   (D) what

7   관계대명사가 잘못 쓰인 문장을 고르세요.

(A) He likes the car whose color is blue.

(B) She found the book whom Sue had lost.

(C) I'll give you these flowers that you wanted.

(D) I said nothing, which made him angry.

8   관계부사가 잘못 쓰인 문장을 고르세요.

(A) I remember the time when we met first.

(B) That is the reason why I came here.

(C) This is where he was born.

(D) I'm proud of the way how you look tonight.

9   밑줄 친 부분과 바꾸어 쓸 수 있는 말을 쓰세요.

(1) You may have anything that you want.

   →You may have (   ) you want.

(2) No matter how young you may be, you'll understand it.

   → (   ) young you may be, you'll understand it.

Vocabulary

□ bookworm: 책벌레

유형 63 관계사 찾기

1 Some mountains are still being made, _____ are volcanoes.

    (A) which   (B) that

    (C) what   (D) but

2 The singer has a beautiful wife _____ he made many songs.

    (A) who   (B) whom she

    (C) for whom   (D) with her

유형 64 관계사절 찾기

1 Animals _____ webbed feet are good swimmers.

    (A) and have   (B) that have

    (C) that they have   (D) to have that

2 The forty-niners were pioneers _____ the new lands and built new cities.

    (A) went to   (B) and who went to

    (C) who did go   (D) who went to

Vocabulary

□ **volcano**: 화산   □ **webbed**: 물갈퀴가 있는   □ **forty-niner**: 미국 서부 개척시대의 광부들

□ **pioneer**: 개척자   □ **land**: 땅

유형 65 관계사를 잘못 쓴 경우

1 Alexander Graham Bell <u>taught</u> in a school <u>for</u> people <u>what</u> could not <u>hear</u>.
                               A   B   C   D

2 Meggy went <u>to the</u> great museum <u>where</u> had <u>been</u> built <u>in</u> 1900.
                        A   B   C   D

유형 66 필요한 관계사가 빠진 경우

1 <u>We</u> have electrical <u>machines can</u> wash and <u>dry</u> clothes <u>automatically</u>.
   A   B   C   D

유형 67 불필요한 관계사가 쓰인 경우

1 The bases in a baseball game <u>that are</u> the four <u>stations</u>, and the players must
                                          A   B

<u>go</u> around <u>them</u>.
 C   D

Vocabulary

□ **museum**: 박물관   □ **electrical**: 전기의   □ **automatically**: 자동적으로

□ **base**: (야구) 루   □ **station**: 위치

1 The mountain is green, ＿＿＿＿＿＿＿＿＿＿＿＿ is always white with snow.

(A) the top   (B) of the top
(C) whose top   (D) what top

2 Henry David Thoreau was <u>a writer</u> and naturalist <u>whom</u> lived <u>in</u> the <u>nineteenth</u> century.
　　　　　　　　　　　　A　　　　　　　　　　B　　　C　　　　D

3 The man ＿＿＿＿＿＿＿＿＿＿＿＿ Buddha was the son of a king in the mountains of India.

(A) that to become   (B) became
(C) and became   (D) who became

4 Christmas <u>which is</u> the day not <u>only</u> for <u>God</u> but also <u>for</u> children.
　　　　　　　　A　　　　　　　　B　　　C　　　　　　D

5 There are many famous portraits in the world, ＿＿＿＿＿＿＿＿＿＿＿＿ was painted by Leonardo da Vinci.

(A) which of   (B) the one
(C) one of which   (D) which is one

6 My brother is <u>in</u> this picture <u>was</u> taken <u>in</u> L.A. <u>last</u> year.
　　　　　　　　A　　　　　　B　　　C　　　D

7 Tornadoes are very strong storms ＿＿＿＿＿＿＿＿＿＿＿＿ perhaps the strongest on earth.

(A) are the winds   (B) the winds are
(C) that the winds are   (D) whose winds are

8 A witness <u>should</u> say <u>that</u> she or he <u>has</u> seen <u>or</u> heard.
　　　　　　　　A　　　　B　　　　　　　C　　　D

9 The U.S. government is often called ＿＿＿＿＿＿＿＿＿＿＿＿ its nickname since the early 1800s.

(A) "Uncle Sam," which has been   (B) "Uncle Sam" has been
(C) it has been "Uncle Sam"   (D) which has been "Uncle Sam"

10 <u>This</u> book contains <u>many</u> interesting stories <u>who</u> can <u>interest</u> children.
　　　　A　　　　　　　　B　　　　　　　　　　C　　　　D

276

1   Benjamin Franklin played an important role _____ of the United States.

    (A) in the early history   (B) the early history

    (C) the history when early   (D) it was early history

2   A glacier in the <u>north of</u> Canada <u>is</u> cutting a <u>newly</u> path down the <u>side</u> of a
                     A   B   C   D

    mountain.

3   Many people are <u>worried</u> about <u>that</u> television <u>has</u> done <u>to</u> children.
                       A   B   C   D

4   Honeybees make <u>their</u> homes <u>of</u> wax, <u>which</u> comes from <u>into</u> the bees.
                          A   B   C   D

5   <u>Of</u> all the <u>animal</u> in the zoo, bears are <u>certainly</u> the <u>favorites</u>.
    A   B   C   D

6   Geese can hear <u>little</u> noises, and <u>theirs</u> honk <u>loudly</u> at strange <u>sounds</u>.
                    A   B   C   D

7   Kathy Arendsen can throw a softball faster _____ almost anyone else who ever played the game.

    (A) that   (B) to   (C) by far   (D) than

8   Many years ago _____ was often the town surgeon.

    (A) the town barber   (B) the town barber who

    (C) is the town barber   (D) there was the town barber

9 Eight <u>out of</u> ten <u>students</u> who come to the United States <u>to succeed</u> <u>because of</u>
                      A   B   C   D
hard work.

10 General Eisenhower, a professional warrior, showed _____ that people considered him a man of peace.

(A) human understand

(B) who understand such human

(C) to understand human

(D) such human understanding

11 _____ of volcanic action is commonly due more to the material blown out than to the flowing lava.

(A) Its destructiveness

(B) It is greatly destructive

(C) The great destructiveness

(D) Destructive

12 In its <u>pure</u> form and in <u>some</u> of its <u>compounds</u>, chlorine <u>has</u> deadly to animals
                  A   B   C   D
and human beings.

Vocabulary

- **play a role**: 역할을 하다
- **honeybee**: 꿀벌
- **honk**: (기러기가) 울다
- **out of ~**: ~중에서
- **warrior**: 전사
- **chlorine**: 염소
- **glacier**: 빙하
- **wax**: 밀랍
- **barber**: 이발사
- **succeed**: 성공하다
- **lava**: 용암
- **path**: 길
- **geese**: goose(거위)의 복수형
- **surgeon**: 외과의사
- **professional**: 직업적인
- **compound**: 합성물

m-TOEFL

LINK

문법편

ANSWER KEY

LinguaForum™

m-TOEFL

LINK

Introductory

Answer Key

Grammar Up
p.10-19

Check-Up

A-1
(1) 부사 (2) 형용사
(3) 전치사 (4) 접속사
(5) 접속사 (6) 명사
(7) 부사 (8) 대명사
(9) 부사 (10) 형용사

A-2
(1) famous (2) kind
(3) give (4) quickly
(5) healthy (6) Though
(7) heavily (8) won
(9) because of (10) discovered

A-3
(1) hard (2) delicious
(3) loudly (4) in
(5) obey

A-4
(1) ① 동사 ② 명사
(2) ① 형용사 ② 부사
(3) ① 명사 ② 동사
(4) ① 동사 ② 형용사
(5) ① 동사 ② 명사

B-1
(1) There is a tower on top of the mountain.
　　　　　　동사　주어

(2) It is raining outside.
　　주어　　동사

(3) He gave me a pretty yellow flower.
　　주어　동사　간접목적어　　직접목적어

(4) What are you going to do this Christmas?
　　목적어　　　주어　　　동사

(5) The food smells good.
　　주어　　동사　보어

(6) I met the boy during my trip to London.
　주어 동사　목적어

(7) Who made this cream soup?
　　주어　동사　　목적어

(8) It is important to keep one's promise.
　가주어 동사　보어　　　　(진)주어

(9) The computer enables us to do many
　　주어　　　　　동사　목적어　목적보어

　things easily.

(10) This is what I wanted.
　　주어 동사　　보어

B-2
(1) go (2) me
(3) interesting (4) Taking
(5) a kind

B-3
(1) is (2) him
(3) is (4) do
(5) is

C-1
(1) 부사구 (2) 명사구
(3) 부사구 (4) 명사구
(5) 형용사구 (6) 명사구
(7) 형용사구 (8) 형용사구
(9) 명사구 (10) 부사구

C-2
(1) 부사절 (2) 명사절
(3) 명사절 (4) 형용사절
(5) 부사절 (6) 명사절
(7) 부사절 (8) 형용사절
(9) 명사절 (10) 부사절

Power Up Test
p.20-21

1
(1) 명사 / 주어   (2) 형용사 / 수식어
(3) 전치사 / 연결어   (4) 감탄사 / 수식어
(5) 대명사 / 주어   (6) 동사 / 술어
(7) 접속사 / 연결어   (8) 부사 / 수식어

2
(1) good box maker   (2) beautiful singer
(3) fast runner

3
(1) different   (2) hungry
(3) easily   (4) died
(5) meeting   (6) When / Because
(7) Wind

4 (C)   **5** (A)

6 (B)   **7** (D)

8
(1) Bikers should follow safety rules.
(2) To be successful does not always mean to be rich.
(3) I allowed my friend to borrow my shirt.

Pattern Drill
p.22-25

유형 1 형용사-명사 혼동
1 A (gratness → great)
2 A (cultural → culture)

유형 2 형용사-부사 혼동
1 D (easy → easily)
2 B (famously → famous)

유형 3 동사-명사 혼동
1 B (a give → a gift)

유형 4 부사-명사 혼동
1 D (peace → peacefully)

유형 5 전치사-접속사 혼동
1 A (Despite → Although)
2 A (While → During)

유형 6 주어 찾기
1 C
2 B
3 B

유형 7 동사 찾기
1 D
2 C

유형 8 주어와 동사 찾기
1 B
2 D

유형 9 보어 찾기
1 B
2 C
3 A

유형 10 목적어 찾기
1 B
2 D

유형 11 문장 성분이 빠진 경우
1 A (Jesse Owens the → Jesse Owens was the)

Pattern Review p.26-27

1 (A) 동사 찾기

2 (C) (healthy → health)
   명사-형용사 혼동

3 (D) (ease → easily)
   부사-명사 혼동

4 (C) 주어 일부 찾기

5 (B) 보어 찾기

6 (C) (kind → kindly)
   형용사-부사 혼동

7 (D) 목적어 찾기

8 (A) (While → During)
   전치사-접속사 혼동

9 (B) 목적어, 목적보어 찾기

10 (C) 목적보어 찾기

11 (D) (develop → development)
   동사-명사 혼동

12 (A) (there a → there is a)
   동사 탈락

13 (A) 주어 찾기

14 (A) (happiness → happy)
   형용사-명사 혼동

15 (D) 동사 찾기

4 (D) (move → moved)
   분사 자리에 동사나 다른 준동사를 쓴 경우

5 (C) (nose red → red nose)
   목적어 찾기

6 (B) 동사 찾기

7 (C) (it forced → forced)
   동사 찾기

8 (A) 접속사 찾기

9 (A) 관계사절 찾기

10 (B) (important industry → important industries) 명사의 수가 잘못된 경우

11 (C) (act → an act or acts)
   동사-명사 혼동

12 (D) 접속사 찾기

Mini Test p.28-29

1 (D) (a umbrella → an umbrella)
   관사를 잘못 쓴 경우

2 (B) 목적보어 찾기

3 (D) (wise → wisdom)
   형용사-명사 혼동

CHAPTER 2 명사와 관사

Grammar Up

Check-Up

A-1

(1) work (U)

(2) money (U), dollar (C)

(3) fruit (U)

(4) desk (C), wood (U)

(5) time (U), hour (C)

(6) sports (C), baseball (U)

(7) languages (C), Korean (U)

(8) snow (U)

(9) homework (U)

(10) idea (C)

A-2

(1) rose → roses

(2) gets → get

(3) many → much

(4) times → time

(5) poem → poems

(6) girl → girls

(7) friend → friends

(8) furnitures → furniture

B-1

(1) cups   (2) piece

(3) sheets   (4) pieces

(5) bottle

B-2

(1) Give me a cup of coffee.

(2) We eat a loaf of bread for lunch.

(3) I will tell you a piece of surprising news

　　[a surprising piece of news]

C-1

(1) question → questions

(2) sample → samples

(3) persons → person

(4) shoe → shoes

(5) 옳은 문장

(6) are → is

(7) bird → birds

(8) fourteen-years-old → fourteen-year-old

(8) dancer → dancers

(10) hobby → hobbies

C-2

(1) a few   (2) books

(3) number   (4) Thousands

(5) were

D-1

(1) foot : feet

(2) taxi : taxis

　　cf) taxies: 'taxi'의 3인칭 단수 현재형

(3) tomato : tomatoes

(4) video : videos

(5) fish : fish

　　cf) fishes: 고기의 여러 종류를 이야기할 때

(6) cow : cows

(7) bench : benches

(8) lady : ladies

(9) leaf : leaves

(10) merry-go-round : merry-go-rounds

(11) woman : women

(12) month : months

(13) datum : data

(14) story : stories

(15) father-in-law : fathers-in-law

(16) thesis (논문) : theses

(17) roof : roofs

(18) photo : photos

(19) house : houses

(20) phenomenon : phenomena

D-2

(1) dishs → dishes

(2) childrens' → children's

(3) passer-bys → passers-by

(4) storys → stories

(5) foots → feet

E

(1) the wall of my room

(2) two pounds' sugar

(3) thirty minutes' walk

(4) girls' shoes

(5) yesterday's newspaper

F-1

(1) 우리는 하루에 세 끼를 먹는다.

(2) 저 두 상자는 크기가 같다.

(3) 잭슨이라는 여자가 널 기다리고 있어.

(4) 차가운 물 한 잔만 주세요.

(5) 한 달에 영화를 몇 편 보니?

F-2

(1) an   (2) a

(3) a   (4) a

(5) a   (6) a

(7) a   (8) a

G-1

(1) the   (2) a

(3) the   (4) the

(5) the   (6) the

(7) a   (8) the

(9) A   (10) The

G-2

(1) an → the

(2) a → the

(3) the → a

(4) the Harvard University → Harvard University

(5) A → The

G-3

(1) the

(2) 옳은 문장

(3) the

(4) The

(5) the

H

(1) X   (2) X

(3) a   (4) X

(5) an   (6) X

(7) X

I-1

(1) a small bag

(2) too good a chance

(3) the book that I told you about

(4) What a small car it is!

(5) quite a good student

I-2

(1) very a useful machine → a very useful machine

(2) 옳은 문장

(3) so a nice man → so nice a man

(4) The all boys → All the boys

(5) a such funny guy → such a funny guy

Power Up Test

p.45-46

1

(1) men   (2) teeth

(3) fish   (4) mice

(5) wives

2

(1) a little   (2) a piece

(3) a few   (4) a glass

(5) a little   (6) a few

(7) a little

3

(1) '내 지갑에 있는 돈' 으로 한정되었기 때문에. 즉, 일반적 의미의 '돈' 이 아닌 특정한 '돈'.

(2) 고유명사에 관사가 붙는 이유 중 하나는 그 사람의 작품을 나타내는 경우. 이 경우에는 멜빌이 '멜빌의 작품' 을 의미하므로 관사를 쓴다.

(3) 추상명사도 한정어의 수식을 받아서 구체적인 행위를 가리키면 관사를 쓴다. 이 문장에서의 의미는 추상적인 '용기' 가 아니라 '(병사의) 용기 있는 행동'

4 (C)　　　　5　(A)

6 (D)

7

(1) 오늘 내 우체통에 내게 온 12통의 편지가 있었다.

(2) 일 달러짜리 지폐에는 미국 대통령의 그림이 들어있다. 그것은 죠지 워싱턴의 그림이다.

Pattern Drill

유형 12 명사의 수가 잘못된 경우

1 C (egg → eggs)

2 D (days → day)

유형 13 명사의 복수형이 잘못된 경우

1 D (wheeles → wheels)

2 A (womens → women)

유형 14 필요한 관사가 빠진 경우

1 D (team → a team)

2 A (First → The first)

유형 15 불필요한 관사가 쓰인 경우

1 D (a historians → historians)

2 B (the first → first)

유형 16 관사를 잘못 쓴 경우

1 D (a → an)

2 D (a → the)

Pattern Review

1 (C) (is → are)

주어와 동사가 일치하지 않은 경우

2 (B) (sings → songs)

동사 – 명사 혼동

3 (D) (farm → farmer)

보어찾기

4 (B) (a last → the last)

관사를 잘못 쓴 경우

5 (D) (wild horse → wild horses)

명사의 수가 잘못된 경우

6 (D) (leafs → leaves)

명사의 복수형이 잘못된 경우

7 (A) (Milk → The milk)

필요한 관사가 빠진 경우

8 (B) (favorite movie → favorite movies)

명사의 수가 잘못된 경우

9 (A) (Best → The best)

필요한 관사가 빠진 경우

10 (B) (question → questions)

명사의 수가 잘못된 경우

11 (B) (a breakfast → breakfast)

불필요한 관사가 쓰인 경우

12 (B) (eye → eyes)

명사의 수가 잘못된 경우

13 (A) (students → student)

명사의 수가 잘못된 경우

Mini Test

p.49-50

1 (C) (interest → interesting)

어휘(형용사 – 명사/동사)를 혼동한 경우

2 (D) 올바른 어순 찾기

3 (C) (have to → has to)

주어와 동사가 일치하지 않는 경우

4 (B) 접속사 찾기

5 (D) (what give → what to give)

준동사 대신 동사를 쓴 경우

6 (A) 동사 찾기

7 (D) (at the night → at night)

불필요한 관사가 쓰인 경우

8 (B) 주어 찾기

9 (A) (bigger → biggest)

비교급 쓰임이 잘못된 경우

10 (C) (what → which/that)

관계사를 잘못 쓴 경우

11 (A) (locating → located)

현재분사와 과거분사를 혼동하여 쓴 경우

12 (D) 관계사절 찾기

CHAPTER 3 대명사

Grammar Up

p.54-61

🧩 Check-Up

A-1

(1) my   (2) her

(3) their   (4) its

(5) he

A-2

(1) him → his   (2) their → her

(3) 옳은 문장   (4) I → me

(5) hers → her

A-3

(1) hers → her   (2) 옳은 문장

(3) your → yours   (4) ours → our

(5) hers → her

A-4

(1) It   (2) It

(3) it   (4) to

(5) It

A-5

(1) It is good for health to exercise regularly.

(2) I think it bad to tell a lie.

(3) It is not important whether she knows it or not.

A-6

(1) myself   (2) himself

(3) yourself   (4) themselves

(5) ourselves

A-7

(1) yourself   (2) 옳은 문장

(3) 옳은 문장   (4) myself

(5) 옳은 문장

B-1

(1) this   (2) those

(3) this   (4) that

(5) that

B-2

(1) This → These   (2) it → that

(3) 옳은 문장   (4) Those → That

(5) 옳은 문장

C

(1) What   (2) Whose

(3) Who   (4) whom

(5) What

D-1

(1) one   (2) it

(3) one's   (4) one

(5) one

D-2

(1) other   (2) some

(3) the other   (4) another

(5) another

Power Up Test

1

(1) He, his, mine   (2) We, our

(3) They, him

2

(1) that   (2) it

(3) One   (4) It

(5) Some   (6) any

(7) others   (8) by

3 (D)   **4** (C)

5 (B)

6

(1) There are four colors in the Korean flag.

(2) another is blue, and the others are black and white.

(3) I will solve this problem for myself.

Pattern Drill
p.64-65

유형 6 주어 찾기

1 A

2 D

유형 10 목적어와 목적보어 찾기

1 C

2 B

유형 17 명사와 대명사의 일치

1 C (they → it)

2 D (its → their)

유형 18 인칭대명사의 격이 잘못된 경우

1 D (him → his)

2 A (hers → her)

유형 19 대명사를 잘못 쓴 경우

1 C (that → it)

2 B (those → they)

Pattern Review
p.66

1 (C) (hers → her)
인칭대명사의 격이 잘못된 경우

2 (B) (another → other)
대명사를 잘못 쓴 경우

3 (D) (its lunch → his lunch)
명사와 대명사의 일치

4 (D) (another → the other)
대명사를 잘못 쓴 경우

5 (C) (it → its)
대명사의 격이 잘못된 경우

6 (D) (of me → of mine)
인칭대명사의 격이 잘못된 경우

7 (A) (Them → Those)
대명사를 잘못 쓴 경우

8 (B) (their → her/his)
명사와 대명사의 일치

9 (D) (one → that)
명사를 잘못 쓴 경우

10 (B) (his → its)
명사와 대명사의 일치

6 (D) to 부정사 찾기

7 (B) (feets → feet)
명사의 복수형이 잘못된 경우

8 (C) (which → on which)
필요한 전치사가 빠진 경우

9 (A) 동사 찾기

10 (B) (it was → he was)
명사와 대명사의 일치

11 (C) (breathe → breath)
동사 – 명사 혼동

12 (D) 관계사절 찾기

Mini Test
p.67-68

1 (A) (separates → is separated)
능동태를 잘못 쓴 경우

2 (D) 주어와 동사 찾기

3 (B) (later → late)
어휘를 잘못 쓴 경우

4 (C) 분사구문 찾기

5 (A) (or → and)
상관접속사를 잘못 쓴 경우

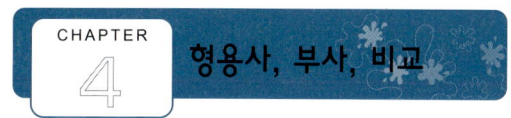

CHAPTER 4 형용사, 부사, 비교

Grammar Up

p.72-84

Check-Up

A-1
(1) elder, delicious
(2) early, second
(3) This, higher, any, other, this
(4) tired, hard, long
(5) American, a few

A-2
(1) the shortest (명사 수식)
(2) interesting (명사 수식)
(3) happy (목적격 보어)
(4) blue (주격 보어), brown (주격 보어)
(5) afraid (주격 보어), all (명사 수식)

A-3
(1) exciting anything → anything exciting
(2) white that sweater → that white sweater
(3) a thing interesting → an interesting thing
(4) ring gold → gold ring
(5) new nothing → nothing new

A-4a
(1) a few   (2) much
(3) woman   (4) number
(5) much

A-4b
(1) score   (2) amount
(3) various   (4) few
(5) No

A-5
(1) nineteen ninety-eight

(2) ten twenty-five in the morning[a.m.]
(3) one and a[one] third
(4) o[zero] one one seven three o[zero] one
    two three four
(5) ten to five
(6) three point one four
(7) March twelfth *or* the twelfth of March

B-1
(1) hard - 동사(tried) 수식
(2) very - 형용사(happy) 수식
(3) Even - 명사(the teacher) 수식
(4) very - 부사(much) 수식
    much - 동사(likes) 수식
(5) Fortunately - 문장 수식

B-2
(1) tomorrow on 2nd Street → on 2nd Street
    tomorrow
(2) 옳은 문장
(3) eats out seldom → seldom eats out
(4) fully was misunderstood → was fully
    misunderstood
(5) go often → often go

B-3a
(1) either   (2) very
(3) ago   (4) much
(5) already

B-3b
(1) 윌리엄은 이틀 전에 돌아왔다고 말했다.
(2) 샌드위치 벌써 다 먹었니?
(3) I like strawberries very much, too.

C

(1) wide — wider — widest

(2) thin — thinner — thinnest

(3) careful — more careful — most careful

(4) little — less — least

(5) necessary — more necessary — most necessary

(6) free — freer — freest

(7) curious — more curious — most curious

(8) well — better — best

(9) pleased — more pleased — most pleased

(10) diligent — more diligent — most deligent

D

(1) Chris is not as tall as Andy.

(2) Mt. Everest is the highest mountain in the world.

(3) Hannah is the smartest of all the students.

(4) The Atlantic Ocean is less large than the Pacific Ocean.

(5) This is the smallest computer that I have ever seen.

E

(1) bigger than any other

(2) No, bigger

(3) No, as, as

F-1

(1) possible, you, can

(2) times, bigger, times, as, big

(3) The, harder, the, better

F-2

(1) 두 소년 가운데 로빈이 더 똑똑하다.

(2) 목성은 지구보다 1,300배 더 크다.

(3) 이만한 크기의 원을 그려라.

Power Up Test
p.85-86

1

(1) strange   (2) slowly

(3) beautiful   (4) happy

(5) interesting   (6) either

(7) few

2 (A)

3

(1) so[as] tall   (2) as tall

(3) not older   (4) oldest

(5) younger than

4 (D) little — later — latest

5 (B)

6

(1) 너는 봄과 가을 중 어느 것을 더 좋아하니? 나는 봄이 더 좋아. 그리고 겨울이 가고 날씨가 더 따뜻해지고 있어서 요즘 무척 행복해.

(2) 저는 위대한 과학자 토마스 에디슨을 존경합니다. 그리고 그 분과 같은 과학자가 되고 싶습니다. 저의 어머님은 제가 노력하면 할수록 더 많이 배울 수 있을 것이라고 말씀하십니다.

Pattern Drill
p.87-88

유형 9 보어 찾기

1 B

2 C

유형 20 형용사를 혼동하여 쓴 경우

1 B (seven → seventh)

2 B (alive → live)

3 D (fatly → fat)

유형 21 부사(구), 형용사(구) 찾기
1 D
2 C

유형 22 원급, 비교급, 최상급 찾기
1 C
2 D
3 B

유형 23 원급, 비교급, 최상급의 쓰임이 잘못된 경우
1 B (than → as)
2 C (as → than)
3 B (most → the most)

유형 24 비교급, 최상급의 형태가 잘못된 경우
1 B (commoner → common)
2 B (most longest → longest)

Pattern Review

1 (C) (sooner → soon)
   비교급의 쓰임이 잘못된 경우

2 (D) 최상급 찾기

3 (B) (bright → brighter)
   원급의 쓰임이 잘못된 경우

4 (A) 비교급 찾기

5 (D) 비교급 찾기

6 (C) (a long → a longer)
   원급의 쓰임이 잘못된 경우

7 (C) (the one → the first)
   형용사(기수–서수)를 혼동하여 쓴 경우

8 (B) 원급 찾기

9 (A) 비교급 찾기

10 (C) 형용사구 찾기

11 (B) 원급 찾기

12 (C) (most largest → largest)
    최상급의 형태가 잘못된 경우

13 (A) 비교급 찾기

14 (C) (still live → still alive)
    형용사를 혼동하여 쓴 경우

15 (B) 부사 찾기

Mini Test
p.91-92

1 (B) (speaking → spoken)
   현재분사와 과거분사를 혼동한 경우

2 (A) 관계사절의 동사 찾기

3 (C) (only not → not only)
   상관접속사가 잘못 쓰인 경우

4 (D) 동격 찾기

5 (A) (idea → ideas)
   명사의 수가 잘못된 경우

6 (D) (tasting → taste)
   병렬 오류

7 (B) 목적보어 찾기

8 (C) (makes → to make)
   준동사 자리에 동사를 쓴 경우

9 (D) 올바른 어순 찾기

10 (C) (whose → who)
    관계대명사의 격을 혼동한 경우

11 (B) 주어–동사 찾기

12 (A) (to supply → of supplying)
    전치사구 찾기

13

CHAPTER 5 동사, 시제

Grammar Up
p.96-108

🚩 Check-Up

A-1

(1) She is a teacher of history in my school.
　　주어 동사　　　　　주격보어　　↘2형식

(2) They eat lunch at a fast food restaurant.
　　주어 동사 목적어　　　　　　　↘3형식

(3) Who wrote this novel?
　　주어 동사 목적어　　　　↘3형식

(4) Tom and I were walking along the beach.
　　주어　　　　동사　　　　　↘1형식

(5) Keeping early hours is good for health.
　　주어　　　　　동사 주격보어　↘2형식

(6) I want to know if he will come.
　　주어 동사 　목적어　　　↘3형식

(7) Did you buy him a bicycle?
　　주어 동사 간접목적어 직접목적어　↘4형식

(8) He must be a foreigner.
　　주어　동사　　주격보어　↘2형식

(9) They consider the man honest.
　　주어　동사　　목적어　목적격보어　↘5형식

(10) You mean everything to me.
　　주어 동사　목적어　　↘3형식

A-2

(1) is　　　　　　(2) 옳은 문장
(3) works[worked][has worked][has been working]
(4) are　　　　　　(5) talk

B-1

(1) reads　　　　　　(2) was
(3) returns 또는 will return
(4) are　　　　　　(5) is

(6) makes　　　　　　(7) had
(8) will go　　　　　　(9) have already seen
(10) was 또는 am

C-1

(1) am needing → need
(2) 옳은 문장
(3) are having → have
(4) is remembering → remembers
(5) 옳은 문장

C-2

(1) I am watching TV now.
(2) I was eating supper alone when my mother came home.
(3) I will be taking a test this time tomorrow.

D-1

(1) have been　　　　(2) has already washed
(3) has lived　　　　(4) went
(5) has worked　　　　(6) had written
(7) have learned　　　(8) have you done
(9) had already left　(10) has gone

D-2

(1) 해리스 부인은 독일에 5년째 살고 있다.
(2) 지난 목요일 이후로 줄곧 비가 내리고 있다.
(3) 극장에 들어갔을 때 이미 영화는 시작했었다.
(4) 헨리는 예전에 본 적이 있기 때문에 그녀를 알아보았다.

D-3

(1) have you gone to → did you go
(2) have arrived → arrived
(3) for three days ago. → for three days.
　　(ago 삭제)
(4) has → had

E-1

(1) ends   (2) returns

(3) will have   (4) make

(5) will have

E-2

(1) will be → is   (2) will leave → leaves

(3) 옳은 문장

F-1

(1) would, study   (2) had, been

F-2

(1) will → would   (2) was → is

(3) 옳은 문장   (4) traveled → travels

(5) 옳은 문장

Power Up Test

1

(1) <u>Debbie</u> <u>woke up</u> in the morning.
    S   V

(2) <u>Tim</u> <u>can't reach</u> <u>the ceiling.</u>
   S   V   O

(3) <u>I</u> <u>like</u> <u>living</u> in Cheju Island in winter.
  S   V   O

(4) <u>I</u> <u>saw</u> <u>the little girl</u> <u>playing</u> with her pretty
  S   V   O   OC

    doll.

(5) <u>The baby sleeping in the bed</u> <u>looks</u>
          S   V

    <u>happy.</u>
     SC

(6) <u>My friend</u> <u>sent</u> <u>me</u> <u>a present</u> by mail.
    S   V   O(간목)   O(직목)

(7) <u>It</u> <u>is</u> <u>important</u> <u>to keep one's promise.</u>
   S   V   SC   S(진주어, it–가주어)

(8) <u>You</u> <u>know</u> <u>that you should stop on the</u>
    S   V   O

    <u>red traffic light.</u>

(9) There <u>are</u> <u>two students</u> in the classroom.
        V   S

(10) <u>My mother</u> always <u>calls</u> <u>me</u> <u>'baby.'</u>
     S   V   O   OC

2 (D)   **3** (B)

4 (A)   **5** (A)

6 (C)   **7** (C)

8 (B)

9

(1) I haven't written a letter to my sister for a long time.

(2) I bought the book the day before yesterday.

Pattern Drill

유형 3 동사-명사 혼동

1 B (building → build)

유형 7 동사 찾기

1 D

유형 25 동사 자리에 준동사를 쓴 경우

1 A (leaving → leaves)

2 B (to be → were)

유형 26 진행 시제의 형태가 잘못된 경우

1 D (increase → increasing)

15

유형 27 완료 시제의 형태가 잘못된 경우

1 B (be → been)
2 C (broke → broken)

유형 28 동사의 시제가 잘못된 경우

1 C (come to → came to)
2 D (was → is)
3 A (sit → sat / was sitting)

Pattern Review

1 (B) (tell → told)
   동사의 시제가 잘못된 경우

2 (C) (to meet → met)
   동사 자리에 준동사를 쓴 경우

3 (A) (is listen → is listening)
   진행 시제의 형태가 잘못된 경우

4 (B) (believe → believed)
   동사의 시제가 잘못된 경우

5 (A) (keep → kept)
   완료 시제의 형태가 잘못된 경우

6 (C) (were already → had already been)
   동사의 시제가 잘못된 경우

7 (B) (is separated → has been separated)
   동사의 시제가 잘못된 경우

8 (D) (visiting → visited)
   동사 자리에 준동사를 쓴 경우

9 (C) (has died → died)
   동사의 시제가 잘못된 경우

10 (A) (will come → comes)
   동사의 시제가 잘못된 경우

Mini Test

1 (B) (wash → washing)
   준동사 자리에 동사를 쓴 경우

2 (A) to 부정사 찾기

3 (C) (vitamin → vitamins)
   명사의 수가 잘못된 경우

4 (C) (being allowed → be allowed)
   조동사 뒤에 동사원형을 쓰지 않은 경우

5 (D) 동사 찾기

6 (B) (attend → attention)
   명사-동사 혼동

7 (C) 진주어 찾기

8 (A) (Half of earth → Half of the earth)
   필요한 관사가 빠진 경우

9 (C) (difficult → more difficult)
   병렬 오류

10 (D) 주어와 동사 찾기

11 (B) 접속사 찾기

12 (C) (their → them)
   인칭대명사의 격이 잘못된 경우

CHAPTER 6 태

Grammar Up
p.118-122

Check-Up

A

(1) The song La Vie en Rose is sung by many singers.

(2) Claude Monet painted this picture.

(3) I was hit on the back by him.

(4) The top of the mountain is covered with snow.

(5) Today cellular phones are used by most people.

B-1

(1) The motion picture was invented by them.

(2) What I tell her is understood by her.

(4) I was surprised at the sight.

(5) The man is looked down on by them.

B-2

(1) The washing machine has been used for 10 years.

(2) We will be taught Japanese by Mr. Murakami.

(3) A snowman is being made by the children.

B-3

(1) Was the house cleaned by her?

(2) Let it be done at once.

(3) By whom was the movie *Christmas in August* directed?

(4) Is the car driven by her?

(5) Let the door never be closed.

B-4

(1) I will be picked up by my husband on his way home.

(2) The matter should be looked into by us.

(3) Her nephew is looked after by her.

(4) The dwarf was laughed at by the bad boys.

(5) His boss is always spoken ill of by him.

B-5

(1) - A surprising story was told to me by him.
   - I was told a surprising story by him.

(2) A bicycle was bought for me by my father.

(3) He is envied his wealth by them.

(4) A cushion was made for me by her.

(5) I was given a skirt by my sister.
   A skirt was given to me by my sister.

B-6

(1) The baby was heard to cry by us all.

(2) Her son was being watched to play on the playground by the mother.

(3) The students were made to read it aloud by the teacher.

B-7

(1) - It is said that Deborah is smart.
   - Deborah is said to be smart.

(2) - It is believed that Mr. Parker will be the president.
   - Mr. Parker is believed to be the president.

(3) - It is thought that the man is guilty.
   - The man is thought to be guilty.

B-8a

(1) at   (2) with

(3) with   (4) in

(5) about

(1) by → about   (2) by → to

(3) by → at   (4) by → with

(5) with → at

Power Up Test
p.123-124

1

(1) I was invited to dinner by Ms. Hopkins.

(2) The door key was kept in the box by Mr. Cart.

(3) The sick child has been examined by the doctor.

(4) My watch is going to be fixed by the jeweler.

(5) Our hotel room will be cleaned by a maid.

2

(1) The bird was not killed by my cat.

(2) The window cannot be broken by Johnny.

(3) Is his car being repaired by your father?

(4) Are clean towels provided by the hotel?

(5) By whom was the radio invented?

(6) He was seen to enter the room.

(7) Let your homework be done now.

(8) It is said that he is kind.

     He is said to be kind.

3

(1) at   (2) to

(3) by   (4) with

(5) with

4 (B)   **5** (A)

6 (C)   **7** (D)

Pattern Drill
p.125

유형 29 능동태와 수동태를 혼동하여 쓴 경우

1 B (knew → was known)

2 B (were looked → looked)

유형 30 수동태의 형태가 잘못된 경우

1 C (call → called)

2 A (is dividing → is divided)

Pattern Review
p.126

1 (B) (are used → use)

능동태와 수동태를 혼동하여 쓴 경우

2 (C) (eaten by → been eaten by)

능동태와 수동태를 혼동하여 쓴 경우

3 (B) (wrote → written)

수동태의 형태가 잘못된 경우

4 (B) (was arrived → arrived)

능동태와 수동태를 혼동하여 쓴 경우

5 (C) (deliver → be delivered)

능동태와 수동태를 혼동하여 쓴 경우

6 (B) (is repairing → is being repaired)

능동태와 수동태를 혼동하여 쓴 경우

7 (B) (invent → invented)

수동태의 형태가 잘못된 경우

8 (C) (crowd → are crowded)

능동태와 수동태를 혼동하여 쓴 경우

9 (B) (interesting → interested)

능동태와 수동태를 혼동하여 쓴 경우

10 (B) (has chosen → has been chosen)

능동태와 수동태를 혼동하여 쓴 경우

Mini Test

p.127-128

1 (B) (ours → our)
인칭대명사의 격이 잘못된 경우

2 (C) (instead → instead of)
필요한 전치사가 빠진 경우

3 (A) 동사와 보어 찾기

4 (B) (so → such)
어휘가 혼동된 경우

5 (A) 동사 찾기

6 (B) (immediate → immediately)
형용사–부사 혼동

7 (D) 보어 찾기

8 (C) (using → used)
현재분사와 과거분사가 혼동된 경우

9 (A) 주어와 동사 찾기

10 (D) (as → than)
비교구문의 쓰임이 잘못된 경우

11 (C) (center → the center)
필요한 관사가 빠진 경우

12 (B) 보어 찾기

CHAPTER 7 조동사

Grammar Up

p.132-137

Check-Up

A
(1) makes → make
(2) mays → may
(3) Do I should → Should I
(4) 옳은 문장
(5) can → be able to

B-1
(1) be   (2) would
(3) have been   (4) to eat
(3) Shall

B-2
(1) ought, to/had, better
(2) need
(3) able, to
(4) would, like
(3) should/must

B-3
(1) had   (2) used
(3) must have   (4) cannot
(3) may

B-4
(1) must be → must have been
(2) may come → may not(약한 의미)[must not/should not] come
(3) Should Mr. Jones pay the bill?
(4) must finish → don't have to[need not] finish
(5) must do → will have to

B-5

(1) I am not used to dancing.
(2) Roger should[must/has to/ought to] go home early today.
(3) We don't have to[need not] go to school tomorrow.
(4) May I enter[come into] your room?
(3) Anne couldn't play the piano when (she was) young.

Power Up Test p.138-139

1

(1) can
(2) would
(3) have
(4) used
(5) must
(6) may/can
(7) had
(8) must
(9) need
(10) cannot

2 (B)   **3** (C)

4 (D)   **5** (A)

6 (C)   **7** (D)

8

(1) A good student should not miss any class.
(2) The baby must be hungry.
(3) I have to wait for Sera here.

Pattern Drill p.140

유형 31 조동사 뒤에 동사 원형을 쓰지 않은 경우

1 B (proves → prove)
2 B (eating → eat)

Pattern Review p.141

1 (A) (helps → help)
조동사 뒤에 동사 원형을 쓰지 않은 경우

2 (C) (seeing → see)
조동사 뒤에 동사 원형을 쓰지 않은 경우

3 (B) (included → include)
조동사 뒤에 동사 원형을 쓰지 않은 경우

4 (A) (to learn → learn)
조동사 뒤에 동사 원형을 쓰지 않은 경우

5 (A) (coming → com)
조동사 뒤에 동사 원형을 쓰지 않은 경우

Mini Test p142-143

1 (D) (fighting → fight)
to 부정사 형태가 잘못된 경우

2 (D) (country → countries)
명사의 수가 잘못된 경우

3 (C) 전치사 찾기

4 (B) (he is → is)
문장성분이 중복된 경우

5 (A) 주어 찾기

6 (D) (self-defensive → self-defense)
명사-형용사 혼동

7 (B) 주어와 동사 찾기

8 (C) (rolling → roll) 병렬 오류

9 (A) 부사(배수 표현) 찾기

10 (A) (many → much)
어휘가 혼동된 경우

11 (D) 동사 찾기

12 (C) (markedly → marked)
형용사-부사 혼동

Grammar Up

p.146-153

Check-Up

A-1
(1) 그가 정직한 사람이라면 그런 일을 하지 않을 텐데.
(2) 내가 남자라면 너 같은 여자랑 결혼할 텐데.
(3) 네가 그 광경을 봤더라면 뭐라고 했을지 궁금하다.
(4) 내가 젊다면 책을 많이 읽고 여행을 많이 하고 많은 사람들을 만날 텐데.
(5) 그녀가 그를 봤더라면 사랑에 빠졌을 텐데.

A-2
(1) As we don't have more money, we can't eat a more expensive lunch.
(2) If it were not raining, I would go out.
(3) As mother isn't at home, she can't make us a delicious meal.
(4) If she were not short, she could take part in the beauty contest.

B-1
(1) had   (2) have gone
(3) do   (4) have gone
(5) were

B-2
(1) 그녀가 좀 더 좋은 가정에서 태어났다면 피아니스트로 성공할 수 있었을지 모른다.
(2) 음악이 없다면 세상은 따분하고 우울할 것이다.
(3) 지구가 내일 멸망한다면 무얼 하겠니?

B-3
(1) be   (2) Were
(3) had saved   (4) hadn't walked

(5) be

B-4
(1) Were I rich, ~
(2) Had she a sister or a brother, ~
(3) Had he gone there by bus, ~
(4) Were it not for air, there ~
(5) Had it not been for his wife's help, he would not ~

C-1
(1) if   (2) wish
(3) if, had, seen (4) were
(5) as, if, were

Power Up Test

p.154-155

1
(1) had, would write
(2) have, will buy
(3) would have met, had come
(4) were, would allow
(5) had not been, could not have solved
(6) had left, would be
(7) buy, will drive
(8) were not, could not live

2
(1) I wish that you did not have to work tonight.
(2) My son treats me as if I were his friend.
(3) As you did not finish high school, you cannot get a better job.

3 (B)   **4** (D)

5 (C)   **6** (A)

7

(1) ~, I could bathe with my mother/father.

(2) ~, I would have a snowball fight with my friends.

(3) ~, I would help poor people.

(4) ~, we will go on a picnic.

(5) ~, I would have been to the concert.

Pattern Drill

p.156

유형 32 가정법 구문 찾기

1 C (had not killed)

유형 33 가정법을 잘못 쓴 경우

1 A (is → were)

Pattern Review

p.157

1 (C) (is → were)
　　가정법을 잘못 쓴 경우

2 (B) 가정법 구문 찾기

3 (D) 가정법 구문 찾기

4 (A) (there were → it were)
　　가정법을 잘못 쓴 경우

5 (C) 가정법 구문 찾기

6 (B) (would have → had)
　　가정법을 잘못 쓴 경우

7 (A) 가정법 구문 찾기

8 (C) (can have → could have)
　　가정법을 잘못 쓴 경우

9 (B) 가정법 구문 찾기

10 (D) 가정법 구문 찾기

Mini Test

p.158-159

1 (B) (eighteen → eighteenth)
　　형용사(기수 – 서수)가 혼동된 경우

2 (B) (sentence → sentences)
　　명사의 수를 잘못 쓴 경우

3 (A) 올바른 어순 찾기

4 (D) (as well → as well as)
　　접속사가 잘못 쓰인 경우

5 (C) 주어 찾기

6 (C) (into → in)
　　전치사가 잘못 쓰인 경우

7 (B) 현재분사 찾기

8 (B) 분사구문 찾기

9 (A) (shocked → shocking)
　　현재분사와 과거분사를 혼동한 경우

10 (B) (speaks → speak)
　　주어와 동사가 일치하지 않는 경우

11 (D) 전치사구 찾기

12 (C) (one → ones)
　　명사의 수가 잘못된 경우

Grammar Up

p.162-172

🦋 Check-Up

A-1
(1) likes   (2) is
(3) have   (4) are
(5) is   (6) is
(7) was   (8) are
(9) are   (10) wins
(11) is   (12) was
(13) was   (14) Is
(15) eats

A-2
(1) his or her   (2) his
(3) its   (4) her
(5) him

B-1
(1) to dance → dancing
(2) a dog → those of a dog
(3) cook → cooking
(4) not do → not to do
(5) 옳은 문장
(6) have → has
(7) beauty → beautiful
(8) him → he
(9) as well → as well as
(10) not → not only (or) but also → but

B-2
(1) and   (2) nor
(3) but   (4) or
(5) but   (6) as
(7) than   (8) and

(9) than   (10) but

C-1a
(1) She always smiles like an angel.
(2) I have nothing special to say.
(3) You should often check up your computer.
(4) I saw him singing in the rain.
(5) Tara looks at her baby sleeping peacefully in the bed.
(6) 옳은 문장

C-1b
(1) 분명히, 그는 그 그림을 그리지 않았다.
(2) 그는 그 그림을 분명하게 그리지 않았다.

C-2a (주절의 주어-밑줄, 종속절의 주어-italic)
(1) There are many fish in the pond.
(2) All *I* want is to sleep right now.
(3) Not until *Jane* heard the news, did she start to cry.
(4) Such was my surprise at his loud voice.
(5) High in the sky fly birds.
(6) Little did I dream *you* would be a doctor!

C-2b
(1) had he seen me
(2) does he write to her

D-1
(1) much more difficult
(2) do pay
(3) What in the world
(4) the very woman
(5) It was Thomas that(who) built the house.
   (It ~ that 강조구문 이용)

E-1 (기준어구-italic, 동격어구-밑줄)

(1) *Mr. Jones*, <u>a writer and critic</u>, will join us.
(2) His suggestion is *this*, <u>to have coffee break</u>.
(3) I know *the fact* <u>that he can't visit his mother</u>.
(4) *Seoul*, <u>the largest city in Korea</u>, is my hometown.

Power Up Test p.173-174

1 (D) **2** (C)

3 (D) **4** (B)

5 (B) **6** (A)

7
(1) Not until our teacher comes can we start the meeting.
(2) It is this book that(which) I have long wanted.
(3) Only in the department store does my wife buy things.
(4) I haven't thought that you would fail at all.

8 (C)

9
(1) a doctor
(2) that Mr. Bak told a lie.
(3) delivering newspapers

10
(1) 만약 네가 기숙사에서 산다면, 네 옷을 직접 세탁해야 한다.
(2) 성공하기 위해서, 너는 일을 열심히 해야 할 뿐만 아니라 정직해야 한다.

(3) 내 모자가 바람에 날아가자마자 사람들이 내 대머리를 보고 웃었다.

Pattern Drill p.175-177

유형 34 주어와 동사의 수 일치
1 C (are → is)
2 C (make → makes)

유형 17 명사와 대명사의 일치
1 D (its → her)

유형 35 병렬 – 열거 구문
1 D (crying → to cry)
2 D (to throw → throw)

유형 36 병렬 – 등위 접속사로 연결된 구문
1 D (danger → dangerous)

유형 37 병렬 – 상관 접속사로 연결된 구문
1 C (helping → in helping)

유형 38 병렬 – 비교 구문
1 D (play → to play)

유형 39 어순 – 문장 성분 및 품사의 위치
1 A (of full → full of)
2 D

유형 40 어순 – 수식어의 위치
1 B (animals strong → strong animals)
2 C

유형 41 도치
1 A
2 D

유형 42 동격어 찾기

1 B
2 C

Pattern Review
p.178-179

1 (C) (it → they)
명사와 대명사의 일치

2 (A) 동격어 찾기

3 (B) (on foot → feet)
병렬 – 열거 구문

4 (C) (tells → tell)
주어와 동사의 수 일치

5 (B) 어순 – 수식어의 위치

6 (D) (home way → way home)
어순 – 문장성분 및 품사의 위치

7 (C) (they → it)
명사와 대명사의 일치

8 (D) (noon until → until noon)
어순 – 문장성분 및 품사의 위치

9 (B) (things living → living things)
어순 – 수식어의 위치

10 (A) 도치

11 (C) (cloud → cloudy)
병렬 – 열거 구문

12 (A) 동격어 찾기

13 (C) (grow → grows)
주어와 동사의 일치

14 (B) (bee small → small bee)
어순 – 수식어의 위치

15 (D) (pollute → pollution)
병렬 – 상관접속사로 연결된 구문

Mini Test
p.180-181

1 (C) (and also → but also)
접속사를 잘못 쓴 경우

2 (A) 어순 – 수식어의 위치

3 (D) (civilized → civilization)
형용사 – 명사 혼동

4 (C) (best dog → best dogs)
명사의 수가 잘못된 경우

5 (D) 보어 찾기

6 (B) (pass down → passed down)
수동태의 형태가 잘못된 경우

7 (D) (commonest → common)
원급, 비교급, 최상급의 형태가 잘못된 경우

8 (A) 분사(구문) 찾기

9 (D) (years wet → wet years)
어순 – 수식어의 위치

10 (C) 주어와 동사 찾기

11 (C) (hunger → hungry)
형용사 – 명사 혼동

12 (B) 분사(구문) 찾기

Grammar Up

p.184-200

Check-Up

A-1
(1) 부사적 용법, 결과
(2) 명사적 용법, 주격보어
(3) 형용사적 용법, 명사 수식
(4) 명사적 용법, 진주어
(5) 명사적 용법, 목적어
(6) 형용사적 용법, 보어—예정
(7) 형용사적 용법, 보어—의도
(8) 부사적 용법, 형용사 수식
(9) 부사적 용법, 조건
(10) 부사적 용법, 목적

A-2
(1) on   (2) how
(3) in   (4) 필요 없음

A-3
(1) to me → for me
(2) for you → of you
(3) for you → you
(4) students → for students

A-4
(1) to be   (2) to have answered
(3) lost   (4) to exercise
(5) had bought

A-5
(1) to enter → enter
(2) to choose → choose
(3) to come → come
(4) wait → to wait
(5) had not better → had better not

(6) stayed → stay
(7) 옳은 문장

A-6
(1) 말하자면   (2) 우선
(3) ~은 말할 것도 없고 (4) 솔직히 말하면

A-7
(1) so   (2) too
(3) enough   (4) to
(5) in order, so as

B-1
(1) John   (2) her
(3) 일반인(생략) (4) I

B-2
(1) There   (2) prevented
(3) reading   (4) without
(5) help

B-3
(1) 비행기가 차보다 빠르다는 것은 말할 필요도 없다.
(2) 그 소식을 듣자마자 그녀는 얼굴이 창백해졌다.
(3) 다음 일요일에 당신을 만나기를 기대하고 있습니다.
(4) 나는 달까지 날아가고 싶다.
(5) 당신의 실수를 후회해봐야 소용 없다.
(6) 당신의 전화를 써도 되겠습니까?
(7) 나는 내가 직접 그린 그림을 자랑스럽게 생각한다.
(8) 나는 매일 아침 조깅을 하고 있다.
(9) 이 방에 들어올 때마다 나는 편안함을 느낀다.
(10) 그 문제는 결코 쉽지 않다.

C-1
(1) boring   (2) interested
(3) cut   (4) broken
(5) quarreling   (6) running
(7) recorded   (8) making

C-2

(1) been   (2) surrounded

(3) running/run   (4) called

(5) standing   (6) doing

(7) boiled   (8) bought

D-1

(1) (Though) (Being) 30 years old

(2) (When) Walking along the street

(3) (If) Turning to the right

(4) gazing at my eyes

D-2

(1) So surprised at the news

(2) (When) Left alone

(3) (After) Having written a letter

(4) Night coming on

(5) It being very cold

D-3

(1) Seeing → Seen

(2) speak → speaking

(3) Being → It being

(4) crossing → crossed

(5) Writing → Written

Power Up Test
p.201-205

1 (1) b   (2) a

    (3) 없음   (4) c

2 (A)   **3** (C)

4 (B)

5 In-su seems to have seen the movie before.

6

(1) My brother was too sick to go to school.

(2) It is impossible for Mr. Kim to come back by midnight.

7 (A)   **8** (C)

9

(1) It is very kind of you to help me.

(2) She heard the dog bark in the room.

10

(1) driving   (2) laughing

(3) eating   (4) participating

(5) coming

11 (D)

12

(1) meeting   (2) to stop

13 (C)   **14** (D)

15 (A)

16 I regret having lent him my car.

17

(1) rolling   (2) living

(3) hidden   (4) looking, exciting

(5) made

18 (B)

19

(1) Judging from his appearance, he seems to be a thief.

(2) Made of glass, the cup is easily broken.

(3) He ate his breakfast and read a newspaper.

20 (D)   **21** (B)

22
(1) Considering his age (or) Taking his age
   into consideration
(2) Frankly speaking

Pattern Drill p.206-208

유형 6 주어 찾기
1 B
2 C

유형 9 보어 찾기
1 A

유형 10 목적어와 목적보어 찾기
1 D

유형 43 to 부정사 찾기
1 B

유형 44 to 부정사 자리에 동사를 쓴 경우
1 C (get → to get)
2 B (what do → what to do)

유형 46 원형부정사 자리에 다른 형태를 잘못 쓴 경우
1 B (waiting → wait)
2 D (to wear → wear)

유형 47 to 부정사의 형태가 잘못된 경우
1 B (to seeing → to see)
2 B (having → have)

유형 48 동명사 찾기

1 D
2 B

유형 49 동명사 자리에 동사를 쓴 경우
1 B (be hurt → being hurt)
2 B (help → helping)

유형 50 분사(구문) 찾기
1 B
2 D
3 C

유형 51 현재분사와 과거분사를 혼동하여 쓴 경우
1 A (surprised → surprising)
2 A (interesting → interested)

유형 52 분사 자리에 동사나 다른 준동사를 쓴 경우
1 D (moves → moving)
2 D (invent → invented)

Pattern Review p.209-210

1 (C) to 부정사 찾기

2 (A) to 부정사 찾기

3 (C) (visit → to visit)
   to 부정사 자리에 동사를 쓴 경우

4 (C) (to try → try)
   원형부정사 자리에 다른 형태를 잘못 쓴 경우

5 (B) (watching → watch)
   to 부정사의 형태가 잘못된 경우

6 (C) (send → to send)
   to 부정사 자리에 동사를 쓴 경우

7 (B) (cook → cooking)
   동명사 자리에 동사를 쓴 경우

8 (C) 동명사 찾기

9 (B) (turn off → turning off)
동명사 자리에 동사를 쓴 경우

10 (D) 동명사 찾기

11 (A) (work → working)
동명사 자리에 동사를 쓴 경우

12 (B) (finished → finishing)
현재분사와 과거분사를 혼동하여 쓴 경우

13 (B) (name → named)
분사 자리에 동사나 다른 준동사를 쓴 경우

14 (A) 분사(구문) 찾기

15 (B) (believing → believed)
현재분사와 과거분사를 혼동하여 쓴 경우

16 (D) (took → taking)
분사 자리에 동사나 다른 준동사를 쓴 경우

17 (B) 분사(구문) 찾기

18 (C) (elects → elected)
분사 자리에 동사나 다른 준동사를 쓴 경우

19 (A) (Being → There being)
분사(구문) 찾기

20 (C) 분사(구문) 찾기

병렬–등위접속사로 연결된 구문

6 (C) 동사 찾기

7 (B) (big → bigger)
원급, 비교급, 최상급의 쓰임이 잘못된 경우

8 (A) (stick → sticky)
형용사–부사 혼동

9 (B) 목적어와 목적보어 찾기

10 (A) (such → so)
형용사–부사 혼동

11 (D) (this → these)
형용사를 혼동하여 쓴 경우

12 (C) 동격어 찾기

Mini Test
p.211-212

1 (A) (they → their)
인칭대명사의 격이 잘못된 경우

2 (D) (waste → wasting)
동명사 자리에 동사를 쓴 경우

3 (C) 주어와 동사 찾기

4 (B) 전치사(구) 찾기

5 (D) (poverty → poor)

CHAPTER 11 준동사

Grammar Up
p.216-219

🧩 Check-Up

B-1
(1) living
(2) smoking / to smoke
(3) playing
(4) to take / taking
(5) to run / running
(6) to make
(7) losing
(8) seeing

C-1
(1) 현재분사
(2) 동명사
(3) 동명사
(4) 현재분사
(5) 동명사

Power Up Test
p.220

1 (A)

2
(1) 그녀는 어제부터 술을 끊었다.
(2) 그녀는 술집에서 술을 마시기 위해 걸음을 멈췄다.

3 (C)   **4** (B)

Pattern Drill
p.221

유형 43 to 부정사 찾기
1 C

유형 45 부정사와 동명사를 혼동하여 쓴 경우

1 D (eating → to eat)
2 C (to follow → following)
3 C (checking → to check)

Pattern Review
p.222

1 (C) (taming → tame)
to 부정사의 형태가 잘못된 경우

2 (A) (traveling → to travel)
to 부정사와 동명사를 혼동하여 쓴 경우

3 (D) to 부정사 찾기

4 (A) (seeing → to see)
to 부정사와 동명사를 혼동하여 쓴 경우

5 (A) 동명사 찾기

6 (D) (to cry → crying)
to 부정사와 동명사를 혼동하여 쓴 경우

7 (D) (blow → blowing)
동명사 자리에 동사를 쓴 경우

8 (B) 동명사 찾기

9 (B) (to live → to living)
동명사 자리에 동사를 쓴 경우

10 (C) 분사(구문) 찾기

Mini Test
p.223-224

1 (B) (principle → principles)
명사의 수가 잘못된 경우

2 (D) 분사(구문) 찾기

3 (A) (secretly → secret)
형용사-부사 혼동

4 (A) 주어와 동사 찾기

5 (C) (always be → always been)

완료시제의 형태가 잘못된 경우

6 (B) (what → who)
관계사를 잘못 쓴 경우

7 (B) 어순 – 문장 성분 및 품사의 위치

8 (D) (much → many)
형용사를 혼동하여 쓴 경우

9 (B) (were → was)
주어와 동사의 수 일치

10 (A) 동사 찾기

11 (B) (link → linked)
분사(구문) 찾기

12 (B) (and they → but they)
접속사를 잘못 쓴 경우

Grammar Up

p.228-237

Check-Up

A-1
(1) 주격 보어(형용사구) (2) 명사 수식(형용사구)
(3) 동사 수식(부사구) (4) 동사 수식(부사구)
(5) 문장 수식(부사구)

B-1
(1) studying (2) him
(3) succeeding (4) me
(5) my father

B-2
(1) speak → speaking
(2) he → him
(3) the desk on → on the desk
(4) to see → to seeing
(5) the about question to think
    → the question to think about
(6) to choose → choose
(7) see → seeing
(8) I → me
(9) 옳은 문장
(10) of that → of 삭제

C-1
(1) by (2) of
(3) in (4) to
(5) sake (6) For
(7) account

D-1

(1) at	(2) for
(3) By	(4) since
(5) on	(6) after
(7) into	(8) During
(9) from	(10) in

D-2

(1) at → in	(2) on → above
(3) in → into	(4) over → up
(5) in → to	(6) 옳은 문장
(7) on → over, across	
(8) in → on	

D-3

(1) 그는 그것이 둘 사이의 문제라고 말했다.
   그는 그것이 그들(셋 이상) 사이의 문제라고
   말했다.
(2) 나는 5시까지 내 숙제를 마칠 것이다.
   나는 5시까지 내 숙제를 하고 있을 것이다.

D-4

(1) into	(2) from
(3) on	(4) of
(5) from	(6) by
(7) with	(8) of
(9) for	(10) at
(11) to	(12) at
(13) for	(14) after
(15) with	

Power Up Test p.238-239

1 (D)	**2** (B)

3 (C)

4
(1) Children were afraid of losing their way
to school.
(2) He was frozen to death.
(3) Nancy has studied German during this
   semester.
(4) She painted the picture from morning till
   night.
(5) Milk is made into cheese.

5 (C)	**6** (A)
7 (C)	**8** (A)

9 (B)

Pattern Drill p.240

유형 53 전치사(구) 찾기
1 A
2 B

유형 54 전치사를 잘못 쓴 경우
1 D (for → during / in)
1 C (than → from)

유형 55 필요한 전치사가 빠진 경우
1 D (because → because of)
1 B (listen → listen to)

유형 56 불필요한 전치사가 쓰인 경우
1 A (married to → married)

Pattern Review p.241

1 (B) (for → on)
   전치사를 잘못 쓴 경우

2 (D) (parts the → parts of the)
   필요한 전치사가 빠진 경우

3 (A) 전치사(구) 찾기

4 (C) 전치사(구) 찾기

5 (C) (at nine → from nine)
전치사를 잘못 쓴 경우

6 (B) (into → within)
전치사를 잘못 쓴 경우

7 (A) (In spite → In spite of)
필요한 전치사가 빠진 경우

8 (C) (place which → place in which)
필요한 전치사가 빠진 경우

9 (C) 전치사(구) 찾기

10 (B) (with her → her)
불필요한 전치사가 쓰인 경우

11 (B) 전치사 찾기

12 (D) (land → landed)
동사의 시제가 잘못된 경우

Mini Test

p.242-243

1 (D) (thinness → thin)
형용사 – 명사 혼동

2 (A) 주어와 동사 찾기

3 (C) 접속사 찾기

4 (D) (a whole → for a whole)
필요한 전치사가 빠진 경우

5 (A) (many → much)
형용사 혼동

6 (B) 부사(구문) 찾기

7 (B) (or → and)
접속사를 잘못 쓴 경우

8 (A) (covering → the covering)
필요한 관사가 빠진 경우

9 (A) 어순 – 수식어의 위치

10 (B) (weakness → weak)
병렬 – 등위접속사로 연결된 구문

CHAPTER 13 접속사

Grammar Up ── p.246-251

Check-Up

A-1
(1) but   (2) or
(3) and   (4) for
(5) or

B-1
(1) or not 삭제 혹은 if → whether
(2) whether → that
(3) will be → is
(4) went → go/should go
(5) He is a Korean → That he is a Korean
(6) 옳은 문장
(7) will succeed → succeeds

B-2
(1) lest   (2) Since
(3) unless   (4) As
(5) while   (6) that
(7) As long as   (8) as
(9) because   (10) that
(11) since   (12) In case
(13) If   (14) before
(15) As

C-1
(1) before → than
(2) and → but
(3) also → but also
(4) or → nor 혹은 Neither → Either

D-1
(1) Therefore   (2) Otherwise
(3) Besides   (4) However

Power Up Test ── p.252-253

1 (C)   **2** (D)

3 (B)   **4** (A)

5 (D)   **6** (A)

7 (B)

8
(1) comes   (2) and
(3) whether   (4) take
(5) lest

9 (C)

Pattern Drill ── p.254-255

유형 57 접속사 찾기
1 B
2 D

유형 58 부사절 찾기
1 A
2 C

유형 59 축약된 부사절 찾기
1 D

유형 60 접속사를 잘못 쓴 경우
1 C (though → for)

2 C (or → and)

유형 61 필요한 접속사가 빠진 경우
1 C (more → more than)

유형 62 불필요한 접속사가 쓰인 경우
1 A

Pattern Review
p.256-257

1 (B) (long → long before)
필요한 접속사가 빠진 경우

2 (C) 접속사 찾기

3 (A) (When cowboys → Cowboys)
불필요한 접속사가 쓰인 경우

4 (D) 부사절 찾기

5 (B) (but → and)
접속사를 잘못 쓴 경우

6 (C) 접속사 찾기

7 (B) 부사절 찾기

8 (A) (also → but also)
필요한 접속사가 빠진 경우

9 (D) 접속사 찾기

10 (A) 축약된 부사절 찾기

Mini Test
p.258-259

1 (A) 관계사절 찾기

2 (B) (man black → black man)
수식어의 위치

3 (C) (slow → slowly)
형용사 – 부사 혼동

4 (D) 도치

5 (C) (turns → turn)
주어와 동사의 수 일치

6 (D) 주어 찾기

7 (A) (flat → a flat)
필요한 관사가 빠진 경우

8 (B) (found → was found)
능동태와 수동태를 혼동하여 쓴 경우

9 (A) to 부정사 찾기

10 (D) (cook → cooking)
동명사 자리에 동사를 쓴 경우

11 (C) 분사(구문) 찾기

12 (D) (elevate → elevating)
분사 자리에 동사나 다른 준동사를 쓴 경우

Grammar Up

p.262-271

🧩 Check-Up

A-1a

(1) I know the boy who likes sports.

(2) I like the girl whose hair is long.

(3) I saw the expensive watch whose chain was made of gold.

I saw the expensive watch of which the chain was made of gold.

I saw the expensive watch the chain of which was made of gold.

(4) This is the boy (whom) I saw there.

(5) This is the letter which arrived yesterday.

(6) My brother, who lives in Busan, is a student.

(7) This is the dog (which) I like.

(8) Bob is the young man (whom) she interviewed.

(9) She put away the book whose cover was missing. (3번 참조)

(10) The farmer burnt out the tree whose fruits had poison. (3번 참조)

A-1b

(1) that	(2) what
(3) which	(4) which
(5) who/that	(6) whom/that
(7) what	(8) which/that
(9) what	(10) what
(11) which	(12) whose
(13) what	(14) that
(15) what	

A-1c

(1) who won the prize (who 삽입)

(2) in that → in which 혹은 (that/which) George is interested in.

(3) which → that

(4) that → which

(5) 옳은 문장

(6) whom → whose

(7) what → which 혹은 that

(8) who → that

A-2

(1) 그녀는 의사가 된 세 명의 아들이 있다.

(2) 그녀는 아들이 셋 있는데, 모두 의사가 되었다.

(3) 수잔은 외국에 가고 싶었지만, 너무 어렸다.

(4) 그녀는 그 집을 사기로 결심했는데, 값이 비싸지 않았기 때문이다.

(5) 그는 그 여자를 발견하고, 그녀와 사랑에 빠졌다.

A-3

(1) (which)	(2) (which was)
(3) 생략할 곳 없음	(4) 생략할 곳 없음
(5) (that)	(6) (who was)
(7) 생략할 곳 없음	(8) (that)
(9) (whom)	(10) 생략할 곳 없음

B-1

(1) Let him have what comfort he can.

(2) Give me what money you have.

(3) You misunderstood what I meant.

C-1

(1) I remember the day when he left.

(2) I don't know the reason why you like her.

(3) He explained the way/how he opened the door.

(4) He met Jane on Friday when he went to the hospital.

(5) She likes the company where she works.

C-2

(1) which → where   (2) how → when
(3) for → why
(4) which 삭제
(5) when → which
(6) at 삭제 (or) at where → at which
(7) the way나 how중의 하나를 삭제
(8) 옳은 문장
(9) where → which
(10) 옳은 문장
(11) for which → in which
(12) which → when
(13) when → where
(14) 옳은 문장
(15) from 삭제 (or) from where → from which

D-1

(1) which   (2) whatever
(3) who   (4) which
(5) Whatever   (6) what
(7) whomever   (8) what
(9) which   (10) Whoever
(11) whom   (12) whichever
(13) Whoever   (14) whatever
(15) Whoever

D-2

(1) No matter where you may go, I'll find you.
(2) No matter how smart you may be, you should study hard.
(3) No matter when I may get up, dad prepares my breakfast.
(4) No matter how late you may come, the door of my house will be kept unlocked.
(5) No matter where you may be, the place is a home.

Power Up Test
p.272-273

1 (B)

2
(1) Is this the pie which was made by Su-mi?
(2) She has a son who will be a dancer.
(3) I'll visit the house where/at which the artist worked and died.

3 (C)   **4** (C)

5 (D)   **6** (A)

7 (B)   **8** (D)

9
(1) You may have (whatever/what) you want.
(2) (However) young you may be, you'll understand it.

Pattern Drill
p.274-275

유형 63 관계사 찾기
1 A
2 C

유형 64 관계사절 찾기
1 B
2 D

유형 65 관계사를 잘못 쓴 경우
1 C (what → who/that)
2 B (where → which/that)

유형 66 필요한 관계사가 빠진 경우
1 B (machines can → machine which/that can)

유형 67 불필요한 관계사가 쓰인 경우

1 A (that are → are)

Pattern Review

p.276

1 (C) 관계사 찾기

2 (B) (whom → who)
관계사를 잘못 쓴 경우

3 (D) 관계사절 찾기

4 (A) (which is → is)
불필요한 관계사가 쓰인 경우

5 (C) 관계사 찾기

6 (B) (was → which/that was)
필요한 관계사가 빠진 경우

7 (D) 관계사절 찾기

8 (B) (that → what)
관계사를 잘못 쓴 경우

9 (A) 관계사절 찾기

10 (C) (who → which/that)
관계사를 잘못 쓴 경우

6 (B) (theirs → they)
대명사의 격이 잘못된 경우

7 (D) 접속사 찾기

8 (A) 주어 찾기

9 (C) (to succeed → succeed)
동사 자리에 준동사를 쓴 경우

10 (D) 목적어와 목적보어 찾기

11 (C) 주어 찾기

12 (D) (has → is)
동사 찾기

Mini Test

p.277-278

1 (A) 부사(구) 찾기

2 (C) (newly → new)
형용사 – 부사 혼동

3 (B) (that → what)
관계사를 잘못 쓴 경우

4 (D) (into → inside)
전치사를 잘못 쓴 경우

5 (B) (animal → animals)
명사의 수가 잘못된 경우

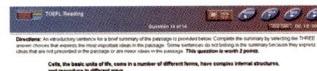